Judicial Dissent in European Constitutional Courts

Dissent in courts has always existed. It is natural and healthy that judges disagree on legal issues of a certain importance and difficulty. The question is if it is reasonable to conceal dissent. Not every legal system allows judges to explain their disagreement to the public in a separate opinion attached to the judgment of the court. Most constitutional courts do. This book presents a comparative analysis of the practice of judicial dissent in constitutional courts from the perspective of the civil law tradition. It discusses the theoretical background, presents the history of the institution and today's practice, thus laying down the basis for an accurate consideration of the phenomenon from a legal perspective.

Katalin Kelemen is Senior Lecturer in Law at Örebro University in Sweden, where she teaches Comparative Law and EU Law. She graduated in Law at Loránd Eötvös University in Budapest, Hungary, and obtained her PhD in Comparative Law at the University of Florence, Italy. She is the author of several articles, book chapters and conference papers in the field of comparative law, in particular on Eastern European legal systems and constitutional courts.

Judicial Dissent in European Constitutional Courts

A Comparative and Legal Perspective

Katalin Kelemen

Routledge
Taylor & Francis Group
LONDON AND NEW YORK

First published 2018 by Routledge

2 Park Square, Milton Park, Abingdon, Oxfordshire OX14 4RN
52 Vanderbilt Avenue, New York, NY 10017

Routledge is an imprint of the Taylor & Francis Group, an informa business

First issued in paperback 2019

British Library Cataloguing-in-Publication Data
A catalogue record for this book is available from the British Library

Library of Congress Cataloging-in-Publication Data
A catalog record for this book has been requested

ISBN: 978-1-4724-8223-5 (hbk)
ISBN: 978-0-367-33683-7 (pbk)

Typeset in Galliard
by Apex CoVantage, LLC

A Gabriele e Anna
és szüleimnek

Contents

Tables

Table of cases

Council of Europe

European Court of Human Rights

Baka v Hungary, App no 20261/12 (ECtHR, 23 June 2016)
Christine Goodwin v the United Kingdom, App no 28957/95 (ECtHR, 11 July 2002)
Cossey v the United Kingdom, App no 10843/84 (ECtHR, 27 September 1990)
I v The United Kingdom, App no 25680/94 (ECtHR, 11 July 2002)
Kress v France, App no 39594/98 (ECtHR, 7 June 2001)
X, Y, and Z v. the United Kingdom, App no 21830/93 (ECtHR, 22 April 1997)
Ždanoka v. Latvia, App no 58278/00 ([First Section] 17 June 2004, [GC] 16 March 2006)

Czech Republic

Constitutional Court

Decision Pl. ÚS 66/04 of 3 May 2006
Decision Pl. ÚS 5/12 of 31 January 2012
Decisions Pl. ÚS 16/14 and Pl. ÚS 19/14 of 27 January 2015
Decision Pl. ÚS 7/15 of 14 June 2016

Estonia

Supreme Court

Decision by the plenary session of 7 July 2001, RT III 2002, 2

European Union

Court of Justice of the European Union

Case 26/62 Van Gend en Loos v Nederlandse Administratie der Belastingen [1963] ECR 1

Case 106/77 Amministrazione delle Finanze dello Stato v Simmenthal SpA [1978] ECR 629

Germany

Federal Constitutional Court

Decision of 8 December 1952, BVerfGE 2, 79
Decision of 5 August 1966, BVerfGE 20, 162
Decision of 4 January 1971, BVerfGE 30, I, 33
Decision of 15 November 1971, BVerfGE 32, 199
Decision of 29 May 1974, BVerfGE 37, 271
Decision of 14 July 1986, BVerfGE 73, 40
Decision of 22 October 1986, BVerfGE 73, 339
Decision of 9 April 1992, BVerfGE 85, 264
Decision of 28 October 1998, 1 BvR 2306/96, 1 BvR 2314/96, 1 BvR 1108/97, 1 BvR 1109/97, 1 BvR 1110/97
Decision of 24 September 2003, 2 BvR 1436/02
Decision of 26 October 2004, 2 BvR 955/00, 2 BvR 1038/01
Decision of 8 December 2004, 2 BvE 3/02
Precautionary measure of 18 July 2001, 1 BvQ 23/01, 1 BvQ 26/01.
State Supreme Court of Bremen (Staatsgerichtshof der Freien Hansestadt Bremen)
Decision of 5 January 1957 (St 2/1956)

Hungary

Constitutional Court

Decision no. 2/1990 (II.18.) AB of 12 February 1990
Decision no. 23/1990 (X.31.) AB of 24 October 1990
Decision no. 31/1990 (XII.18.) AB of 11 December 1990
Decision no. 16/1991 (IV.20.) AB of 18 April 1991
Decision no. 24/1991 (V.18.) AB of 7 May 1991
Decision no. 44/1991 (VIII.28.) AB of 15 August 1991
Decision no. 48/1991 (IX.26.) AB of 23 September 1991
Decision no. 48/1991 (IX.26.) AB of 23 November 1991
Decision no. 57/1991 (XI.8.) AB of 5 November 1991
Decision no. 64/1991 (XII.17.) AB of 9 December 1991
Decision no. 8/1992 (I.30.) AB of 28 January 1992
Decision no. 64/1992 (XII.11.) of 8 December 1992
Decision no. 4/1993 (II.12.) AB of 8 February 1993
Decision no. 5/1993 (II.12.) AB of 8 February 1993
Decision no. 26/1993 (IV.28.) AB of 19 April 1993
Decision no. 38/1993 (VI.11.) AB of 8 June 1993
Decision no. 20/1994 (IV.16.) AB of 12 April 1994
Decision no. 35/1994 (VI.24.) AB of 21 June 1994

Decision no. 55/1994 (XI.10.) AB of 8 November 1994
Decision no. 43/1995 (VI.30.) AB of 30 June 1995
Decision no. 56/1995 (XI.15.) of 12 September 1995
Decision no. 1079/H/1995 AB of 22 April 1996
Decision no. 874/B/1994 AB of 29 April 1996
Decision no. 1067/B/1993 AB of 17 June 1996
Decision no. 42/1996 (X.9.) AB of 7 October 1996
Decision no. 4/1997 (I.22.) AB of 21 January 1997
Decision no. 277/B/1997 AB of 27 May 1997
Decision no. 18/1999 (VI.11.) AB of 7 June 1998
Decision no. 48/1998 (X.2.) AB of 29 September 1998
Decision no. 1/1999 (II.24.) AB of 23 February 1999
Decision no. 39/1999 (XII.21.) of 21 December 1999
Decision no. 23/2000 (VI.28.) AB of 26 June 2000
Decision no. 24/2000 (VII.6.) AB of 4 July 2000
Decision no. 2/2001 (I.17.) AB of 16 January 2001
Decision no. 50/2001 (XI.29.) AB of 26 November 2001
Decision no. 54/2001 (XI.29.) AB of 26 November 2001
Decision no. 55/2001 (XI.29.) AB of 26 November 2001
Decision no. 58/2001 (XII.7.) AB of 3 December 2001
Decision no. 35/2002 (VII.19.) AB of 12 July 2002
Decision no. 37/2002 (IX.4.) AB of 3 September 2002
Decision no. 62/2003 (XII.15.) AB of 15 December 2003
Decision no. 827/B/2000 AB of 16 February 2004
Decision no. 7/2004 (III.24.) AB of 23 March 2004
Decision no. 9/2004 (III.30.) AB of 29 March 2004
Decision no. 25/2004 (VII.7.) AB of 6 July 2004
Decision no. 43/2004 (XI.17.) AB of 15 November 2004
Decision no. 44/2004 (XI.23.) AB of 22 November 2004
Decision no. 620/B/1998 AB of 10 January 2005
Decision no. 1/2005 (II.4.) AB of 1 February 2005
Decision no. 42/2005 (XI.14.) AB of 12 November 2005
Decision no. 2/2006 (I.30.) AB of 30 January 2006
Decision no. 261/D/2005. AB of 21 February 2006
Decision no. 12/2006 (IV.24.) AB of 24 April 2006
Decision no. 28/2006 (VI.21.) AB of 16 June 2006
Decision no. 29/2006 (VI.21.) AB of 16 June 2006
Decision no. 1053/E/2005 AB of 16 June 2006
Decision no. 27/2006 (VI.21.) AB of 19 June 2006
Decision no. 88/B/1999 AB of 27 June 2006
Decision no. 103/B/1999 AB of 16 October 2006
Decision no. 576/D/2000 AB of 7 November 2006
Decision no. 63/2006 (XI. 23) AB of 20 November 2006
Decision no. 70/2006 (XII.13.) AB of 11 December 2006
Decision no. 72/2006 (XII.15.) of 12 December 2006
Decision no. 8/2007 (II.28.) AB of 27 February 2007

Decision no. 11/2007 (III.7.) AB of 6 March 2007
Decision no. 26/2007 (IV.25.) of 24 April 2007
Decision no. 47/2007 (VII.3.) AB of 3 July 2007
Decision no. 99/2007 (XII.6.) of 4 December 2007
Decision no. 55/2008 (IV.24.) AB of 22 April 2008
Decision no. 148/2008 (XII.3.) AB of 1 December 2008
Decision no. 149/2008 (XII.3.) AB of 1 December 2008
Decision no. 150/2008 (XII.3.) AB of 1 December 2008
Decision no. 151/2008 (XII.3.) AB of 1 December 2008
Decision no. 17/2010 (II.18.) AB of 16 February 2010

Italy

Constitutional Court

Judgment no. 393/2006 of 23 October 2006

Latvia

Constitutional Court

Decision no. 2000–03–01 of 30 August 2000
Decision no. 2005–13–0106 of 15 June 2006

Poland

Constitutional Tribunal

Decision no. K 24/98 of 21 October 1998
Decision no. K 39/97 of 10 November 1998
Decision no. K 31/04 of 26 October 2005
Decision no. K 9/11 of 20 July 2011

Romania

Constitutional Court

Decision no. 38/1993 of 7 July 1993
Decision no. 1 of the Plenary Session of 7 September 1993
Decision no. 86/2003 of 27 February 2003

Slovakia

Constitutional Court

Decision no. 43/99 of 20 December 1999

Slovenia

Constitutional Court

Decision no. U-I-51/90 of 14 May 1992
Decision no. U-I-4/92 of 28 May 1992
Decision no. U-I-135/92 of 30 June 1994
Decision no. U-I-77/93 of 6 July 1995

United Kingdom

DPP v. Smith (1961) AC 290 (H.L.)
Grindley v Barker (1798) 1 Bos and Pul 229, 238
Millar v. Taylor (1769) 4 Burrows 2302, 98 ER 201

United States

Adair v. United States (1908) 208 U.S. 161
Adkins v. Children's Hospital (1923) 261 U.S. 525
Baldwin v. State of Missouri (1930) 281 U.S. 586
Bas v. Tingy (1800) 4 U.S. (4 Dallas) 37
Blackstone v. Miller (1903) 188 U.S. 189
Bolling v. Sharp (1954) 347 U.S. 497
Brown v. Barry (1797) 3 U.S. (3 Dallas) 365
Brown v. Board of Education of Topeka (1954) 347 U.S. 483
Buck v. Bell (1927) 274 U.S. 200
Bunting v. State of Oregon (1917) 243 U.S. 426
Bush v. Gore (2000) 513 U.S. 98
Dred Scott v. Sandford (1856) 60 U.S. (How.) 393
Farmers' Loan & Trust Co. v. State of Minnesota (1930) 280 U.S. 204
Furman v. Georgia (1972) 408 U.S. 238
Gregg v. Georgia (1976) 428 U.S. 153
Head & Amory v. Providence Ins. Co. (1804) 6 U.S. (2 Cranch) 127
Huidekoper's Lessee v. Douglass (1805) 7 U.S. (3 Cranch) 1
Keene v. United States (1809) 9 U.S. (5 Cranch) 304
License Cases (1847) 46 U.S. (5 How.) 504
Little v. Barreme (1804) 6 U.S. (2 Cranch) 170
Lochner v. New York (1905) 198 U.S. 45
Marine Insurance Company of Alexandria v. Young (1809) 9 U.S. (5 Cranch) 187
Marks v. United States (1977) 430 U.S. 188
National Labor Relations Board v. Jones & Laughlin Steel Corp. (1937) 301 U.S. 1
Obergefell v. Hodges (2015) 576 U.S. ___
Ogden v. Sanders (1827) 25. U.S. (12 Wheat.) 213

Pierce v. Turner (1809) 9 U.S. (5 Cranch) 154
Plessy v. Ferguson (1896) 163 U.S. 537
Rose v. Himely (1808) 8 U.S. (4 Cranch) 241
Simms & Wise v. Slacum (1806) 7 U.S. (3 Cranch) 300
Southern Pacific Co. v. Jensen (1917) 244 U.S. 205
State Tax Commission of Utah v. Aldrich (1942) 316 U.S. 174
Talbot v. Seaman (1801) 5 U.S. (1 Cranch) 1
Union Refrigerator Transit Co. v. Commonwealth of Kentucky (1905) 199 U.S. 194
West Coast Hotel v. Parrish (1937) 300 U.S. 379

Introduction

Dissent in courts has always existed. It is natural and healthy that judges disagree on legal issues of a certain importance and difficulty. The question is if it is reasonable to conceal dissent. Judges undoubtedly discuss the cases among each other and influence one another's opinions. These discussions are fundamental for reaching the right solution (if one right solution exists). Even so, not every legal system allows judges to explain their disagreement to the public in a separate opinion attached to the judgment of the court. Most constitutional courts do. Still, European constitutional judges are more reluctant to write separately than common law judges. Even when they have the possibility to do so, they show considerable loyalty towards their colleagues and the court as an institution.

This book does not offer to develop new theories about or approaches to judicial dissent. It aims to observe, compare and systematise the practice of dissenting opinions in European constitutional courts within the existing theoretical framework. Judicial dissent is discussed from the perspective of the civil law tradition. Questions specific to this tradition, such as the nature of constitutional courts and the principle of legal certainty, are given special weight in the discussion. The idea behind this work is that an understanding of the practice of separate opinions helps clarify the essential nature of judging within the civil law tradition. An in-depth study of continental European practice allows us to make a careful comparison with the common law tradition, where these studies have already been conducted.

The study of constitutional courts has come into vogue among European political scientists. A few of them have specifically analysed the practice of dissenting opinions.[1] Political scientists are interested in understanding the extent to which courts, or one particular court, might be considered to be 'political'.[2]

1 Christoph Hönnige measured the relation of distance between the constitutional court and the political opposition in Germany and France, analysing the results of cases of abstract review, in his article 'The Electoral Connection: How the Pivotal Judge Affects Oppositional Success at European Constitutional Courts' (2009) 32 *West European Politics* 963. Chris Hanretty analysed and compared the non-unanimous decisions of the Spanish and Portuguese Constitutional Courts in his article 'Dissent in Iberia' (2012) 51 *European Journal of Political Research* 671. He also studied the practice of the Constitutional Chamber of the Estonian Supreme Court in his essay 'Judicial Disagreement Need Not Be Political: Dissent on the Estonian Supreme Court' (2015) 67 *Europe-Asia Studies* 970.

2 Hanretty 2015 (n 1) 971.

Their studies use quantitative methods and focus on what separate opinions reveal about particular judges' ideological background and party alignment. They look for correlations between voting behaviour on the bench and factors such as the political party which appointed the judge and or the career path (professional background) of the judge before appointment to the bench. These questions, though not entirely irrelevant, are not at the centre of the discussion. This book looks at the practice of judicial dissent from the perspective of legal science.

The use of quantitative and empirical methods is an emerging trend also in legal scholarship.[3] This book does not adhere to this trend, but I believe that it offers a necessary basis and background for a future quantitative analysis. This work does offer some statistical data on certain constitutional courts and a quite detailed presentation and discussion of data concerning the Hungarian Constitutional Court, but since the data on the other constitutional courts are very limited and sporadic, they are not compared systematically. The book, instead, tells the story of judicial dissent in European constitutional courts. The approach is heavily historical and often operates with examples. Moreover, it is a comparative story, meaning a story from a comparative perspective. So the approach is that of traditional comparative law (Zweigert-and-Kötz-generation style), rather than embracing the recent popular trend of quantitative analysis. In essence, the approach and the language of this book is that of a comparative lawyer.

It is also important to state beforehand that the comparison does not aspire to be comprehensive. No single researcher can claim to be able to carry out an entirely comprehensive comparison. It would be a cumbersome, though not impossible, task even for a larger research group. Therefore, a selection of legal systems had to be made. Some of the legal systems of the civil law and common law traditions are involved in this comparative exercise. Since the civil law tradition is the main focus of this work, the common law tradition serves only as a basis for comparison and the choice among common law jurisdictions is quite straightforward: England is the motherland of the common law and of its judicial style, while the United States represents a common point of reference for comparative studies today. Chapter 3 will present the practice of dissenting opinions in these two common law systems. Chapter 4 will then focus on discuss judicial dissent in the civil law tradition. First I will examine dissenting opinions from a historical perspective (Section 1), then I discuss judicial dissent in Germany, Spain and Italy from Western Europe (Section 2) and in the two European courts (Section 3), give an overview of the phenomenon in East-Central Europe (Section 4),[4] and

3 The first Conference on Empirical Studies in Europe was held in Amsterdam in June 2016.

4 I use the expression 'East-Central Europe' in the broadest possible sense, including those Eastern European states which were not part of the Soviet Union at its original setup. Thus, East-Central Europe comprises the Baltic states, the formerly socialist Central Europe, and Southeast Europe. Other Eastern European constitutional courts, such as the Russian or the Turkish one, are not involved in the study. About the classification of Eastern European legal systems see Katalin Kelemen and Balázs Fekete, 'How Should the Legal Systems of Eastern Europe Be Classified Today?' in Attila Badó et al (eds), *International Conference for the 10th Anniversary of the Institute of Comparative Law, Lectiones Iuridicae 11* (Universitätsverlag 2014) 197, <https://ssrn.com/abstract=2614944> accessed 9 December 2016.

finally analyse in detail the practice of the Hungarian Constitutional Court in the first two decades of its activity (Section 5).

The choice of civil law legal systems included in Chapter 4 has been a more subjective one. The German Federal Constitutional Court was the first one in Europe to allow the publication of dissenting opinions, moreover it served as a model for most European constitutional courts created later. Thus, it could not be excluded from the discussion. The Spanish Constitutional Court represents the second generation of European constitutional courts,[5] and there exists a modest literature and available statistical data on judicial dissent. The Italian Constitutional Court represents those few European constitutional courts that do not disclose dissent. The French Constitutional Council could have been another choice, but linguistic considerations and the amount of scholarly literature on the topic led me to opt for Italy. Moreover, while the French Constitutional Council until the recent reform represented a special model of constitutional review, the Italian Constitutional Court, similarly to the other constitutional courts involved in the comparison, is based on the Kelsenian model. The two European courts, the European Court of Human Rights and the Court of Justice of the European Union, are involved in the comparison, as it will be explained later, for at least two reasons. First, they also exercise constitutional functions. Second, they engage in a mutual dialogue with domestic constitutional courts and have a direct influence on the domestic legal system of the member states.

Finally, while a broader general overview is offered on the practice of the third generation of constitutional courts in this book,[6] only the Hungarian Constitutional Court has been object of a careful examination and empirical analysis. I chose the Hungarian Constitutional Court for an in-depth analysis for at least two reasons. First, it is the constitutional court of my home legal system in which I am able to move about with greater certainty and competence, have access to all sources and have the contacts necessary for the collection of empirical data.[7] Second, the Hungarian Constitutional Court became famous in the circles of constitutional scholarship worldwide in the 1990s for its especially activist stand.[8] Consequently, there is an astonishingly extensive amount of scholarly literature in English on the constitutional court of this country.[9] This may help readers to

5 Or the third, if we consider the Austrian and Czechoslovak Constitutional Courts established in 1920 to be the first generation.

6 The constitutional courts established in the formerly socialist countries are usually considered to belong to the third generation. See Chapter IV, Section 4.1.

7 I conducted interviews with seven former judges of the Hungarian Constitutional Court, and four law clerks shared their insights with me. In this book reference is made to these interviews anonymously. They have not been tape-recorded, instead I took notes by hand. I conducted the interviews in a semi-structured way, on the basis of a pre-established set of questions, following the leads offered by the subjects and being prepared to ask the questions in any order.

8 Wojciech Sadurski, 'Introduction' in Wojciech Sadurski (ed), *Constitutional Justice, East and West* (Kluwer Law International 2010) 3.

9 The Hungarian Court once again attracted international attention after the 2010–12 reforms which curtailed its competences. However, this book does not deal with the post-2010 period.

compare the findings of this book with other works on the Hungarian Constitutional Court. Moreover, examining the practice of dissenting opinions in a court that enjoyed high prestige may help up us reflect on the relationship between judicial dissent and a court's authority.

The Nordic legal tradition of publishing dissent is not reflected in this study, since the Nordic countries (the Scandinavian countries plus Finland) do not have separate constitutional courts. The practice of their respective supreme courts on constitutional questions may, however, be of additional value in a follow up to this work. Nordic courts have a long history of publication of judicial dissent, and they also have the power of judicial review. Thus, though Nordic countries do not have specialised constitutional courts, they could teach us much about the relationship between judicial dissent and constitutional justice.

This book was born over many years and at two different universities: *Università degli Studi di Firenze* in Italy and *Örebro universitet* in Sweden. An earlier version of the central chapters was defended as part of a doctoral dissertation at the former in April 2008. Since then, the content and the arguments have been revisited and updated. I also published two essays in English and one in Hungarian concerning judicial dissent,[10] and benefited from discussions with colleagues at seminars, workshops and conferences in Budapest, Florence, Pisa, Trento, Berlin, Örebro and New York.

Many thanks are due. I am grateful to Professors Vittoria Barsotti, Vincenzo Varano and Wojciech Sadurski for their mentorship, and for guiding me with their advices and illuminating observations during these years. I am thankful to the judges and law clerks who participated in the interviews for sharing their knowledge and experiences with me, and the staff at the various constitutional courts who helped me to collect materials and data. I am grateful for comments, if not endorsement from, Aryeh Amihay, Eszter Bodnár, Camilla Cordelli, Alessandra Di Martino, Fruzsina Gárdos-Orosz, Gianluca Gentili, Maria Haimerl, Gábor Halmai, Michael Hein, Tarik Radwan, and Imre Vörös, who read and kindly commented on the various chapters. The comments and suggestions of the Publisher's anonymous reviewer were also greatly appreciated. Finally, thanks go to the Swedish Wallenberg Foundation's *Stiftelse för Rättsvetenskaplig Forskning* for supporting this research with an Author Grant, and the Faculty Board of Humanities and Social Sciences (*HS-nämnden*) of Örebro University for financing its final stage.

10 A conference paper and a law journal article: 'The Road from Common Law to East-Central Europe. The Case of the Dissenting Opinion' (2010) in Péter Cserne and Miklós Könczöl (eds), *Legal and Political Theory in the Post-National Age* (Peter Lang 2011) 118–34, and 'Dissenting Opinions in Constitutional Courts' (2013) 14 *German Law Journal* 1345. The latter, in particular, is incorporated into this book in a revised form, divided between Chapters I and V. The Hungarian article discussed the history of dissenting opinions in the Western legal tradition: 'A bírói különvélemény története a nyugati jogrendszerekben' (2008) 9 *Jogtudományi Közlöny* 413.

1 Judicial dissent

What is it and why does it matter?

1. Judicial dissent and dissenting opinions: a definition

By 'dissenting opinion' we mean a separate opinion that diverges from the opinion of the majority of a group. Naturally, dissent can only exist if the decision is taken by multiple actors. It means that in a court it can exist only if there is a collegial body that decides the case. In other words, dissent can occur in a judicial panel. It cannot occur if the judgment is delivered by a single judge. In this book, the expressions 'judicial dissent' and 'dissenting opinion' will be used as synonyms. The former refers to the phenomenon of judges writing separately, while the latter points to its product. It is also important to clarify that the expression 'dissenting opinion' can be used in a broad or a strict sense. In the broad sense a dissenting opinion is any separate opinion of a member of a judicial panel. A dissenter, however, may disagree with the majority only in part. He may 'concur' in the outcome of the case but indicate different reasons for reaching such conclusion. In this case her/his separate opinion is called, more technically, 'concurring opinion'. A dissenting opinion in the strict sense, on the other hand, disagrees with the majority also as regards the ruling. A dissenting judge would have decided the case differently. Conversely, a concurring judge would have simply written the judgment differently, without changing the outcome of the case. Thus, a concurring opinion generally offers an alternative reasoning to the decision, but it may also simply add further arguments (supplementary reasoning) or aim to explain better the opinion of the court (explanatory opinion).[1] If not stated otherwise or made clear from the context, this book will use the expression 'dissenting opinion' in the broad sense, thus also referring to concurring opinions.

1 For a different, partly coincident, categorisation of concurring opinions see Igor Kirman, 'Standing Apart to Be a Part: The Precedential Value of Supreme Court Concurring Opinions' (1995) 95 *Columbia Law Review* 2083, 2088. Kirman defines four types of concurring opinions. For him an alternative reasoning is a *doctrinal concurrence*, and an *emphatic concurrence* is equivalent to the explanatory opinion. Separate opinions which concur both in the outcome and in the reasoning of the majority are also called *'two-cents' concurrences.* See Lewis A Kornhauser and Lawrence G Sager, 'The One and the Many: Adjudication in Collegial Courts' (1993) 81 *California Law Review* 1, 8, fn 14. The practice of concurring opinions is discussed specifically in Chapter 5, Section 4.2.

There are several expressions in the European languages which translate the concept of 'dissenting opinion' and, quite interestingly, they all put the institution in a different light. Examining these expressions represents a good starting point to achieve a deeper understanding of the nature of dissenting opinions. The Spanish expression *voto particular* shows that it is an extraordinary ('particular') opinion, meant to be used exceptionally. The German term *Minderheitsvotum* literally means 'minority vote', which sheds light on the majority rule of judicial decision-making. The European Court of Human Rights uses the French term *opinion individuelle*, emphasising the personal character of a separate opinion. The Latin term *votum separatum*, used in Polish civil procedure, is equivalent to the German *Sondervotum*, both meaning 'separate vote', thus referring to the distinctness of a separate opinion. The Italian *voto di scissura*, used with reference to the historical experience of dissenting opinions in certain regions of the Italian peninsula,[2] gives prominence to the conflictual nature of decision-making in judicial panels. A *scissura* is a rift between two people, a strong difference in opinion. Finally, the finest curiosity among the foreign expressions is the Portuguese *voto de vencido*, meaning 'vote of the loser'.[3] The dissenter is a loser, in the sense that he was unable to convince her/his colleagues of the quality of her/his position.

The term 'judicial dissent' could be meant in a broader sense, including divergence of opinion between judges who are not members of the same panel. Judicial dissent may well emerge between different chambers of the same court or between different courts. This kind of disagreement is not at all uncommon. Especially in large jurisdictions, such as the United States, courts of appeal do contradict each other, and it is the job of the supreme court(s) to solve these contradictions and to ensure a uniform interpretation of the law. The system of appeals itself, inherent to any modern court system, provides for the possibility of disagreement. When the reversal of a lower court's judgment is not based on new factual evidence submitted during the appeal procedure, but solely on legal interpretation, the nature of disagreement between the superior court and the inferior one does not differ substantially from the other forms of judicial dissent.[4] In this

2 Today Italian legal scholars use the term '*opinione dissenziente*'. Vittorio Denti, 'Per il ritorno al "voto di scissura" nelle decisioni giudiziarie' in Costantino Mortati (ed), *Le opinioni dissenzienti dei giudici costituzionali ed internazionali* (Giuffrè 1964) 1–20. See also Chapter 4, Section 2.3.

3 The term dates back to a Portuguese tradition, according to which the judge could express his dissent by affixing the word '*vencido*' to his signature on the judgment. The possibility to publish a dissenting opinion was granted only to constitutional judges in 1982, when the Portuguese Constitutional Court was established. See Saulle Panizza, *L'introduzione dell'opinione dissenziente nel sistema di giustizia costituzionale* [The Introduction of Dissenting Opinions in the System of Constitutional Justice] (Giappichelli 1998) 115.

4 As Karl Llewellyn put it, '[t]he very fact that there is an appeal usually proves that doubts exist among professionals, unless the attorney is using the appeal merely as a dilatory tactic'. Karl N Llewellyn and Paul Gewirtz, 'The Case Law System in America' (1988) 88 *Columbia Law Review* 989, 992. He also explains that such is the nature of authority that a reversed opinion (the opinion of the lower court) is 'virtually invisible', unlike dissenting opinions which are published together with the judgment.

book, however, judicial dissent will be examined only in the context of judicial panels, so in a more limited sense. The expression 'judicial dissent' will be used as a synonym for 'dissenting opinion' and 'separate opinion', referring to the same phenomenon: a member of the judicial panel decides to write separately from her/his peers in order to express publicly her/his disagreement or to supplement the opinion of the majority.

2. Dissenting opinions in legal research: an object or a tool?

Dissenting opinions may play a double role in legal research.[5] They can be, of course, in and of themselves the object of research aiming to analyse court practice and case-law. At the same time, they may also serve as a tool for researchers who study a given legal institution or phenomenon. The practice of dissenting opinions, as judicial decision-making process in general, calls for an empirical research. This is due to the secrecy of deliberations prevalent in courts and to the confidentiality of the records from which we could learn more about the decision-making process. In this field, research cannot be exclusively based on written documents, since these are not generally available to researchers, and even when they are, they do not necessarily reveal all the relevant facts. Certainly, a thorough investigation of the decisions and separate opinions may reveal a good deal about how judges decide the cases before them. It may bring to light the interactions between the various members of a court and possible personality clashes among them.[6] However, judicial opinions alone cannot offer a complete picture. If not stated in the opinion itself, it will be hard to understand the circumstances that motivated its writing. There may be speculation, but the only reliable source of information comes from inside the court. In the United States, for example, despite the duty of confidentiality, law clerks have sometimes served as a source of information for journalists.[7] Moreover, judges themselves at times reveal important facts in scholarly articles or interviews given to researchers or journalists. During my doctoral research, I interviewed several current and former members of the Hungarian Constitutional Court, and I realised that judges are usually willing to share their personal experiences on the court and are very open with researchers who want to inquire into the internal dynamics of their court.[8]

5 I discussed these questions in my article Katalin Kelemen, 'Dissenting Opinions in Constitutional Courts' (2013) 14 *German Law Journal* 1345.

6 For example, Edward McGlynn Gaffney Jr, 'The Importance of Dissent and the Imperative of Judicial Civility' (1994) 28 *Valparaiso University Law Review* 583 <http://scholar.valpo.edu/vulr/vol28/iss2/5/> accessed 16 January 2017 (reporting the study by an American scholar analysing the personal relationship between Justices of the US Supreme Court).

7 This was the case for example in relation to the *Bush v. Gore* (2000) judgment. See Chapter 3, Section 3.2.

8 Other researchers had similar experiences when interviewing judges. For example, Alan Paterson, *Final Judgment: The Last Law Lords and the Supreme Court* (Hart 2013) 5–6.

In relation to the practice of European constitutional courts, other factors make the task of researchers even more complex. First, constitutional courts do not make public the results of voting. Even though in Germany it is possible for the Court to make public the number of votes in a decision, the Court rarely does so, and, in any case, the identity of the judges who voted in favour and against the decision is not revealed.[9] Other constitutional courts do not allow this type of disclosure, making it impossible to gather complete statistics for the voting behaviour of constitutional judges. This circumstance severely restricts the scope of research. However, there is still space for an analysis based on written opinions (majority decisions and separate opinions) and on personal accounts by judges and their clerks. Second, if we wish to study specific aspects of the decision-making process of constitutional courts, a comparative approach is necessary, since it is not possible to draw reliable conclusions if we base them on the practice of only one or two constitutional courts. However, a comprehensive study of European constitutional courts runs into linguistic difficulties. This is especially true in the study of decision-making processes, as this involves the analysis of judicial opinions written in the official language of the court and not necessarily translated into other languages. As a rule, constitutional courts translate only a small number of their decisions, namely those that they consider to be potentially relevant to comparative research due to their significance for the legal system or to the importance of the issue at hand. Researchers cannot investigate the overall practice of writing dissenting opinions if they are provided only with a few separate translated opinions. A comprehensive study is needed. This means that a comparatist carrying out research of this kind must be able to read texts in German, Spanish, Portuguese, Czech, Hungarian, Polish, and so on.[10] This is a difficult, if not impossible, task. Consequently, as I mentioned in the Introduction, I had to make a selection among European constitutional courts according to my linguistic barriers. At the same time, this book does not aim at being comprehensive. Rather, it wants to provide a basis for future research which should be carried out by a larger research group.

While an analysis of the internal effects of dissenting opinions is restricted by the confidentiality of court records, a study of the external effects does not encounter the same limits. In this respect, it is sufficient to study the published dissenting opinions and unpublished dissents. In fact, in regards to external effects, unpublished dissents are not even relevant, since these by definition do not have external effects. Only published dissents do.[11] In any case, research on

9 See Chapter 4, Section 2.1.

10 I mentioned languages in which dissenting opinions can be found. There are no dissenting opinions available for example in Italian, as Italian constitutional judges are not allowed to write separately.

11 Indeed, there are examples of dissenting opinions in Europe which later became the opinion of the majority. See Chapter 4, Sections 4.3.2 and 5.5, providing a few examples from East-Central European constitutional courts; and Maria Theresa Rörig and Carmen Guerrero Picó, *L'opinione dissenziente nella prassi del* Bundesverfassungsgericht *e del* Tribunal Constitucional *spagnolo* (2009) 23 <www.cortecostituzionale.it/documenti/convegni_seminari/CC_SS_opinione_dissenziente_12012010.pdf> accessed 16 January 2017 (providing Spanish examples).

the practice of dissenting opinions has been very limited in Europe. The interest of scholars for separate opinions is not necessarily dependent on their actual existence in the constitutional court of their country. In Italy, for example, despite the fact that the Corte Costituzionale is not allowed to publish dissent, legal scholars are traditionally in favour of the publication of dissenting opinions. Piero Calamandrei, a renowned scholar and member of the Italian constituent assembly, wrote already in the 1930s that 'the secrecy of deliberation is the institutional consecration of conformism'.[12] Moreover, the Corte Costituzionale itself has debated the issue on several occasions.[13] However, the legislature has never approved any proposal for introducing dissenting opinions in the practice of the Court. Despite this fact, Italian scholarship has made a considerable contribution to (the limited) European literature on dissenting opinions.[14]

Regarding the possible place for separate opinions in legal research, it is noteworthy that, besides being subjects of research, they may also be used as tools. Looking at constitutional courts through the lens of separate opinions may indeed reveal the complexity of their decision-making processes and grant particularly eye-opening and thought-provoking insights into the internal debates between judges. This might enrich the range of arguments used in relation to a given constitutional issue. In fact, scholars usually include observations and analysis of separate opinions in their comments to a judicial decision. Concurring opinions may be especially useful in understanding a case, being frequently used by judges not to give an alternative reasoning, but to supplement the majority judgment.[15] They often reveal facts concerning the internal dynamics of the court. Moreover, they frequently aim to better explain the opinion of the court or some aspects of it, given that majority opinions usually emerging from a compromise are of deliberately vague or narrow language. A majority judgment is prone to represent the opinion of everyone, but it may end up representing the opinion of no one fully.[16]

To mention a possible example, for research on how the constitutional courts of the new EU Member States (those that acceded to the EU since 2004) interpret the principle of supremacy of EU law, it may be instructive to take into

12 Translation by the Author. Piero Calamandrei, *Elogio dei giudici scritto da un avvocato* (Ponte alle Grazie 1935) 274.

13 The question emerged from time to time in the Italian legal doctrine, culminating in the publication of a book by Saulle Panizza, Professor of law in Pisa. See Saulle Panizza, *L'introduzione dell'opinione dissenziente nel sistema di giustizia costituzionale* (Giappichelli 1998). The most recent seminar on dissenting opinions was organised by the Constitutional Court in Rome on 22 June 2009. The papers are available on the website of the court: <www.cortecostituzionale.it/convegniSeminari.do> accessed 16 January 2017.

14 Panizza (n 13); See also Lorenzo Luatti, *Profili costituzionali del voto particolare. L'esperienza del tribunale costituzionale spagnolo* (Giuffrè 1995) (discussing Spanish practice from a comparative perspective); Costantino Mortati, *Le opinioni dissenzienti dei giudici costituzionali ed internazionali* (Giuffrè 1964).

15 See the previous section.

16 John Alder, 'Dissents in Courts of Last Resort: Tragic Choices?' (2000) 20 *Oxford Journal of Legal Studies* 221, 242.

consideration the dissenting opinions written by Central and Eastern European constitutional judges. A researcher in that case would find that the Estonian Supreme Court judge Villu Kõve held that the Chamber 'overestimated the principle of supremacy of the European Union law over [the] Estonian legal order'.[17] Another interesting example is the opinion that Czech constitutional judge Stanislav Balik delivered in the European Arrest Warrant case, which takes the form of a short story full of empathetic arguments aiming to detail the situation of a man held in a foreign prison.[18] Additionally, the complete lack of separate opinions in a case may also hint at certain conclusions and require deeper examination. In any case, taking into consideration separate opinions when analysing case-law on any constitutional issue is an instructive and eye-opening exercise.

3. The *sui generis* nature of constitutional courts

An historical overview reveals that examples of disclosure of judicial dissent, even if few and isolated, are nonetheless present even in the civil law tradition.[19] A comparative overview, furthermore, shows that the publication of dissent is not limited to the practice of common law judges anymore. Today it is a widespread practice even in continental Europe. However, it still represents an exception for judges of ordinary courts. Estonia, Spain and Portugal are among those countries which represent the exception that proves the rule. At the same time, the overwhelming majority of European constitutional courts provide for the publication of dissent.[20]

At this point a few questions emerge. First, why is the publication of dissent basically a privilege of constitutional courts in many civil law countries? Second, does this confirm the *sui generis* nature of constitutional courts? Third, what are the consequences?

Constitutional courts are *sui generis* institutions, since they merge judicial (dispute resolution) and political (lawmaking) functions.[21] As Wojciech Sadurski observes, constitutional courts, both in Western and in East-Central Europe, 'in many respects resemble legislative chambers sitting in judgment on the laws enacted by the lower chambers'. At the same time, they behave in a judicial way in many other respects. First of all, they prefer to use technical legal arguments, 'mimicking the reasoning of "ordinary" judges, instead of moral and other

17 See his dissenting opinion attached to an Opinion of the Constitutional Review Chamber of the Supreme Court on the interpretation of the Constitution of 11 May 2006, no 3-4-1-3-06. Its English translation is available at <www.nc.ee/?id=663> accessed 16 January 2017.

18 See Decision no Pl. ÚS 66/04 of 3 May 2006 on the European Arrest Warrant from which three judges dissented (Justices Eliška Wagnerová and Vlasta Formánková wrote a joint opinion). The English translation of the judgment (including dissenting opinions) is available at <www.usoud.cz/en/decisions/> accessed 16 January 2017.

19 See Chapter 4, Section 1.

20 Western European practice will be examined in Chapter 4, Section 2.

21 See generally Mauro Cappelletti, *Judicial Review in the Contemporary World* (Bobbs-Merrill 1971) 55 (becoming one of the first scholars theorising the models of judicial review).

non-legal arguments that legislative chambers are accustomed to'.[22] It is common practice in comparative legal research to involve both constitutional courts and supreme courts in the comparison, but it is important to bear in mind that constitutional courts differ from supreme courts in several aspects. It is not simply a question of jurisdiction. They are not special supreme courts. First, they are not supreme, in the sense that there are no lower courts below them and there is no hierarchy in the administration of constitutional justice.[23] In the American model, all judges have the power of judicial review. In the European model, on the other hand, this is the sole privilege of the constitutional court. That is why the European (or Austrian) model is also called 'centralised' or, less often, 'concentrated'. An important consequence of this difference is that constitutional issues in civil law countries are addressed by ordinary judges only to the extent that, when some requirements are met, they file a reference to the constitutional court. Ordinary judges do not decide constitutional issues themselves and do not deliver judgments declaring the unconstitutionality of public acts or actions. This means that there is no variety of judicial voices on these issues. Constitutional courts, as described by Ferreres Comella, have a 'dialogic disadvantage'[24] compared to common law supreme courts, which have not only the final word on constitutional questions but also at least one other judicial opinion on the matter available to them.

In the European model, however, the time for debate is shortened. In this context, separate opinions may play an important role in enriching the constitutional debate and may help the evolution of constitutional law. In the same line of thought, Julia Laffranque considers dissenting opinions instructive commentaries especially important for legal culture that are not yet fully developed, as was the case of her own country, Estonia.[25] Her observation can be extended to all transitional contexts where interpretive gaps are frequent and an established interpretation of new rules has not yet emerged. This is especially true for constitutional law, which is much more affected by political regime changes than other, more technical areas of law. In fact, this may be a potential explanation for the introduction of dissenting opinions in the formerly socialist countries of Central and Eastern Europe.

The fact that constitutional courts have a monopoly on constitutional review does not only mean that they do not share this power with lower courts. The lack

22 Wojciech Sadurski, *Rights Before Courts: A Study of Constitutional Courts in Postcommunist States of Central and Eastern Europe* (2nd edn, Springer 2014) 161. Sadurski argues this is especially problematic from the perspective of rights-adjudication, as the public transparency of the reasons underlying a particular decision is seen as a maximising factor of rights-orientation. Ibid. 162.

23 There is no hierarchy in federal states either. German state constitutional courts cannot be considered the first instance courts of the German constitutional justice system.

24 Víctor Ferreres Comella, *Constitutional Courts and Democratic Values* (Yale UP 2009) 58.

25 Julia Laffranque, 'Dissenting Opinion in the European Court of Justice. Estonia's Possible Contribution to the Democratisation of the European Union Juridical System' (2003) 9 *Juridica International* 14, 17.

of hierarchy in the administration of constitutional justice also signifies that there is no other court above them. The fact that the decisions of constitutional courts are final and cannot be appealed may have an impact on their argumentative style. Interesting empirical research carried out in French administrative courts showed that, for many judges, reason-giving is mainly an activity directed towards the appellate court so as to avoid reversal.[26] This observation certainly does not apply to supreme courts and constitutional courts. So, the motivations of judges in their reason-giving practices must necessarily be found elsewhere.

Even though constitutional courts must be considered separately from supreme courts, it is quite common for comparative constitutional studies to compare the case-law and the functioning of European constitutional courts to that of supreme courts of countries belonging to the common law tradition, in particular and primarily to the US Supreme Court. Such a comparison is motivated by functional reasons: the compared courts exercise the power of constitutional review. Moreover, both models of constitutional review (centralised and decentralised) struggle with the so-called counter-majoritarian difficulty, or as it is addressed in European constitutional theory, with democratic legitimacy.[27] In addition, their composition shows similarities. According to the results of an empirical study carried out by a German political scientist examining the connection between the composition of European constitutional courts and how they make decisions, European constitutional judges exhibit their political preferences and act as policymakers just as their US counterparts do.[28] However, there are still important differences that distinguish constitutional courts from common law supreme courts, and they are relevant to a study on the practice of dissenting opinions.

First, constitutional courts in civil law systems actually co-exist with ordinary supreme courts and special supreme courts. Political scientists suggested that constitutional courts, as other courts, care about their legitimacy as perceived either by society at large, or by other judicial organs.[29] Even if they do not have a superior court above them, constitutional courts often face competition from courts at the top of the ordinary judiciary. In Germany, for example, there are five

26 Mathilde Cohen, 'Reason-Giving in Court Practice: Decision-makers at the Crossroads' (2008) 14 *Columbia Journal of European Law* 257, 264.

27 See, for example, Michel Rosenfeld, 'Constitutional Adjudication in Europe and the United States: Paradoxes and Contrasts' in Georg Nolte (ed), *European and US Constitutionalism* (Cambridge UP 2005) 184. The argument of counter-majoritarian difficulty is addressed against the power of judicial review on the ground that the judiciary, not being elected by the people, lacks democratic legitimacy; therefore, its power to set aside unconstitutional legislation is unjustified. The expression 'counter-majoritarian difficulty' was coined by Alexander Bickel in his famous book *The Least Dangerous Branch* (Bobbs-Merrill 1962).

28 Christoph Hönnige, 'The Electoral Connection: How the Pivotal Judge Affects Oppositional Success at European Constitutional Courts' (2009) 32 *West European Politics* 963. See also Chapter 4, Section 2.1.2.

29 Nuno Garoupa and Tom Ginsburg, 'Building Reputation in Constitutional Courts: Political and Judicial Audiences' (2011) 28 *Arizona Journal of International and Comparative Law* 539, 542.

supreme courts besides the Bundesverfassungsgericht. It means that constitutional courts do not give the final word on every legal question. Their jurisdiction is limited to constitutional adjudication, while other matters are decided by the other courts. Obviously, a controversy may raise both constitutional and other legal questions. In this case, these parallel judicial bodies have to share the work and decide the questions in their respective jurisdiction. Today every European constitutional court combines abstract and concrete review.[30] After the 2008 French constitutional reform[31] every centralised model in Europe now provides for incidental review as well. Moreover, since the creation of the German Federal Constitutional Court, several constitutional courts also hear constitutional complaints challenging ordinary judicial decisions.[32] This 'judicial cohabitation' not only results in a dialogue between ordinary and constitutional judges but also implies a potential conflict between the parallel supreme jurisdictions, since a truly genuine separation of jurisdictions is not possible.[33] Dissenting and concurring opinions may play a role in this dialogue as well, and this interaction could be a subject for further specific research.

Second, constitutional courts are often able to intervene in the legislative process, which is not the case for common law supreme courts. Indeed, when a constitutional court exercises preventive (or *a priori*) review, it decides on the constitutionality of a draft statute before its promulgation. In that case the review procedure is necessarily initiated by a political actor (a member of the parliament or a group of members of the parliament; the government or one of its members), and the decision is the result of a tripartite dialogue between the court, the proponent of the bill and the actor who challenged it. In fact, the centralised model of judicial review facilitates the right of the governmental majority to defend the constitutional legitimacy of the challenged statute.[34] In the United States, however, notwithstanding the decentralised system of judicial review, the legislature is able to intervene in the proceedings, as courts must notify the US Attorney General – or the relevant State attorney general – if the constitutionality of an act of the Congress or a statute of a State becomes an issue in litigation, permitting intervention for presentation of evidence and for argument on the question of constitutionality.[35]

30 Abstract review means that the court compares two normative texts and assesses their compatibility without regard to their concrete application. Concrete review, on the other hand, implies that there is a controversy from which the constitutional question has arisen.

31 Federico Fabbrini, 'Kelsen in Paris: France's Constitutional Reform and the Introduction of *a Posteriori* Constitutional Review of Legislation' (2008) 9 *German Law Journal* 1297, 1297.

32 Gianluca Gentili, 'A Comparative Perspective on Direct Access to Constitutional and Supreme Courts in Africa, Asia, Europe and Latin America' (2010) 29 *Penn State International Law Review* 705, 707.

33 Lech Garlicki, 'Constitutional Courts versus Supreme Courts' (2007) 5 *International Journal of Constitutional Law* 44, 47.

34 Ferreres Comella (n 24) 65.

35 28 U.S.C. § 2403 (2012).

Third, abstract review is traditionally listed among the features that determine the *sui generis* nature of constitutional courts. As mentioned above, abstract review means that the court compares two normative texts and assesses their compatibility without regard to their concrete application.[36] It is abstract because there is no litigation from which the question of constitutionality emerged. What in the European model is called 'concrete review', on the other hand, is initiated by an ordinary judge, so there is a concrete controversy behind the constitutional issue. However, as Alec Stone Sweet observed, in the European model even concrete review 'remains meaningfully abstract in an overt and formal way'[37] since the constitutional court does not dispose of the litigation in which the question of constitutionality emerged. Deciding the litigation on the merits is a task left to the ordinary judge who referred the question of constitutionality to the constitutional court. The predominantly abstract nature of European constitutional review induces us also to think that the style of argumentation of constitutional courts differs considerably from the style of common law supreme courts, whose main function is to dispose of the litigation. In the American model of judicial review, the decision on the conformity of a statute with the Constitution is incidental to dispute resolution. However, abstract review is not unknown to the American legal system. Preliminary injunctions and declaratory judgments, first developed by the courts of equity, have become instruments of rights adjudication. They have been especially used in relation to the First Amendment's freedom of expression guarantee, a field in which the restrictive doctrines on standing and justiciability have been relaxed.[38] In such cases, American judges act like their European colleagues in constitutional courts: they make authoritative guesses about how a law would likely be enforced by public officials and how a statutory provision would likely be construed by the courts. The techniques of abstract review developed by American judges are strikingly similar to their European counterparts: they use balancing tests, and they try to save the 'uncontaminated' provisions of the challenged statute or the entire statute by interpreting it in a way that is compatible with the Constitution.[39] To conclude, both American and European constitutional judges routinely engage in abstract reasoning and decision-making. In this respect the differences may not be as striking as we might expect at first sight.

Finally, an important distinguishing feature of constitutional courts in comparison to supreme courts is their age. Unlike traditional supreme courts,

36 See n 21. With reference to the French *a priori* review it was also called 'constitutional review of objective law' (controllo di costituzionalità di diritto obbiettivo). See Gustavo Zagrebelsky,*Il diritto mite* (Einaudi 1992) 78–79.

37 Alec Stone Sweet, 'Why Europe Rejected American Judicial Review: And Why It May Not Matter' (2003) 101 *Michigan Law Review* 2744, 2771.

38 Stone Sweet (n 37) 2773–4. Abstract review has become the 'normal' mode of adjudicating also in the domain of reproductive rights. Ibid. 2777.

39 This latter technique is called the 'saving construction' in American parlance, 'strict reserves of interpretation' in France, and 'verfassungskonforme Auslegung' in German. Ibid. 2778.

constitutional courts are relatively new institutions. With the exception of their prototype, the Austrian Constitutional Court, all were created after the Second World War,[40] and the most recent generation has just recently reached its 20s. This creates several consequences that a researcher may consider when analysing the decision-making process. First, constitutional courts are institutions that often have had to face transitional issues and which, in the period immediately following their establishment, could not rely on an established body of domestic case-law. They have had to build a new, coherent system from its very foundations. As already indicated above, in such circumstances, dissenting – and maybe to an even greater extent concurring – opinions can be of great help in establishing a body of constitutional law. Second, the constitutional courts, as newly created institutions in their first years of existence, often struggle with asserting their own authority and legitimacy.[41] In a context of initial distrust in the public institutions, the publication of dissenting opinions can be seen as a way to ensure transparency in the decision-making processes of the new court, thereby enhancing its credibility and legitimacy.[42] Constitutional courts created after the breakdown of an authoritarian regime were faced with this challenge. On the one hand a lack of confidence in the legislative power increased the need for judicial review,[43] and on the other hand mistrust in a new institution composed of members appointed by politicians increased the need for transparency. However, in times when the court's authority and legitimacy are still weak, the publication of seemingly unanimous opinions can serve to protect the newly established court. Consequently, in a transitional period, it may also be argued that a ban on dissenting opinions would serve exactly the same goal as permitting dissents.[44]

40 The Czechoslovakian Constitutional Court, established in 1920, is another exception, even if in its 20 years of functioning it delivered only 65 decisions. See Jiři Přibaň, 'Judicial Power vs. Democratic Representation: The Culture of Constitutionalism and Human Rights in the Czech Legal System' in Wojciech Sadurski (ed), *Constitutional Justice, East and West* (Kluwer Law International 2002) 373, 374. Moreover, Austrian constitutional judges are not allowed to publish dissenting opinions, so there is no century-long experience of dissenting opinions in European constitutional justice.

41 Ruti Teitel, 'Transitional Jurisprudence: The Role of Law in Political Transformation' (1997) 106 *Yale Law Journal* 2031.

42 I am thankful to Wojciech Sadurski for this suggestion.

43 László Sólyom, 'The Role of Constitutional Courts in the Transition to Democracy: With Special Reference to Hungary' (2003) 18 *International Sociology* 133, 135.

44 This was the opinion expressed by Hjalte Rasmussen in relation to the European Court of Justice. He argues in favour of the introduction of dissenting opinions into the practice of the Court, but at the same time he recognises that the ban on the publication of dissent served a legitimate purpose at the time of the adoption of the foundational treaties of the European Communities. Hjalte Rasmussen, 'Legal Opinion About the European Court of Justice's Competence Transgressions, Poor Reasonings and the Complete Non-Transparency of *Willensbildung*' (2009) 8–9 <http://curis.ku.dk/ws/files/18105617/Doc> accessed 16 January 2017. The situation of the European Court of Justice was, however, peculiar, because it did not emerge in a context of transition from an authoritarian regime to democracy but as a new supranational court which had to operate in a completely new legal system and affirm the legitimacy of EC law. More recently, in June 2012, the European Parliament's

This apparent contradiction was solved in different ways by different countries. In Germany and in Lithuania, as it will be explained later,[45] the publication of dissent was not allowed in the first period of the respective courts' existence on the ground that it might compromise the authority of the newly established institution. In both countries it took approximately two decades to acknowledge that the constitutional court's authority was sufficiently established to introduce dissenting opinions.[46] Other countries (Spain, Portugal and Central and Eastern European countries with the exceptions of Lithuania and Romania), on the other hand, allowed constitutional judges to publish their dissent from the very beginning. Therefore, in these countries the institution of dissenting opinion has 'grown up' together with the constitutional court itself, and it is more difficult to examine whether dissenting opinions had a negative effect on the court's authority.

All these features distinguishing constitutional courts from supreme courts point in the direction that when carrying out research on the practice of dissenting opinions in constitutional courts, it is important to be aware of these differences in order to properly use and interpret the results of American studies. It seems that the *sui generis* nature of constitutional courts in continental Europe is confirmed, among others, by the fact that their judges are allowed to publish dissenting opinions. Constitutional judges are less attached to the traditional judicial mentality than ordinary judges, and they use different interpretative techniques and style of argumentation.[47] That is also the reason why the publication of dissent, with a few exceptions, is a privilege reserved only to constitutional courts in continental Europe. As to the third question set out at the beginning of this section, we established that there are several factors that bring us to consider the decision-making process of constitutional courts. All these factors affect the practice of dissenting opinions.

Committee on Legal Affairs requested the Directorate General for Internal Policies a study on the practice of dissenting opinions in the Member States of the European Union, with the aim of assessing the appropriateness of the introduction of separate opinions for the European Court of Justice. The study, authored by Rosa Raffaelli, is available in its entirety at the EP's official website: Directorate-General for Internal Policies, *Dissenting Opinions in the Supreme Courts of the Member States* (PE 462.470, November 2012) <www.europarl.europa.eu/committees/en/supporting-analyses-search.html> accessed 16 January 2017. The study has had no sequel so far.

45 See Chapter 4, Section 2.1 for Germany, and Chapter 4, Section 4.2 for Lithuania.

46 In Germany they were introduced after 19 years (in 1970), in Lithuania after 15 years (in 2008).

47 According to András Jakab, constitutional courts are able to develop a system of concepts considerably more sophisticated than that of the actual text of the Constitution in order to serve as a 'helping toolkit' for the solution of future cases. Moreover, this conceptual system is not always based on the text of the Constitution. It can also be the result of a text-independent abstract speculation. András Jakab, 'Judicial Reasoning in Constitutional Courts: A European Perspective' (2013) 14 *German Law Journal* 1215, 1258.

2 The decision-making process in constitutional courts

The first in-depth interdisciplinary studies of the decision-making process of judges were conducted in the United States in the 1940s. These were stimulated mainly by the dissatisfaction with the traditional legalistic explanations concerning the resolution of controversies. The proliferation of dissenting and concurring opinions generated discontent among legal scholars who started to ask themselves why the members of a judicial panel reach different conclusions on the basis of the same factual background and applicable legal rules.[1] Thus research was carried out in order to investigate the extralegal factors of judicial decision-making, and a new field of study was born in the area of political science, called 'behaviouralism'.[2] Later on, the problem attracted the attention of psychologists and sociologists (and of social psychologists in particular) and, to a lesser extent, of anthropologists and economists.[3] Besides psychological and social factors, judicial behaviour was examined from the point of view of political factors, as it had been acknowledged that courts are not free of political pressure. The study of political factors consists of analysing the influence exercised by public opinion and by groups of interests on judicial decisions and the position of the judiciary in the scheme of checks and balances.[4]

The concept of 'decision-making process' is not to be confused with that of 'judicial process' which refers to 'a set of interrelated procedures and roles for deciding disputes by an authoritative person or persons whose decisions are regularly obeyed'.[5] It is both a means of resolving disputes and a process for making

1 Thomas G Walker and Lee Epstein, *The Supreme Court of the United States: An Introduction* (St Martin's Press 1993) 125.

2 The term 'behaviouralism' is a typical English one, which is difficult to translate into other languages. In Italian, for example, the Anglicism 'behavioralismo' or its literal translation 'comportamentismo' is used.

3 The most important subbranches of behaviouralism are cultural anthropology, systems theory, psychometrics, games theory and statistics used for predicting decisions. Glendon Schubert, 'Judicial Behavior' (1968) 8 *International Encyclopedia of the Social Sciences* 307.

4 Walker and Epstein (n 1) 131–39, and Richard A Posner, *How Judges Think* (Harvard UP 2008).

5 Definition by JW Peltason, 'Judicial Process. Introduction' (1968) 8 *International Encyclopedia of the Social Sciences* 283.

public policies, i.e. for affirming certain values and principles. The decision-making process is, therefore, a particular aspect of the ampler judicial process and concerns those factors and rules which determine the forming of a judge's opinion.

Mathilde Cohen, in her study on supreme and constitutional courts' organisational cultures, convincingly hypothesised that there is a reciprocal influence between a court's institutional design and the style of its opinions.[6] In keeping with Cohen, prior to exploring the phenomenon of judicial dissent I will address the institutional and procedural contexts. For this purpose the most relevant aspect of the decision-making process is represented by its personal dimension: the role of the judicial panel's most prominent members (its president, the rapporteur judges and the opinion-writer) and that of law clerks. This chapter will focus on the Western and East-Central European constitutional courts and make a few comparative remarks on the US Supreme Court.

1. Internal court structure in comparative perspective

As argued in the previous chapter, constitutional courts in many respects represent a special combination of a common law supreme court and a civil law supreme court since they have certain characteristics of both.[7] This is true also with regard to their internal structure. A constitutional court is composed of a relatively limited number of judges (between seven and 15),[8] like a common law supreme court, and it often decides in smaller panels, similarly to civil law supreme courts, but unlike the US Supreme Court.[9] There are, however, a number of constitutional courts that take any decision in full court.[10] In some constitutional courts smaller panels adjudicate on admissibility only,[11] while in others they can also decide on the merits. Some of the latter operate with two types of panel: a larger one for decisions on the merits and a smaller one for decisions on admissibility.[12] So, we can find a great variety of solutions. That is true also for the

6 Mathilde Cohen, 'Ex Ante Versus Ex Post Deliberations: Two Models of Judicial Deliberations in Courts of Last Resort' (2014) 62 *American Journal of Comparative Law* 401, 452. She adds that further research should be done to elaborate this hypothesis.

7 See Chapter 1, Section 3.

8 See Table 2.3 at the end of this section.

9 The US Supreme Court is actually an exception even among common law supreme courts. The UK Supreme Court, composed of 15 members, typically decides in panels of five, but at least three judges (Rule 3 of the Supreme Court Rules 2009 (SI 2009/1603) and UKSC Practice Direction 3). Neil Andrews, 'The United Kingdom's Supreme Court: Reflections on the Role of the British Nation's Highest Tribunal' (2009) 14 *ZZP Int. – Zeitschrift für Zivilprozess International* 33.

10 Namely, the Bulgarian, Italian, Lithuanian, Luxembourgish, Macedonian, Montenegrin, and Romanian Constitutional Courts. See Table 2.1.

11 Namely, the Albanian, Austrian, Kosovar, and Latvian Constitutional Courts. See Table 2.1.

12 Namely, the Belgian, Croatian and Spanish Constitutional Courts. See Table 2.1.

possibility of writing separately. In certain courts it is a prerogative of the plenary session only, while in others it is extended to the panels.[13]

In any event, constitutional courts always decide collectively on the merits of a case, either in smaller or larger panels, or in full court. Only a few countries allow single-judge formations to make decisions, and their decisions are never on the merits. In Hungary and in the Czech Republic, for example, a single constitutional judge may reject a petition on formal grounds.[14] Formal grounds (such as expiration of a filing deadline, lack of standing or lack of jurisdiction) are usually simple procedural questions and do not require a debate among judges. Thus, entrusting a single judge with this function helps the court to dispose of these cases more expeditiously. Naturally, single judges, when adjudicating in a single-judge formation, do not write dissenting opinions.

The German Bundesverfassungsgericht, which often serves as a model in other countries when creating a new constitutional court, has a unique structure which has not been adopted by any other country. Its sixteen members are grouped into two permanent panels, in German called *Senate*. They have different competences established by law,[15] and a plenary session is summoned only when a contrast arises in the jurisprudence of these two panels and to issue rules on judicial administration.[16] In fact, the German senates are often considered to be two separate constitutional courts.[17] An increase in the number of constitutional

13 Bulgaria, the Czech Republic, Hungary, and the Slovak Republic allow for the publication of dissent in panels. In Hungary, after the 2012 reform, only the five-member panels may publish dissent, not the three-member panels (art 49 (4) of the Constitutional Court Act requires unanimity from three-member panels). A complete citation of the relevant constitutions, constitutional court acts and rules of procedure can be found in the Appendix after the last chapter. The creation of 3-member panels is, however, only a possibility. No three-member panel has been established yet. I thank Johanna Fröhlich, former clerk at the Hungarian Constitutional Court, for this information.

14 Art 43 of the Czech Constitutional Court Act and art 55 (5) of the Hungarian Constitutional Court Act. In Hungary it is a novelty introduced by the new Constitutional Court Act. Only two members of the Court act as solo judges at a time, appointed by the President for three months. Art 11 of the Rules of Procedure.

15 See art 14 of the German Federal Constitutional Court Act (BVerfGG). At the beginning the First Senate was designed to deal with all constitutional complaints, while the Second Senate was supposed to decide conflicts of power and other cases of political nature like the pre-existing Staatsgerichtshof of the Weimar Republic. However, the especially conspicuous number of constitutional complaints made it necessary to re-distribute the caseload, and today the Second Senate also decides complaints. The division of work between the two panels is determined by the plenary session at the beginning of every term. Sarang Vijay Damle, 'Specialize the Judge, Not the Court: A Lesson From the German Constitutional Court' (2005) 91 *Virginia Law Review* 1267, 1298.

16 See Table 2.1 and arts 1(3), 7a(2), 14(4), 16(1) and 105 BVerfGG.

17 The idea of this two-halved structure represented a compromise between a court of 24 judges deciding in small panels and a united court following in the footsteps of the US Supreme Court. Donald P Kommers, *Judicial Politics in West Germany: A Study of the Federal Constitutional Court* (Sage 1976) 86.

complaints (the famous *Verfassungsbeschwerden*) made it necessary to create also smaller panels.[18] The so-called *Kammern* or chambers, composed of three judges, work as a filter. They decide on the admissibility of constitutional complaints and applications by ordinary courts.[19] Moreover, since 1986, if they find that a complaint is either manifestly unfounded or manifestly founded, they may also decide the case on the merits.[20] Three chambers operate within both senates, and their decisions shall be taken by unanimity.[21] This means that dissent is allowed only in the plenum of either senate.

The Belgian Constitutional Court's internal organisation also shows a double structure but in a sense different from that of the Bundesverfassungsgericht and for different reasons. The Belgian Court is composed of 12 judges, divided equally into Dutch and French speakers. They form two language groups, each with its own president. The Court even has two registrars to ensure equal treatment of the two linguistic groups.[22] However, there are no two permanent panels, as in Germany, but the two language groups are both represented in all cases. The decision-making panels are composed of three French-speaking and three Dutch-speaking judges plus the president of the linguistic group whose language is that of the case to be heard.[23] This strictly double internal organisation, like the very existence of the Constitutional Court itself, is due to the development of the Belgian unitary state into a federal state in the 1970s. The then Court of Arbitration, created in 1983, had the task of watching the division of legislative powers between the different legislative assemblies.[24] Three years after the Court delivered its first judgment, it was granted power to review compliance with certain constitutional rights and principles.[25] This historical

18 The Senates were authorised to set up preliminary examining 'chambers' in 1956. Donald P Kommers and Russell Miller, 'Das Bundesverfassungsgericht: Procedure, Practice and Policy of the German Federal Constitutional Court' (2009) 3 *Journal of Comparative Law* 194, 198.

19 Arts 81a and 93b BVerfGG. However, the admissibility of applications by state constitutional courts or by a federal supreme court are examined by the senate.

20 However, the authority to declare a statute unconstitutional or in conflict with federal law is reserved to the panel. Arts 93b(2) and 93c(1) BVerfGG. In practice only about 5% of the individual complaints reach the full panel. Dieter Grimm, 'The German Constitutional Court' in Pasquale Pasquino and Barbara Randazzo, *Come decidono le corti costituzionali (e altre Corti). How Constitutional Courts Make Decisions* (Giuffrè 2009) 41, 47.

21 Arts 81a and 93d(3) BVerfGG. Also Peter E Quint, 'Leading a Constitutional Court: Perspectives From the Federal Republic of Germany' (2006) 154 *University of Pennsylvania Law Review* 1853, 1862–63.

22 Arts 31, 33 and 40 of the Belgian Constitutional Court Act. Moreover, one of the judges has to speak German as well (art 34(4)).

23 Art 55 of the Belgian Constitutional Court Act.

24 The Court of Arbitration (Cour d'Arbitrage) was established by the Act of 28 June 1983, and became operative on 1 October 1984.

25 The first judgment was delivered on 5 April 1985, while the constitutional amendment extending the Court's competences was adopted on 15 July 1988. Accordingly, in 2007, the name of the Court of Arbitration was changed to Constitutional Court.

and political background, together with the strong influence of the French legal tradition on Belgian law, might explain the lack of dissenting opinions in Belgian constitutional justice.

The double structure of the German Federal Constitutional Court is also unknown to those East-Central European constitutional courts which adopted the German model.[26] Their structure either follows the simple and united model of the Italian Constitutional Court and of the US Supreme Court, both of which sit in full court in every case, or represents a middle ground between this and the German solution. In the latter group of constitutional courts the most important cases are decided by the plenary session, while the others are assigned to panels composed of three or five judges.[27] Usually, the constitutional review of parliamentary acts and international treaties is reserved for the plenary session, whereas the panels have a residual competence. The Polish Constitutional Tribunal is an exception, as it decides on the constitutionality of parliamentary acts and international treaties in plenary session only at certain conditions. A case is decided by the plenum convened it is of particular complexity, and upon proposal by the Tribunal's president or a panel, or if the particularly complex aspect is concerned with financial outlays not provided for in the budgetary act; finally, when the adjudicating panel intends to depart from the legal opinion expressed in the Tribunal's judicial decision given earlier in plenary session.[28]

An interesting solution is offered by the Romanian model which represents a unique combination of the French and the Italian constitutional courts.[29] The Court's composition is clearly inspired by the French Constitutional Council,[30] and cases of preventive review are always decided in plenary session. On the other hand, in the first years, cases referred by ordinary judges were assigned to chambers of three judges, whose decisions could be appealed to a chamber of five judges. This system of internal appeal, however, generated inconsistencies in

26 About the predominance of the German model in Central Europe see Allan F Tatham, *Central European Constitutional Courts in the Face of EU Membership* (Brill 2013) 41 ff.

27 The panels are composed of three or five members both in Poland (art 25 of the Constitutional Tribunal Act) and in Hungary (art 49 of the Constitutional Court Act and art 5 of the Rules of Procedure). However, in Hungary only five-member panels have been set up so far. In Croatia there are five and six-member panels (art 68 of the Constitutional Court Act). In all the other East-Central European constitutional courts they are composed of three members.

28 Art 25(1) point 1.e of the Constitutional Tribunal Act.

29 See Chapter 4, Section 4.2.

30 The Romanian Constitutional Court is composed of nine members. Three are appointed by the head of the state, three are elected by the upper and three by the lower house of the Parliament. This method of appointment is not identical to the French solution, where two thirds of the judges are appointed by the presidents of the two houses and not by the houses themselves. In Romania constitutional judges are elected by absolute majority. Another similarity with the French model is that one third of the members are replaced every three years. See art 5 of the Romanian Constitutional Court Act. On the French Constitutional Council's composition see Alec Stone, *The Birth of Judicial Politics in France: The Constitutional Council in Comparative Perspective* (Oxford UP 1992) 46–59.

the Court's case-law and was abolished by the legislature in 1997. Since then, all cases have been decided in plenary session.[31]

As with the *Kammern* of the German Federal Constitutional Court, most of the panels of European constitutional courts, where they exist, decide by unanimity. The German solution is understandable if we consider that the panels operate as a filter and decide on the merits only when the case is manifestly founded or unfounded. Clearly, foundedness or unfoundedness is not manifest if there is a disagreement between the judges. The same logic is applied by the Czech, Croatian, Latvian and Slovenian laws which assign to three-member panels the decision on the admissibility of constitutional complaints and require unanimity.[32] The Austrian Constitutional Court, which does not hear constitutional complaints against judicial decisions, also applies this rule with regard to all cases. Manifestly unfounded petitions are to be rejected by smaller panels and unanimity is required. However, dismissal of the application on formal or procedural grounds does not require a unanimous decision.[33] The Hungarian Constitutional Court is an exception, as it allows the five-member panels to make their decisions by majority. The reason may lie in the fact that Hungarian panels are not simple filters of constitutional complaints (even if they have this function as well), but they have residual competence. All cases not reserved for the plenary session are decided in panels. In a similar manner, panels of other constitutional courts decide on the constitutionality of sub-legislative acts and have other residual competences.[34] From a legal-technical point of view, the constitutional review of sub-legislative acts is not necessarily less complex than questions of constitutionality of legislative acts.

Even if the law allows publication of dissents for the panels, the actual practice may be different. In Hungary, three-member panels could issue judgments by majority vote,[35] but in practice they never did so. If there was disagreement

31 See more in detail in Renate Weber, 'The Romanian Constitutional Court: In Search of Its Own Identity' in Wojciech Sadurski (ed), *Constitutional Justice, East and West* (Kluwer Law International 2002) 283, 287–89.

32 Art 55c of the Slovenian Constitutional Court Act and art 68(3) of the Croatian Constitutional Court Act. In Croatia also decisions on the merits of constitutional complaints have to be taken by unanimity in the six-member panels. See art 23(2) of the Rules of Procedure. In Latvia art 20(7)1 provides that if one of the three members of the panel considers the petition admissible, a decision on the merits must then be taken by the plenary session, to which the case is transferred. The three-member panels of the Czech Constitutional Court also decides cases on the merits, but unanimity is required only for the rejection of manifestly ill-founded petitions. Arts 19(2) and 43(2) of the Czech Constitutional Court Act.

33 Arts 19 (3)–(4) and 31 of the Austrian Constitutional Court Act. The Austrian law, instead of providing for panels of a given number of judges, determines a lower quorum for certain types of cases (the president and four other judges, art 7(2) of Constitutional Court Act).

34 These other courts are the Croatian, the Polish, the Czech, the Slovak and the Spanish constitutional courts. See Table 2.1.

35 See art 25(3) of the previous Constitutional Court Act (Act no XXXII of 1989). Art 49(4) of the new Constitutional Court Act, which entered into force on 1 January 2012, requires unanimity for the decisions of three-member panels, while upholds the majority rule for five-member panels.

Table 2.1 The internal structure of Western and East-Central European constitutional courts

	Plenary session	*Panels*	*Single-judge formations*
Albania	(nine judges) on the merits always (art. 133 Const. and art. 20 CC Act) – quorum: two-thirds (six judges) – art 32 CC Act	*three-member* panels on admissibility (art 31 CC Act)	no
Austria	(14 judges) as a rule (art 7(1) CC Act)	smaller panels of at least five members (art 7(2) CC Act): – rejection of a manifestly unfounded complaint – dismissal on formal or procedural grounds – dropping of the proceeding (withdrawal or accepted complaint) – motions for execution of the decisions – motions to define the costs in dropped cases(art 19 CC Act)	no
Belgium	(12 judges) art 56 CC Act: 1) in organisational and disciplinary cases 2) on request by the president 3) on request by two of seven judges of the bench	– deliberation in *seven-member panels* (art 55 CC Act): composed of three Dutch-speaking, three French-speaking judge and the president of the linguistic group whose language is that of the case to be heard – preliminary procedure in *three-member* panels (art 69 CC Act): examines admissibility, manifest foundedness and unfoundedness and jurisdiction	no
Bosnia and Herzegovina	(nine judges) art 9 CC Act – conflicts of competence – referrals by ordinary courts – challenge against legislation on the basis of art IV(3)(f) Const.	Grand Chamber (art 10 CC Act): residual competence *three-member* panel (art 12 CC Act): requests for interim measures and administrative issues	no

(*Continued*)

Table 2.1 (Continued)

	Plenary session	*Panels*	*Single-judge formations*
Bulgaria	(12 judges) always – art 151(1) Const.: ruling by absolute majority	none	no
Czech Republic	(15 judges) art 11(2) CC Act	four *three-member panels* (art 15 CC Act) – the President and the two Vice-Presidents are not a permanent member of any panel – residual competence – rejecting manifestly unfounded petitions (art 43 CC Act)	rejection of a petition on formal grounds (art 43(1) CC Act)
Croatia	art 27 CC Act art 10 Rules of Proc	– *six-member panels* on const. complaints (art 68 CC Act) and impeachment of judges (arts 97–98) – *three-member panels*: reject const. complaint on procedural grounds (art 68), decide electoral disputes (art 92)	no
France	(nine judges) always – quorum of seven judges (art 14 CC Act)	three *three-member panels* for prior examination of cases on electoral issues (art 36 CC Act)	no
Germany	(16 judges) – resolution of conflicts between the two senates (art 16(1) CC Act) – issuing rules on judicial administration (arts 1(3), 7a(2), 14(4) and 105 CC Act)	– two eight-member permanent panels (*Senates*):as a rule – *three-member panels*: admissibility of applications by lower ordinary judges (art 81a CC Act), admissibility of constitutional complaints (art 93b CC Act)	no

Hungary	(15 judges) (art 50(2) CC Act) – constitutional review of legislative acts and international treaties, – preventive review, – constitutional interpretation, – review of constitutional amendments, etc. – other important cases on proposal by the President of the Court or five judges *Rules of Procedure*, art 2(2): – *ex officio* procedure, – omission of the legislator, etc.	*five-member panels*: residual competence (art 50(1), CC Act) The plenary session may also create *three-member panels* (none set up yet).	rejection of a petition on formal grounds or for manifest unfoundedness (art 55(5) CC Act) – only two judges act as solo judges at a time, appointed for three months (art 11 Rules of Proc)
Italy	(15 judges) always (art 16(1) CC Act)	none	no
Kosovo	(nine judges) on the merits always (art 19 CC Act: quorum of seven judges)	one *three-member review panel*: filters referrals on formal grounds (art 22 CC Act) – for refusal unanimity required	no
Latvia	(seven judges)as a rule two *three-member panels* on the admissibility of petitions → may also reject manifestly unfounded complaints (art 20 CC Act)	no	
Lithuania	(nine judges) always	none	no
Luxembourg	(nine judges) never	deliberation always in *5-member* panels (art 4 CC Act)	no
Macedonia	(nine judges) always (art 6 RoP: quorum of six judges)	none	no
Montenegro	(seven judges) always (art 29 CC Act)	none	no

(*Continued*)

Table 2.1 (Continued)

	Plenary session	*Panels*	*Single-judge formations*
Poland	(15 judges) – conflicts between central state organs – vesting the temporary performance of the duties of the President of the Republic of Poland in the Marshal of the Sejm – constitutionality of the purposes and/or activity of political parties – preventive review – cases of a particularly complicated nature (art 25(1) CC Act)	*five-member panels:* – constitutionality of statutes and international treaties – conformity of statutes to ratified international agreements whose ratification requires prior consent granted by statute *three-member panels:* – conformity of other normative acts to the Constitution, ratified international agreements and statutes – complaints in relation to the refusal to proceed with the application for the confirmation of the conformity of other normative acts to the Constitution, ratified international agreements and statutes as well as complaints concerning constitutional infringements – challenging of a judge (art 25(1) CC Act)	no
Portugal	(13 judges) a) preventive review (art 59 CC Act) b) on order by the president, with the agreement of the Court: – if it is necessary to avoid a divergence in the case-law – because of the nature of the question to be judged (art 79-A(1) CC Act) c) appeal from the panels by the complainant or the state attorney): if decision contradicts a precedent (art 79-D(1) CC Act) d) removal from office and dismissal of the President of the Republic (arts 90(2) and 91(2) CC Act) e) general balloting of election (art 100(4) CC Act) f) other minor competences (arts 102-C(4), 103-A(3), 107(2), 112(2) CC Act)	*five-member panels*: three panels, each one comprising the president or the vice-president – residual competence preliminary and summary decisions (art 78-A CC Act) can be appealed before the conference (composed of the president or the vice-president, the rapporteur judge and one other judge)	no

Romania	(nine judges) always	*Until 1997: three-member panels* decided references from ordinary judges	no
Serbia	(15 judges) list of competences in art 42a CC Act	two *Grand Chambers*: composed of seven members and the President (art 42b CC Act) *three-member* panels: (art 42c CC Act) – dismissing constitutional complaints on procedural grounds – other procedural decisions	no
Slovakia	(13 judges) art 131(1) Const. – declaring the post of President of the Republic vacant – impeachment of the President of the Republic – constitutional review of legislative, sub-legislative acts and international treaties – decision on the conformity of legislative and sub-legislative acts with international treaties – constitutional review of referendum subjects – interpretation of the Constitution – constitutional review of elections – decision on the conformity of a declaration of state of emergency – impeachment of judges and the General Prosecutor – disciplinary proceedings against own members	*three-member panels*: residual competence (art 131(2) Const.)	no
Slovenia	(nine judges) – constitutional complaints on the merits and all other cases	*three-member panel:* on the admissibility of constitutional complaints, on the protection of the privacy of the petitioner(s), and on penalty payment for abuse of rights (art 54 CC Act) – by unanimity (art 55c CC Act)	decision on the discontinuation of proceedings due to the withdrawal of a constitutional complaint (art 54(3) CC Act)

(*Continued*)

Table 2.1 (Continued)

	Plenary session	*Panels*	*Single-judge formations*
Spain	(12 judges) art 10(1) CC Act: – constitutionality of international treaties; – constitutional appeals against laws (may be deferred to the panels); – reserved questions of constitutionality; – conflicts of competence between the state and autonomous communities or between the autonomous communities; – actions by the Government against decisions of autonomous communities; – conflicts in defence of the local self-government – conflicts between the constitutional bodies of the state – annulments in defence of the Court's jurisdiction provided by art 4(3)	two *six-member panels* (Salas) appointed by the plenary session (*Pleno*) (art 7(1) CC Act) *three-member panels* (*Secciones*) decide on admissibility and appeals of constitutional protection (amparo) deferred by the appropriate panel (art 8(1) CC Act)	no

between the judges they used to refer the case to the plenary session.[36] There was just one concurring opinion published in a case decided by a panel, and authored by Judge Zlinszky. The peculiarity of this case is that Judge Zlinszky was also the author of the opinion of the court.[37] Obviously his separate opinion did not state different reasons for the judgment, but it supplemented the panel's opinion with additional grounds for the annulment of the challenged provision.[38]

2. The prominent figures of the decision-making process

2.1. The president of the court

In those constitutional courts that embraced the publicity of internal disagreements, the traditional civil law principle of impersonality of judicial decisions is losing its strength. In these courts the personal views of the single judges are increasingly given consideration. Consequently, I will first examine the position of the judicial panels' most prominent members, their tasks and role in the decision-making process.

As regards the most prominent members of the judicial panel, constitutional courts differ considerably from the US Supreme Court. Even if, as previously indicated, these organs are comparable to each other, it is important to bear in mind certain differences. First, the US Supreme Court is at the top of the hierarchy of the country's entire court system, while a constitutional court co-exists with a supreme court and has special competences. Furthermore, the latter, technically, is not part of the hierarchy of a country's court system.[39] Consequently, the president of a constitutional court is a relatively less important figure in the legal life of a country than the Chief Justice of the United States, even if s/he still presides over the court that reviews the constitutionality of legislation and decides other questions of constitutional importance. Moreover, s/he definitely plays a key role in the life of the court s/he presides. As we shall see in more detail further, the personality of the president of the court has had a great impact on the practice of opinion-writing, just as in the United States.

It is a well-known fact that the Chief Justice of the United States is appointed by the President with the advice and consent of the Senate, the upper house of the Congress.[40] The majority of the presidents of European constitutional courts, on the other hand, are chosen by the judges from among themselves. The former starts his career in the court as its chief, while the latter are first appointed as ordinary members of the court and become presidents later for a shorter term. Thus,

36 According to Judge Y his panel referred approx. 3–5% of the cases to the plenary session because of internal disagreement. Interview with Judge Y (Budapest, 14 November 2006).

37 Decision no 44/1991 (VIII.28.) AB of 15 August 1991.

38 On concurring opinions of Hungarian constitutional judges see more in Chapter 4, Section 5.4.

39 See Chapter 1, Section 3.

40 Art II, Section 2 of the US Constitution.

they often stay on the court after their presidential mandate ends, if this moment does not coincide with the end of their term as a member of the court. This is true even when the president of the court is appointed not by the court itself but by the head of the state or by the parliament. She is usually chosen from among the sitting members of the court.[41]

As regards the role of the president, the Bundesverfassungsgericht is again unique in the European panorama. The special internal structure of the German Court, divided into two permanent panels,[42] seems to give the president less power compared to the Chief Justice of the United States and the presidents of East-Central European constitutional courts. The president of the Bundesverfassungsgericht only presides over one of the two Senates. The other Senate is presided by the vice-president of the Court.[43] Consequently, the possible influence of the Court's president is limited to only one of the panels. Moreover, since there are three *Kammern* composed of three judges within each senate and the senate has only eight members, one judge has to be part of two chambers. During the 2000s, the president and the vice-president assumed this task in their respective senate. On the one hand, this practice increases their role as filters of constitutional complaints, a function performed by the chambers.[44] On the other hand, however, it also increases their workload, so they act as rapporteur in fewer cases. This second circumstance limits their influence on the overall case-law.[45]

The Belgian model is also unique in its internal organisation due to its linguistic demarcation. As indicated earlier, the Belgian Constitutional Court's internal organisation reflects the division of the country between French-speaking and Dutch-speaking citizens.[46] Each linguistic group within the Court chooses its own president. One of the two presidents represents the Court in its external relations on a rotary basis, but in the decision-making process they are on equal footing.[47]

The casting vote (or presidential veto) is a good indicator of power of the court president. Its presence usually indicates a strong presidential role. In European constitutional courts we can find two different solutions in case of tie votes. The first is that the president casts the deciding vote (for example in Austria,[48] Belgium, Bosnia and Herzegovina,[49] France, Hungary, and Italy), so her/his vote weighs

41 See Table 2.2.
42 See Section 1.1.
43 Arts 9(1) and 15(1) BVerfGG. Out of eight presidents of the German Court's history between 1951 and 2006 six presided over the First Senate and two the Second Senate. Quint (n 21) 1856. Currently, the president is a member of the Second Senate (Andreas Vosskuhle, in office since March 2010).
44 See Section 1.1.
45 Quint (n 21) 1863.
46 See text to nn 22–23.
47 Arts 56(2), 56(4) and 59 of the Belgian Constitutional Court Act.
48 The Austrian practice is peculiar. As a rule, the president, who sits in all cases, does not participate in the voting. He does so only if there is a tie of votes, and in this case his vote is decisive (art 31 of the Austrian Constitutional Court Act).
49 In the Bosnian Constitutional Court the president has a casting vote as an *extrema ratio.* In the event of a tie, first the Court has to postpone the decision-making for no more than six

Table 2.2 Methods of appointment and term of office of constitutional court presidents

	Appointment by the Parliament	*Appointment by the Head of the State*	*Election by the members of the Constitutional Court*
Albania	Art 125(4) Const. and art 7 CC Act: Appointed by the President of the Republic with the consent of the Assembly – for three years		
Austria	Art 147(2) Const.: appointment by the Federal President on the recommendation of the Federal Government		
Belgium	Art 33 CC Act: two presidents (one of each language group, elected by the respective language group) Art 54 CC Act: Presidency of the Court assumed by each president for a one-year term on a rotating basis		
Bosnia and Herzegovina			Arts 81 and 83 CC Act – by secret ballot – rotation between the judges appointed by the different entities Art 84 CC Act – for three years
Bulgaria			Art 147(4) Const. – by secret ballot – for three years, re-eligible Art 7 CC Act – by simple majority
Czech Republic		Art 62(e) Const. Art 2 CC Act	

(*Continued*)

Table 2.2 (Continued)

	Appointment by the Parliament	*Appointment by the Head of the State*	*Election by the members of the Constitutional Court*
Croatia			Art 125 Const. Art 15 CC Act – by secret ballot – for four years – by absolute majority
France	Art 56(3) Const.		
Germany	Art 9(1) CC Act: The Bundestag and the Bundesrat shall alternately elect the President and the Vice-President		
Hungary	Since 2012: Art 24(8) FL: the Parliament from among the members of the Court by two-thirds majority		Until 2011: Art 4(2) CC Act – for three years, – re-eligible
Italy			Art 135(5) Const. – for three years – re-eligible Art 7(1) Rules of Proc. – by secret ballot
Kosovo			Art 114(5) Const. – for three years – by secret ballot
Latvia			Art 12 CC Act – by secret ballot and absolute majority – for three years

Lithuania	Art 103(2) Const. – by the Parliament (Seimas) upon submission by the President of the Republic – from among the sitting members of the Court		
Luxembourg		Art 3(2) CC Act: – appointment by the Grand Duke Art 3(5) CC Act: – the President of the Supreme Court is at the same time the President of the Constitutional Court	
Macedonia			Art 109(3) Const. – for three years, not re-eligible Art 7 Rules of Procedure – by two-thirds majority and secret voting
Montenegro		Art 153(3) Const. – for three years	
Poland			Art 194(2) Const. – candidates proposed by the General Assembly of the Const. Court Art 15 CC Act – candidates nominated by the General Assembly from among the judges of the Tribunal – by secret ballot
Portugal		Art 222(4) Const.	
Romania			Art 142(4) Const. – by secret ballot – for three years Art 7 CC Act – by majority vote – re-eligible

(*Continued*)

Table 2.2 (Continued)

	Appointment by the Parliament	*Appointment by the Head of the State*	*Election by the members of the Constitutional Court*
Serbia			Art 172(6) Const. – for three years – by secret ballot Art 23(2) CC Act – by majority vote
Slovakia		Art 135 Const. – from among the sitting members of the Court	
Slovenia			Art 163(3) Const. – three-year term Art 10 CC Act – elected by secret ballot
Spain		Art 160 Const. – appointment by the King from among the judges, on the recommendation of the plenum of the Court – for three years Art 9 CC Act – by secret ballot – re-eligible only once	

more than that of the other members of the panel. This is sometimes also called presidential veto. The second is that a constitutional challenge cannot be sustained by a tie vote, in other words the challenged law cannot be declared unconstitutional in absence of a majority (for example in Germany and Latvia). Finally, in some systems there is no explicit rule for the circumstance of tie votes (for example in Poland and Romania), which implies that the majority rule applies.[50]

A court president may, however, play an important role even without the presidential veto. In the United States, the Chief Justice is, in theory, *primus inter partes* whose vote has the same value as that of the other eight members of the Court. However, in practice, he plays a very important role in the Court's life.[51] He is the Supreme Court's public face and voice, as he represents the body in public relations. More importantly, he has the power to assign cases to the single Justices. This means that he decides who will be the author of the opinion of the Court. This, in practice, allows him to influence the outcome of a case. It should be underlined that in the US Supreme Court the case is assigned to a Justice after the first voting only, and the Chief Justice is requested to choose among those Justices who were part of the majority (herself/himself included, if that is the case). If s/he voted against the decision, however, s/he loses his right to assign the case.[52] This exception has two important consequences. First, certain Chief Justices used their power to assign what they perceived to be pivotal cases to themselves.[53] Second, the Chief Justice may circumvent the rule by tactical voting. If s/he does not want to lose her/his power to assign the case, s/he can vote with the majority, even if s/he actually disagrees with it.

Also, roughly half of the presidents of the considered European constitutional courts have the power to choose the rapporteur judge,[54] even if in practice they rarely have complete discretion. There are different methods for appointing the rapporteur judge. In Belgian practice, cases are assigned on the basis of a complex rotation system established by law. In German practice this is done on the basis of the judges' expertise,[55] which is the case also in Austria, even if it is not required

---

months. Since all judges have the duty to vote, this situation can occur only if one judge is prevented from sitting in the case due to prolonged illness. Art 42(3) and (5) of the Bosnian Constitutional Court Act.

50 See Table 2.3.

51 Chief Justice Charles Evans Hughes once suggested that 'by virtue of the distinctive function of the Court [the Chief Justice of the United States] is the most important judicial officer in the world', as quoted in *New York Times* (24 June 1969) 25, cited in Henry J Abraham, *The Judicial Process* (7th edn, Oxford UP 1998) 215.

52 In that case it is the Senior Associate Justice on the side of the majority who either writes the opinion of the Court herself/himself or assigns it to one of the other members among the majority. Abraham (n 51) 221.

53 This practice characterised the presidency of Chief Justices Taft and Hughes, but not that of Burger. Peter G Fish, 'Office of the Chief Justice' in Kermit L Hall (ed), *The Oxford Companion to the Supreme Court of the United States* (2nd edn, Oxford UP 2005) 162, 163.

54 See Table 3.

55 See Kommers (n 17) 176–77. The Federal Constitutional Court Act provides that the panels decide at the beginning of every term upon the division of the proceedings and constitutional complaints among the rapporteurs (art 15a(2)).

Table 2.3 Powers of the presidents of Western and East-Central European constitutional courts

	Casting vote	*Choosing the rapporteur judge*	*Sitting in all cases*
Albania	No (art 72(2) CC Act)	Yes (art 27(2) CC Act)	No (but on the merits yes)
Austria	Yes – but she votes only in case of a tie of votes. (art 31 CC Act)	Yes – among the permanent reporters elected by the plenum (art 16 CC Act)	Yes – even in the panels (arts 3(1) and 7 CC Act)
Belgium	Yes (art 56(4) CC Act)	No – rotation system established by law (art 68 CC Act)	Yes – even in the panels (art 59 CC Act)
Bosnia and Herzegovina	Yes (art 42(5) CC Act)	No – in alphabetic order, but the president can change it (art 24(1) CC Act)	Yes – even in the panels (art 12(1) CC Act)
Bulgaria	No (art 151(1) Const.)	Yes (art 8(1)(4) CC Act)	Yes (no panels)
Czech Republic	No, but the chairperson of the panel yes (art 21(2) CC Act)	No – random distribution, but he distributes the caseload among panels (art 16 CC Act)	No
Croatia	No	Yes (art 41 CC Act)	No
France	Yes (art 56(3) Const.)	Yes (art 37 CC Act)	Yes (no panels)
Germany	No (art 15(4) CC Act)	No	No
Hungary	Yes (art 48(5) CC Act)	Yes (art 17(1)(e) CC Act)	No
Italy	Yes (art 17(3) CC Act)	Yes (art 7(1) CC Act)	Yes (no panels)
Kosovo	No	No – system of random raw (Rule 8 of RoP)	No (but on the merits yes)
Latvia	No (art 30(3) CC Act)	Yes (art 22(1) CC Act)	No (but on the merits yes)

Lithuania	No (since 2015)[56]	Yes (art 24 and 27 CC Act)	Yes (no panels)
Macedonia	No – majority rule (art 25(4) RoP)	No – alphabetic order (art 17(3) RoP)	Yes (no panels)
Montenegro	No – majority rule (art 151(1) Const.)	No – alphabetic order (art 42(1) RoP)	Yes (no panels)
Poland	No explicit rule	Yes (art 25(3) CC Act)	No
Portugal	Yes (art 42(3) CC Act)	No (art 50(1) CC Act)	No
Romania	No explicit rule	Yes (art 9(1)(c) CC Act)	Yes (no panels)
Serbia	No – majority rule (art 58(4) RoP)	No – assignment according to a preset algorithm (art 41 RoP)	No (but on the merits yes)
Slovakia	Yes (art 28(2) CC Act)	No – random choice (art 29(1) CC Act)	No
Slovenia	No	No – in alphabetic order (art 11(4) RoP)	No (but on the merits yes)
Spain	Yes (art 90(1) CC Act)	No	No (presides the plenum and the First Chamber only) (art 7 CC Act)

56 The casting vote of the president was abolished in 2015 as a consequence of the modification of the rule on the calculation of majority. While before 2015 a majority of the participating judges was required, today the majority of all judges (thus five out of nine) is required for a decision to be adopted (art 19(3) of the Constitutional Court Act). Consequently, a tie vote is not possible anymore and the casting vote of the president has lost its purpose. I thank Vaidas Lubauskas, Head of the Division of Legal Research of the Lithuanian Constitutional Court, for this explanation.

by the law which is silent on how this presidential power shall be exercised. The president of the Austrian Constitutional Court, however, cannot assign a case to herself/himself, as s/he must choose among the so-called 'permanent reporters' elected by the plenum.[57]

A further indicator of presidential power is if s/he sits in all cases decided by the court. If s/he does, s/he can clearly have a greater influence on the court's jurisprudence. It depends primarily on the internal court structure whether the president sits in all cases. In courts which take all decisions in full court, the president can play a more influential role. This is the case, for example, in Bulgaria, France, Italy, and Romania.[58] However, there are also constitutional courts in which the president participates in the decision-making both in the plenum and in the smaller panels. This is the case in Austria, Belgium, and Bosnia and Herzegovina. In the remaining constitutional courts the president does not sit in all cases, but since in many of these courts the smaller panels only decide admissibility and other procedural issues, the president still participates in all decisions on the merits. This is the case, for example, in Albania, Latvia, and Serbia. Finally, those courts where panels may decide cases on the merits, and the participation of the president is not required, the latter has fewer occasions to influence the jurisprudence than other court presidents. This is the case in Germany, Hungary, and Spain.

If we consider all three examined indicators of presidential power, it seems that the most powerful presidents are those of the Austrian, French and Italian constitutional courts. Interestingly, none of these courts allow for the publication of dissent. Thus, while they are bound by the principle of collegiality and the greatest possible extent of secrecy on the court's decision-making, the president is considered to be a *primus inter partes*, who has certain privileges compared with her/his colleagues during her/his presidential mandate. While the presidents of the French Constitutional Council served for seven years on average, on the Italian Constitutional Court the president is appointed for a shorter term of three years, and it is an unwritten custom that the most senior sitting member of the court is chosen.[59] Consequently, Italian constitutional court presidents usually do not fill their entire mandate of three years. On the other hand, the Czech and German Constitutional Courts' presidents seem to be the less powerful. They do not have a casting vote, cannot choose the rapporteur judge, and do not participate in the decision of every case.

While the aforementioned rules offer a good ground for a guess about the role and influence of a court's president, other factors, such as a particular president's personality, also come into play. The Hungarian experience can illustrate this point. While the three examined indicators do not suggest that the Hungarian Constitutional Court's president would be an especially powerful one, the Court's first president, László Sólyom, played a very important role in the

57 See more below in Section 2.2.

58 See Tables 2.1 and 2.3.

59 Interview with Judge Marta Cartabia (Rome, Italy, 15 September 2016).

Court's life and left his mark on Hungarian constitutional justice.[60] The president may also influence the practice of dissenting opinions. In Hungary, statistics show a clear increase in the number of separate opinions from 1998, after Sólyom left the Court.[61] According to a former member of the Hungarian Constitutional Court, President Sólyom, just like the famous Chief Justice Marshall of the US Supreme Court, had set the goal of delivering mostly unanimous decisions and his efforts can be seen in the statistics.[62] After the appointment of János Németh as President, the number of separate opinions doubled. Despite his strong and dominant personality, President Sólyom never wanted to exercise his casting vote as provided by law.[63] András Holló, instead, during his short presidency, made use of it once. In that case, in which the Court had been requested by the head of state to interpret the constitutional provisions determining the powers of that office, the discussion came to a halt. The Court was composed of ten members at the time, and the judges split evenly over the decision.[64] President Holló supported the opinion of fellow judges with an expertise in public law, and his vote decided the issue. In similar cases President Sólyom postponed the debate until a majority was achieved.[65]

2.2. *The most prominent member of the decision-making panel: the rapporteur judge and the opinion-writer*

A majority of the presidents of European constitutional courts enjoy, as the US Chief Justice, the power to assign cases.[66] This way, they choose the so-called 'rapporteur judge'.[67] Within these constitutional courts, in fact, the cases are

60 See Chapter 4, Sections 5.5 and 5.6.
61 Table 4.3 in Chapter 4, Section 5.3.
62 Interview with Judge I (Budapest, Hungary, 27 April 2007). A similar policy was pursued by President Paczolay after his appointment in July 2008, which in part explains the remarkably low dissent rate in 2010. See Chapter 4, Section 5.1 and Table 4.3.
63 Art 30(3) of the old Constitutional Court Act. The new Constitutional Court Act has upheld the same solution (art 48(5)).
64 Decision no 62/2003 (XII.15.) AB of 15 December 2003. This case was particular because eight judges out of ten expressed their separate opinion, three concurring in and five dissenting from the judgment. The concurring judges (Kiss, Czúcz and Kukorelli), however, just supplemented the majority's opinion and did not state alternative reasons for the decision. The five dissenters were Judges Bagi, Erdei, Harmathy, Strausz and Tersztyánszkyné.
65 During Németh's Presidency the problem never emerged. Interview with Judge M (Budapest, Hungary, 26 September 2007).
66 An exception is represented by the Constitutional Court of Kosovo, where the president appoints the rapporteur without choosing her/him. The rapporteur judges are assigned to a case by a system of random draw. See Rule 8 of the Rules of Procedure.
67 See above Table 2.3 on the powers of constitutional court presidents. While this office takes on different names in the English translation of the various laws (for example, 'judge-informer' in the Macedonian Rules of Procedure or 'reporter' in the Austrian Constitutional Court Act), they all refer to the same function. I chose to use the term 'rapporteur', which is borrowed from French but very common in English as well.

assigned before any discussion, immediately after being considered admissible. Thus the office of the rapporteur judge is different from that of the US opinion-writer. The former is the 'master' of the case from the very beginning and during the whole procedure, while the latter assumes that role only after the first voting.[68] The author of the opinion of the US Supreme Court is, therefore, not a central figure of the discussion of the case. All justices participate in the discussion in the same way. The rapporteur judge, conversely, is vested with the task of presenting the case to the court. To this purpose, s/he collects materials and information, prepares a draft judgment before the voting, and keeps contacts with the petitioner.[69] Thus s/he also makes important procedural decisions.

Nonetheless, the difference between the two models might not be as significant as it seems at first sight. Cohen, in her comparative analysis of the internal organisational cultures of French supreme courts, the US Supreme Court and the two European courts, demonstrated that both models may present institutional obstacles to deliberation.[70] She calls these two models *ex ante* and *ex post* deliberations. In the former, prevalent in the French and European courts, where a rapporteur judge is designated at an early stage of the proceedings, judges draft and deliberate the court's opinion *before* the case is orally argued and scheduled for the conference meeting. In the latter model, typical of Anglo-American supreme courts, judges do most of the deliberative work *after* the case has been orally argued and a vote on the merits has taken place at the conference. According to Cohen, both models diverge from the deliberative ideal in at least three ways. First, decision-makers are not always on equal footing. Some court members are considered worthier than others, for example because they have a specific expertise, as rapporteur judges often do.[71] Second, collective face-to-face meetings are relatively rare events. The deliberative importance of the conference has been overstated, in both *ex ante* and *ex post* courts.[72] Third, docket pressure sometimes interferes with full-fledged deliberations. This is especially true for *ex ante* courts that typically have mandatory jurisdiction.[73]

68 William P McLauchlan, 'Assignment and Writing of Opinions' in Hall (n 53) 705–6.

69 András Holló, former judge of the Hungarian Constitutional Court, compares these tasks to the activity of a solo judge. See András Holló, *Az Alkotmánybíróság. Alkotmánybíráskodás Magyarországon* [The Constitutional Court: Constitutional Justice in Hungary] (Útmutató Kiadó 1998) 54.

70 Cohen (n 6).

71 In this sense, courts are elitist not because judges are unelected, but because they constitute a professional environment revolving around expert knowledge. Cohen (n 6) 443.

72 In *ex ante* courts, the conference is an end point. By the time they get together, the judges have already pre-deliberated. In *ex post* courts, the conference is a starting point. Judges begin to deliberate in small groups afterwards. As Cohen explains, in both judicial cultures the conference remains a forum for decision-making, but not so much for deliberating. In *ex ante* courts, the conference serves to confer a collective stamp of approval on an opinion prepared by a sub-group of the panel. In *ex post* courts, the conference serves to determine a majority in favour of a disposition and to assign the writing of opinions. Cohen (n 6) 447.

73 Cohen (n 6) 449–52.

Cohen did not, however, involve any Kelsenian constitutional court in her study. The French Constitutional Council and the two European courts differ from other constitutional courts in many respects. Thus, it is questionable to what extent do other European constitutional courts fit within these two models. For example, in the Bundesverfassungsgericht the rapporteur judge's pre-conference memo does not include a draft opinion, only a suggested solution (whether the challenged act is unconstitutional or not). According to a former member of the Court, many judges read the full file of the case, not only the rapporteur's memo.[74] Moreover, in most cases there is no need for a formal voting, because the result emerges clearly from the discussions.[75] A similar practice is followed in the Italian Constitutional Court.[76]

In the *ex ante* courts, as indicated earlier, the rapporteur is chosen either by the president of the court or on the basis of a pre-established system, sometimes even randomly. In Belgian practice, for example, as mentioned earlier, the distribution of cases is not random but it is made according to a complex rotation system provided by law. In Czech practice, on the other hand, cases are distributed randomly in order to avoid subjective choices and any speculation over the probable future opinion of the rapporteur judge.[77] The Slovenian Constitutional Court offers a third alternative: an administrative session prepares the Court's schedule twice a year.[78] In Austria, where the assignment of cases is a presidential prerogative, and the law does not provide for any criteria to be followed, in practice the rapporteur judge is chosen considering the specific experience and expertise of the judges and ensuring a fair distribution of the workload.[79] As a rule, cases can be assigned only to judges who assume also the office of 'permanent reporter', and only in exceptional cases may the president choose another member of the court.[80] Permanent reporters are elected by the members of the Court from among themselves for a three-year period. Today, actually, all judges and the vice-president act as permanent reporters. Re-election is allowed and is, in fact,

74 Grimm (n 20) 49.
75 Grimm (n 20) 50.
76 Gustavo Zagrebelsky, 'La Corte costituzionale italiana' in Pasquale Pasquino and Barbara Randazzo (eds), *Come decidono le corti costituzionali (e altre Corti)* [How Constitutional Courts Make Decisions] (Giuffrè 2009) 59, 78 ff.
77 Art 40 of the Czech Constitutional Court Act. The full plenum gives an abstract guideline on distribution and the President issues a concrete work schedule accordingly. Judges do not specialise which means that the schedule merely states that the cases are distributed in the alphabetical order, plus deals with situations of newly appointed judges and judges who are not present for a longer period (for example for medical issues). I thank Ľubomír Majerčík from the Analytics Department of the Czech Constitutional Court for this information. (In Czech terminology the rapporteur judge is called *soudce zpravodaj*.)
78 Art 11 of the Slovenian Constitutional Court's Rules of Procedure.
79 Art 16 of the Austrian Constitutional Court Act and the official website of the Court at <www.vfgh.gv.at/kompetenzen-und-verfahren/decision_process.en.html> accessed 18 January 2017.
80 However, the law does not provide for any definition of 'exceptional case'. Art 16 of the Austrian Constitutional Court Act.

a common practice.[81] In Germany, too, rapporteurs are chosen on the basis of the experience and expertise and, like in Austria, it has not been imposed by the legislature, but rather established by practice.[82]

In continental European court practice the author of the opinion of the court is usually, although not always, the rapporteur judge. If the latter remains in the minority, s/he is allowed to refuse to write the judgment and or the task may be passed to a judge of the majority.[83] In such a case the draft already written by the rapporteur, originally meant to be the opinion of the court, may then become a dissenting opinion.[84] In most cases, however, the rapporteur judge does not remain in the minority.[85] The reason may lay in the fact that the president usually chooses the rapporteur judge according the judges' area of specialisation, so the rapporteur is an expert on the issue. In addition, the pressure of time often prompts judges to defer to the rapporteur's opinion.[86] In these circumstances the

81 See the official website of the Court <https://www.vfgh.gv.at/verfassungsgerichtshof/organisation/the_courts_bench.en.html> accessed 26 September 2016. Permanent reporters earn almost double their fellow judges (art 4(1) of the Constitutional Court Act).

82 Art 15a(2) of the German Federal Constitutional Court Act simply states that prior to the beginning of a business year the panel shall decide, for the duration of that year, upon the division of proceedings and constitutional complaints among the rapporteurs.

83 In Portugal, for example, the Constitutional Court Act provides clearly that if the solution proposed by the rapporteur is not accepted, the judgment is drawn up by another judge (art 59(3)). Similarly in Kosovo, where if the rapporteur is not among the majority, the president shall assign the preparation of the draft decision to any judge of the majority. Interestingly, precedence is to be given to members of the review panel that decided on admissibility (Rule 14(4) of the Rules of Procedure). In Italy, instead, the unwritten rule is that the rapporteur (*relatore* in Italian) writes for the majority even if s/he is not part of it. S/he passes the task to a fellow judge only in exceptional cases. Interview with Judge Marta Cartabia (Rome, Italy, 15 September 2016).

84 This happened, for example, to Judge Erdei of the Hungarian Constitutional Court in case no 43/2004 (XI.17.) AB of 15 November 2004. Even though Judge Erdei did not succeed in convincing his peers (apart from Judge Kukorelli who joined his dissent), his argumentation persuaded the legislator who followed his opinion and modified the Code of Criminal Procedure. Interview with a former law clerk (Budapest, Hungary, 26 September 2007). Interestingly, however, the explanatory memorandum attached to the bill does not make reference to the dissenting opinion but to the opinion of the court (Explanation attached to art 83 of Act no 51 of 2006 modifying Act no 19 of 1998 on criminal procedure). Another example is case no 48/1998 (X.2.) AB of 29 September 1998, in which the original rapporteur was President Sólyom, who remained in minority with his position which he explained in a dissenting opinion (joined by two other judges). The majority opinion was authored by Judge Holló, who is indicated as rapporteur of the case in the judgment. Judge Holló also wrote a separate concurring opinion in order to explain his disagreement with the dissenters. The change of rapporteur in this case is revealed by Gábor Halmai, in 'Az aktivizmus vége? A Sólyom-bíróság kilenc éve' [The End of Activism? Nine Years of the Sólyom Court] (1999) 2 *Fundamentum* 5.

85 This is confirmed by the personal account of a former member of the Bundesverfassungsgericht, Dieter Grimm, who admittedly never wrote the opinion of the other side during his 12 years on the Court. Grimm (n 20) 50–51.

86 Kommers and Miller (n 18) 205 and Cohen (n 6) 445.

other members of the panel are less likely to conduct their own research.[87] So, in most cases the rapporteur's opinion becomes the opinion of the court, and s/he is also the author of the judgment. The primary importance of the rapporteur's opinion is also recognised by the legislature when the law provides, as it happens in Italy, that the rapporteur judge shall cast her/his vote first, before all other judges.[88]

The system of assigning the cases to a rapporteur may be one of the reasons behind the low dissent rate in constitutional courts. First, as indicated above, the rapporteur is often a specialist in the issue at hand in the case, and, as such, her/his opinion has a greater weight in the eyes of the other judges. Second, the rapporteur holds a near monopoly over knowledge of facts and other materials concerning the case, including the competing arguments, so the other judges may be left at an informational disadvantage, which discourages them from writing separately.[89] On the other hand, one may argue that in a court with a heavy workload the system of the rapporteur judge helps maintaining the quality of the jurisprudence of the court and ensures a more effective distribution of the workload.[90]

Special reference also needs to be made to the publicity or confidentiality of the rapporteur's identity. Does the public know the name of the judge who handled the case as rapporteur and/or wrote the judgment? The role of rapporteur judge exists in all European constitutional courts, including the French Constitutional Council.[91] In France, however, her/his identity is not revealed. This practice is not surprising. In the French context judgments have always been considered impersonal decisions of the court.[92] What may be surprising is that not even the German Federal Constitutional Court's decisions reveal the identity of the rapporteur judge (*Berichterstatter*).[93] Among the second generation of constitutional courts, the Italian Corte costituzionale is the only one that opted to require that the identity of the rapporteur judge be made public. However, the

87 Also Amos Tversky and Daniel Kahneman, 'The Framing of Decisions and the Psychology of Choice' (1981) 211 *Science* 453.

88 Art 17(3) of the Supplementary Rules (*Norme integrative*) for the Procedure before the Constitutional Court of 7 October 2008 (SR[2008]). Alternatively, or in addition, the law may provide for voting in inverse order of seniority. This is the case for example in Austria, where seniority means age (art 30(3) of the Austrian CC Act) and in Italy, where seniority is based on the length of service (art 17(3) of the Italian Supplementary Norms).

89 Benjamin Bricker, 'Breaking the Principle of Secrecy. An Examination of Judicial Dissent in European Constitutional Courts' (2017) 39 *Law & Policy* 170, 174.

90 Grimm (n 20) 49.

91 The President of the Conseil designates the rapporteur judge in each case. He takes into consideration the judges' expertise and distributes the work fairly among all the members. Paolo Passaglia, 'La giustizia costituzionale in Francia' in Jörg Luther, Roberto Romboli and Rolando Tarchi (eds), *Esperienze di giustizia costituzionale*, Vol 1 (Giappichelli 2000) 199. Since this office is absent in common law jurisdictions, the French term 'rapporteur' is usually used also in English legal discourse.

92 See also Section 3 in this Chapter.

93 Kommers and Miller (n 18) 205.

practice changed in 1987, when the Court amended the Rules of Procedure.[94] Since then, judgments are no longer drafted and signed by the rapporteur, but by the opinion-writer,[95] a change that made it clear that the two figures do not necessarily coincide within the decision-making process.[96] If we look at the third generation of constitutional courts, the Portuguese court reveals the rapporteur's identity, while the Spanish Tribunal Constitucional does not. Therefore, there seems to be no correlation between the publicity of the rapporteur's identity and the publicity of judicial dissent.

Almost all East-Central European constitutional courts include the name of the rapporteur judge in their judgments. This practice largely contributes to present the decisions as personal to the public. An exception is represented by the Lithuanian and Romanian constitutional courts, which chose the French-German way and do not reveal the identity of the rapporteur. It is also worth mentioning that in Hungarian legal history the publicity of the rapporteur judge is not unprecedented. Before the rise of socialism, it had been common practice to specify the name of the rapporteur in the judgments of the *Kúria*, the ordinary Supreme Court.[97] Today the Hungarian Supreme Court (called *Kúria* again after the 2012 constitutional reform) makes public the name of the rapporteur only in its 'uniformity decisions'.[98] Despite this historical precedent, the Hungarian Constitutional Court in the first year did not reveal the identity of the rapporteur judge. The practice changed, however, very early on in 1991.[99] The fact that the Hungarian Constitutional Court showed greater collegiality in the beginning, and that there has been a gradual shift towards individualisation of decision-making, is also demonstrated by the first collective separate opinions. In the first two years there was no case of simple joining. Instead, if a judge decided to join the separate opinion of a colleague, s/he was indicated as co-author. Indeed, among the separate opinions from that period, we can find several ones co-authored by three of four judges.[100]

94 Art 18(5) of the Rules of Procedure, Decision of 16 March 1956 of the Italian Constitutional Court (in *Gazzetta Ufficiale*, 24 March 1956, no 71, special edn), modified by the Decision of 7 July 1987 (in *Gazzetta Ufficiale*, 9 July 1987, no 158). The rule has been upheld by the new Rules of Procedure as well (art 17(6), Decision of 7 October 2008 of the Italian Constitutional Court).

95 Alessandro Pizzorusso, 'Dal "relatore" al "redattore" delle sentenze della Corte costituzionale' (1988) *Il Foro italiano*, I, cols 2–3.

96 This new practice and the phenomenon of the so-called 'creeping' dissenting opinions (*opinioni dissenzienti 'striscianti'*) will be explained in Chapter 4, Section 2.3.

97 Interview with Judge G (Budapest, Hungary, 19 October 2007).

98 'Uniformity decisions' are adopted by the supreme court to ensure the uniform application of the law on the initiative of the court's president, the president of one of its panels, the president of a court of appeal, or the prosecutor general. Arts 32–33 of Act No CLXI of 2011 on the organisation and administration of courts.

99 This fact was explained to me by Judge M who also added that at the same time the Court abandoned the practice of specifying the name of the petitioner(s) in the published judgments. Interview with Judge M (Budapest, Hungary, 9 November 2006).

100 For example, Decision no 48/1991 (IX.26.) AB of 23 November 1991, in which there is a dissenting opinion co-authored by three judges, a concurring opinion co-authored by four

2.3. Non-judicial offices: law clerks and the secretary general

As explained in the previous section, the president assigns the case to a rapporteur judge who is usually, but not necessarily, the author of the judgment. The final decision is taken by the judicial panel, whose members vote after a long and thorough discussion of the case. Sometimes it may take several meetings to reach an agreement, and drafts are circulated among judges. Judges, however, do not work in isolation: in their work, they are supported by collaborators, or law clerks,[101] who play a very important role in the decision-making and give their personal contribution to the development of the court's case-law. Thus, if we want to thoroughly understand a constitutional court's decision-making process, the role of law clerks cannot be ignored.

The very existence of law clerks shows the influence of the American model in Europe. All European constitutional courts employ lawyers who assist judges as clerks, even if their title and number varies from court to court.[102] Their main task is to research legal questions under the court's supervision and to prepare draft judgments. Law clerks not only write a report for each case, but they also analyse precedents, study foreign solutions to similar questions, present the leading legal doctrine and other opinions. In a few constitutional courts they also play an important role in filtering the petitions. Each judge has his or her own team including a few clerks, usually three or four. A law clerk, therefore, works for a given judge, not for the court in general. The same system is applied in the

---

judges and another concurring opinion co-authored by two judges. The first case in which a judge simply declared the intention to join at the bottom of the separate opinion of a colleague dates back to November 1991 (Judge Schmidt joining the dissenting opinion of Judge Kilényi in Decision no 57/1991 (XI.8.) AB of 5 November 1991). Interestingly, the second time this happened, one-and-a-half years later, Judge Kilényi chose to join Judge Schmidt's dissent (Decision no 5/1993 (II.12.) AB of 8 February 1993), and the opinion is written in first-person plural, showing that they co-authored it.

101 'Law clerk' is the American term which I chose to use consistently throughout the book also for European constitutional courts in order to facilitate reading and understanding. These positions serve a comparable function, even if they may be called with different names in the English translation of the various European constitutional court acts, and there are some differences as regards their tasks and career structure.

102 In Germany, each federal constitutional judge is entitled to four clerks, called 'scientific collaborators' (*wissenschaftliche Mitarbeiter*) of his or her own choosing. German clerks are already experienced lawyers (judges, civil servants, professors) and usually serve for two or three years. Kommers and Miller (n 18) 203 and 206. Similarly in Italy, where law clerks (three working for each judge) are usually experienced legal scholars or judges themselves. In Slovenia 34 law clerks work at the Constitutional Court. In Poland each constitutional judge has two *asystents*. At the Czech Constitutional Court every judge collaborates with three *asistents* employed full-time, as at the Slovak Constitutional Court where they are called *súdny poradca* (judicial advisor). At the Hungarian Constitutional Court, since 2000, there are three *tanácsadós* (advisors) working for each judge. Until 2006, one of them had the title of 'personal secretary' (*személyi titkár*) and was chosen among the best recent law graduates by the judge herself/himself. This office could be considered analogous to that of the American law clerk.

Court of Justice of European Union, where both judges and Advocates General are entitled to three clerks.[103]

Unlike their American counterparts, European law clerks are not employed for one year; rather, they work for the same judge for several years, usually for her/his whole term of office. Actually, it is not uncommon for them to remain at the court even after the retirement of the judge who originally employed them, so that they can continue to work in the team of another judge.[104] It is therefore possible to make a lifetime career as a clerk at a constitutional court, even if many also work in academia at the same time. This circumstance has an impact on the practice of opinion-writing as well. European constitutional judges are more prone to delegate opinion-writing to their clerks than their American colleagues, as law clerks are more experienced than a fresh graduate. It is especially true when a newly appointed constitutional judge 'inherits' a law clerk from a retired judge. In this case, at least in the first period, the law clerk has more experience in preparing constitutional court judgments and separate opinions than the judge herself/himself.[105]

Besides clerks, another non-judicial office supports the work of constitutional judges: the secretary general of the court. S/he is the head of a special department: the Secretariat.[106] Neither of these can be found within the US Supreme Court. The secretary general of the constitutional court assists the president in the assignment of cases and often acts as a first filter of petitions. The rapporteur judge may be designated either before or after the decision on admissibility. Each constitutional court has its own specific method of filtering petitions. At the Czech Constitutional Court, for example, judges may delegate to their clerks the task of rejecting defective petitions and to give notice of it to the petitioner. In this case the clerk also sets a deadline by which the petition may be cured.[107] German law clerks also play an important role in filtering constitutional

103 Both at the General Court and at the Court of Justice. Judges with management responsibilities are entitled to four clerks, called *référendaires* at the CJEU. Judges at the Court of Justice have additional help from lawyers, the so-called *administrateurs juristes*, who however do not work on cases directly. Angela Huyue Zhang, 'The Faceless Court' (2015) King's College London Law School Research Paper No 2015–45, 8 <https://ssrn.com/abstract=2640861> accessed 18 January 2017. For a detailed account on the *référendaires* from a comparative perspective see Sally J Kenney, 'Beyond Principals and Agents: Seeing Courts as Organizations by Comparing *Référendaires* at the European Court of Justice and Law Clerks at the U.S. Supreme Court' (2000) 33 *Comparative Political Studies* 593.

104 Béla Pokol, 'Az alkotmánybíráskodás szociológiai megfigyelése' [Sociological Observation of Constitutional Justice] (2014) 3 *Alkotmánybírósági Szemle* 158, 181.

105 At the CJEU it is even more accentuated, as when appointed some judges lack a background in EU law or struggle with the working language of the Court (or both), while clerks are fluent in French, well-versed in EU law and familiar with the institutional workings of the Court. Zhang (n 103) 31.

106 For the functions of the Secretariat see, for example, arts 25–26 of the Rules of Procedure of the Hungarian Constitutional Court.

107 Art 41 of the Constitutional Court Act. Czech constitutional judges may also delegate other procedural tasks to their clerks, such as preparing the matter for consideration on the merits by the plenum or the panel.

complaints. Their allegedly substantial influence on the Court's decisions has been subject to serious criticism. Some commentators affirmed that they actually form a secret third chamber (*Dritter Senat*) within the German Federal Constitutional Court.[108] The Hungarian Constitutional Court's method is different. There are four lawyers working at the Secretariat who filter the petitions before they are assigned to a rapporteur judge. Only roughly half of the petitions pass this first filter and reach a judge at all.[109]

The German and Czech solutions are closer to the decision-making process of the US Supreme Court, where clerks play an important role in the selection of 'certworthy' cases.[110] They analyse petitions and prepare the so-called 'pool' memos which summarise the case and recommend a certain decision. In German and Czech constitutional justice, however, there is no writ of certiorari, and the Court is mandated to adjudicate all petitions deemed admissible. Only those petitions that are deemed defective or manifestly unfounded are rejected. This means that neither law clerks nor judges have any discretionary power in selecting cases. The Court has to decide all petitions which fulfil the legal requirements. Even so, law clerks review all cases, especially those in which the judge they work for is not the rapporteur,[111] and they recommend a certain outcome.

The tasks performed by a clerk and her/his influence on the court's decisions may differ considerably even within the same court. It lies within the discretionary power of the judge to decide how to distribute tasks within her/his team and to what extent make use of her/his clerks' assistance. At the Hungarian Constitutional Court, for instance, Judge Attila Harmathy was known for writing most of the opinions alone (irrespective of whether he wrote for the majority or just for himself) and never left any draft prepared by a clerk unchanged.[112] Generally speaking, judges involve their clerks in the preparation of judgments rather than in that of separate opinions. Indeed, separate opinions usually have a more personal tone and character. The judge speaks for herself/himself and not for the court, and therefore s/he is less willing to delegate this task. In the United States, legal commentators have observed that the increasing involvement of law clerks in the preparation of judgments in the last decades has largely contributed

108 For example, Friedrich Karl Fromme, 'Die Mitarbeiter der Verfassungsrichter sind nich mehr en Korps wie enst' *Frankfurter Allgemeine Zeitung* (24 August 1995), cited in Adele Anzon, 'Gli assistenti di studio dei giudici costituzionali' in Pasquale Costanzo (ed), *L'organizzazione e il funzionamento della Corte costituzionale*, vol 1 (Giappichelli 1996) 215, 225.

109 Official statistics of the Hungarian Constitutional Court <http://alkotmanybirosag.hu/letoltesek/statisztika_ossz.pdf> accessed 18 January 2017.

110 A 'certworthy' case in American legal jargon describes a case worthy of being granted a writ of certiorari, i.e. of being admitted to the court.

111 The same is true for the Hungarian Constitutional Court. In general, with a few exceptions, the cases are not distributed among all clerks of the judge, but they are assigned to one clerk according to their expertise.

112 Interview with a former law clerk (Budapest, Hungary, 26 September 2007). According to her, Judge Harmathy was the last one to write all opinions on his own.

to the proliferation of separate opinions and to a perceived worsening quality of the judgments.[113] As regards East-Central European constitutional courts, sufficient information on a sufficiently long period of time is still unavailable, and, therefore, it is not possible to make any similar claim. However, what can be observed is that at the Hungarian Constitutional Court it has become common practice under the presidency of János Németh[114] to delegate the task of preparing draft judgments to clerks. Even if there is no evidence that a causal link exists, it emerges clearly that the period of increased involvement of law clerks in the preparation of judgments coincides with a rise in the number of separate opinions. However, if we consider that Judge Harmathy himself – a judge who notoriously made a more limited use of his clerks' assistance than his colleagues – is considered one of the Great Dissenters of the Hungarian Constitutional Court, the aforementioned possible correlation is called into question. Thus, it could be argued that a larger involvement of clerks in the preparation of judgments does not necessarily entail an increase in the number of separate opinions. During Mihály Bihari's presidency, at the beginning of 2006, the practice was consolidated in a new unwritten rule, according to which the draft judgment had to be signed with the initials of its author, i.e. of the clerk who prepared it.[115]

In the formerly socialist countries, in the first period, most of the law clerks had a consolidated background of academic excellence in legal science. Péter Paczolay's career at the Hungarian Constitutional Court is noteworthy and illustrates this point well. He was a clerk to the first president, László Sólyom, and later became the Court's secretary general, then a member judge and the President of the Court.[116] Only after some time, space was given also to fresh graduates, as in the United States.[117] The reason probably lies in two circumstances. First, it took a decade for the courts to develop their own case-law, after which they did not have a compelling need for the advice of experienced scholars anymore. Second, there has been a general increase in the number of clerks, which may also explain the changing composition.[118]

113 Artemus Ward and David L Weiden, *Sorcerers' Apprentices. 100 Years of Law Clerks at the United States Supreme Court* (New York UP 2006) 231. See more in Chapter 3, Section 3.2.

114 János Németh was the second president of the Hungarian Constitutional Court, from November 1998 to August 2003.

115 Interview with a former law clerk (Budapest, Hungary, 26 September 2007).

116 Péter Paczolay sat on the Court from 2006–2015 and was its president from July 2008 until the end of his term.

117 In the Czech Republic, for example, in 1993, at the moment of the establishment of the Constitutional Court, the majority of the clerks had come from the Law Faculty of Masaryk University located in the same city as the Court (Brno). I thank Mark Gillis, advisor of the Czech Constitutional Court in comparative and European law, for this information.

118 In the Czech Republic, for example, the need for law clerks increased even more because in 1999–2000 also the Supreme Court introduced this position, previously unknown at that Court. Today, all 50 Supreme Court judges have a clerk. This rule was later extended also to the Supreme Administrative Court upon its establishment in 2003. Finally, the ombudsman has its seat in Brno too, a circumstance that further limits the number of available lawyers for the office of law clerk.

3. The style of constitutional court decisions

Judicial style is an essential part of the spirit of a legal system, because it reveals the legal thinking at the basis of a legal culture.[119] The style of judgments emerged as a popular theme for comparatists in the 1960s.[120] It is difficult to propose a general definition of 'style'. As Richard Posner aptly pointed out, style is 'one of those words that we are entirely comfortable in using but that is devil to define'.[121] Matters of style call into question both the formal and substantial characteristics of a given object or of an individual. In the case of judgments, the formal dimension of style is concerned with the structure of the decision. The recurring parts of a judgment are the verdict, the reasoning and the judges' signatures. In the civil law tradition, the verdict typically precedes the reasoning, while in the common law tradition the decision is presented in the reverse order. Separate opinions are, needless to say, a possible but not necessary element of the judgment. The substantive dimension of style, on the other hand, concerns language and tone. The opinion of the court is the result of a decision taken by multiple actors and as such is written in an impersonal tone. It usually also resorts to more technical language compared to a separate opinion. Generally speaking, the latter tends to be markedly individual and personal, revealing the personality of its author.

In this short section I will focus on the formal aspects of style, while I will discuss the substantive dimension in the following chapters. While the former display a few common features, even though with some notable exceptions, such as a similar structure and the potential presence of separate opinions, the latter shows a more heterogeneous picture. As András Jakab found in his illuminating essay, there is no 'European' style of constitutional reasoning. He points out that rather than common features we can talk about different emphasis in European constitutional reasoning which distinguish it from the style of the US Supreme Court, such as the less frequent use of substantive moral, sociological, or economic reasons, less concern about the use of comparative law arguments, and the absence of radically originalist interpretation of the constitution.[122]

119 Konrad Zweigert and Hein Kötz, *An Introduction to Comparative Law* (Weir tr, 3rd edn, Oxford UP 1998) 4. According to Zweigert and Kötz to compare the diverse styles of judicial opinions is an exercise in macrocomparison.

120 Beginning with Karl N Llewellyn, *The Common Law Tradition: Deciding Appeals* (Little 1960) and J Gillis Wetter, *The Styles of Appellate Judicial Opinions* (Sythoff 1960), two representatives of American legal realism. On the Italian style see three essays by John H Merryman, *The Italian Style I: Doctrine* (1965) 18 *Stanford Law Review* 39, *The Italian Style II: Law* (1966) 18 *Stanford Law Review* 396, and *The Italian Style III: Interpretation* (1966) 18 *Stanford Law Review* 583. From a comparative perspective Folke F Schmidt, 'The Ratio Decidendi. A Comparative Study of a French, a German, and an American Supreme Court Decision' (1965) 6 *Acta Instituti Upsaliensis Iurisprudentiae Comparativae* 12, and Jean Louis Goutal, 'Characteristics of Judicial Style in France, Britain and the U.S.A.' (1976) 24 *American Journal of Comparative Law* 43.

121 Richard A Posner, 'Judges' Writing Style (And Do They Matter?)' (1995) 62 *University of Chicago Law Review* 1420, 1421–22.

122 András Jakab, 'Judicial Reasoning in Constitutional Courts: A European Perspective' (2013) 14 *German Law Journal* 1215, 1274.

As regards the formal style of judgments, the most common distinction made by comparatists within the civil law tradition is that between the French and the German judicial styles. The former is still much anchored in the Montesquieuan ideal that judges are the 'mouth of the law', consequently their decisions are characterised by a syllogistic structure. French judgments typically consist of a *phrase unique*, one long single sentence.[123] German judgments, on the other hand, are more articulate. They are close to an academic style due to the historical links between the judiciary and legal doctrine. Constitutional courts do not follow faithfully the style of the ordinary judiciary. Their decisions are not addressed to the parties and the lawyers only, but to a larger public, including the legislature and the citizens, since they touch upon issues of general interest.[124] This makes the style of constitutional court judgments more discursive than that of ordinary courts. However, the structure still resembles that of ordinary court decisions. Thus, the reasoning of the French Constitutional Council usually consists of a long chain of statements introduced with the phrase '*considérant que*', while the German Federal Constitutional Court's decisions look like a long scholarly essay. The Italian Constitutional Court's style is close to its German counterpart's style, but with a less systematic analysis of precedents and without explicit references to legal doctrine.[125]

Most European constitutional courts follow rather faithfully the style of German constitutional judgments. These usually contain a long and well-organised reasoning, and look more like a scholarly article rather than a judgment. The same is true even for the Romanian Constitutional Court, which, established under the influence of the French and Italian models, does not follow the concise style of the Conseil Constitutionnel but the more diffuse style of the Italian Constitutional Court. However, in a way, the structure of both the Romanian and the Italian Constitutional Courts' decisions is reminiscent of the French style, as the reasoning precedes the verdict, unlike in the Kelsenian courts' decisions. Thus, Italian and Romanian constitutional judgments are structured in a French way (the reasoning precedes the verdict), but their reasoning is much more developed, similar to German judgments. They do not consist of a *phrase unique* as the French judgments. Similarly, in the Latvian Constitutional Court's judgments the verdict is preceded by the reasoning, but the latter is usually quite long and well-developed, as the Italian and Romanian constitutional judgments.[126] Consequently, French judgments can still be considered unique in Europe, with only

123 This syllogistic style characterises the whole French judiciary, including both ordinary courts and the Constitutional Council. About the French judicial style in English see Mitchell de S.-O.l'E. Lasser, *Judicial Deliberations* (Oxford UP 2004) 27–61, 166–202; and Michal Bobek, *Comparative Reasoning in European Supreme Courts* (Oxford UP 2013) 97–119.

124 Jakab (n 122) 1219.

125 Alessandra Di Martino, *Le opinioni dissenzienti dei giudici costituzionali. Uno studio comparativo* (Jovene 2016) 442.

126 For example, the two Latvian judgments presented in Chapter 4, Section 4.3.2, which are 25 and 37 pages long, respectively. Decision no 2000–03–01 of 30 August 2000 and Decision no 2005–13–0106 of 15 June 2006.

Belgium imitating their very concise style.[127] None of the other constitutional courts do.

The style of the East-Central European constitutional courts, in particular, has been especially strongly influenced by the German model.[128] A concrete example may be seen in the Hungarian practice. For the Hungarian Constitutional Court it has become common practice to formulate so-called 'constitutional requirements' (*alkotmányos követelmények*). These requirements are analogous to the German *Leitsätze*. However, unlike their German counterparts, in Hungarian constitutional judgments they are included in the verdict, not in the reasoning part, with the consequence that they become binding.[129] The fact that constitutional requirements are part of the verdict can also be deduced from the practice of defining the separate opinion of a disagreeing judge as 'dissenting' and not 'concurring' opinion.[130] This formal qualification in this case is of substantive relevance.

Concluding, even if there is a dialogue and mutual influence between European constitutional courts, and the German Federal Constitutional Court exerts a strong pull on many other constitutional courts, especially in East-Central Europe, we can talk about a convergence of styles rather than a common European style of constitutional adjudication.[131]

127 Antonio Gambaro, 'Lo stile della sentenza francese' in Letizia Vacca (ed), *Lo stile delle sentenze e l'utilizzazione dei precedenti* (Giappichelli 2000) 121.

128 Bobek (n 123) 255, 270.

129 László Sólyom, *Az alkotmánybíráskodás kezdetei Magyarországon* [The Dawning of Constitutional Justice in Hungary] (Osiris 2001), 56–57 and 225, fn 4. Moreover, as Judge G observed, sometimes even the grammatical structure of the sentences follows the rules of German language (predicate at the end, which is not at all usual in Hungarian language). Interview with Judge G (Budapest, Hungary, 2 November 2006).

130 An example is Decision no 42/1996 (X.9.) AB of 7 October 1996, to which Judge Ödön Tersztyánszky attached his separate opinion, entitled 'dissenting opinion'. He agreed with the majority on the rejection of the petition but did not agree with the constitutional requirement established by the Court.

131 Even if contrary opinions are not lacking. For example, Patricia Popelier, 'An Italian or a European Style of Judicial Review? Setting the Agenda for Comparative Research on Courts' (2016) 8 *Italian Journal of Public Law* 72.

3 Judicial dissent in the common law tradition

1. Introductory remarks

This chapter tells the story of dissenting opinions in its natural habitat: the common law tradition. Getting to its roots leads us to better understand each legal rule and institution. The phenomenon of judicial dissent is not an exception. In this case a historical investigation brings us to medieval England where legal disputes, if argued before a panel of judges, were decided separately by each member of the panel. This practice of delivering judicial opinions '*seriatim*' (separately)[1] was a natural consequence of the orality of English court procedure.[2] On the continent, on the other hand, medieval court procedure was prevalently written, and even if a few jurisdictions allowed their judges to write separately, the separate opinions were usually kept in a secret book.[3]

The institution of dissenting opinions is an especially suitable object of study for a comparatist, as it spread gradually in the Western legal tradition. It first appeared in the United States in the baggage of common law, then moved to Germany and Spain where it upheld and renewed judicial traditions, and finally arrived in East-Central Europe to help the building of constitutional democracy. In each legal system dissenting opinions grew out of different needs and were embedded in different surroundings. A comparative study must look into these needs and surroundings in order to adequately evaluate the practice. This and the following chapters follow and explain the spread of the institution.

2. The origins of the dissenting opinion

2.1. The historical roots: England

By examining the roots of dissenting opinions in medieval English court practice we discover that in that context it is actually not correct to refer to the dissenting

1 *Seriatim* means 'separately' in Latin.

2 The principle of orality is, on the other hand, attributable to the trial by jury, predominant in English procedure. Members of the jury were typically illiterate commoners who could not write or read. Geoffrey Samuel, *A Short Introduction to the Common Law* (Edward Elgar 2013) 29.

3 See Chapter 4, Section 1.

opinion as a legal institution. At least historically, it is a phenomenon rather than an institution.[4] There were no (written or unwritten) rules regarding the expression of dissent in the English legal tradition. Judicial opinions were necessarily delivered separately, as they were announced orally at the end of the trial by the single judges and not written down by one of them as opinion of the court.[5] These opinions were written down by a clerk, rather than by the judges, in order to be collected and published in the Reports. The English Reports are therefore an original product of the clerks, different from the collections of case-law that we can find on the continent simply reproducing texts written by the judges themselves.[6] In fact, English judges traditionally did not discuss the cases at all, as that would have violated the principle of orality. This principle also aimed to ensure that judges did everything in public so that their behaviour could be monitored.[7]

The opinion of the single judge, delivered orally at the end of the trial, could be either a full judgment or a simple formal concurrence. The latter consists of a short declaration of sharing the opinion of another member of the panel.[8] Full judgments, on the other hand, could be identified as a majority, dissenting or concurring opinion only after all judges expressed their judgment. Thus, historically, a judicial opinion was not dissenting or concurring *a priori*, but it could be qualified as such after a comparison between the different opinions. The very fact that the opinions of the single judges, even if in minority, have been considered as judgments, and not simply opinions, demonstrates the particular approach to judicial decision-making in England. Each judge expresses her/his own judgment. The opinion of the court emerges from a joint reading of these judgments. No judgment is 'entitled' dissent, concurrence or opinion of the court, as in the American system, but they are regarded such by interpretation. Thus, it may happen that different interpretations emerge in relation to the same judgment, which may be considered either as concurring or as dissenting opinion. For example, Alan Paterson in his book on the highest court of the English legal

4 'Legal institution' (in the sense of a set of norms which concern the same matter) is itself, in fact, a civil law concept unknown to the common law tradition. John Henry Merryman and Rogelio Pérez-Perdomo, *The Civil Law Tradition* (3rd edn, Stanford UP 2007) 91 ff.

5 Michael D Kirby, 'Judicial Dissent – Common Law and Civil Law Traditions' (2007) 123 *Law Quarterly Review* 379.

6 Gino Gorla, 'La struttura della decisione giudiziale in diritto italiano e nella "Common Law": Riflessi di tale struttura sull'interpretazione della sentenza, sui "Reports" e sul "Dissenting"' (1965) Giurisprudenza italiana I/1, 1239, 1254.

7 Richard A Posner, *How Judges Think* (Harvard UP 2008) 2–3.

8 Thus a concurrence is different from a concurring opinion which expresses alternative or additional reasons for the decision. The English sometimes call the concurring opinion 'assenting judgment'. Louis Blom-Cooper and Gavin Drewry, *Final Appeal: A Study of the House of Lords in its Judicial Capacity* (Clarendon Press 1972) 79–95. Others, however, use the terms 'concurrence' and 'concurring opinion' as synonyms. Alan Paterson, *Final Judgment: The Last Law Lords and the Supreme Court* (Hart 2013) 11. In the practice of the Court of Appeal today it is common to have only one full judgment and two formal concurrences (the decision-making panel is composed of three judges). Patrick S Atiyah, 'La sentenza in Inghilterra' in *La sentenza in Europa. Metodo, tecnica e stile* (Cedam 1988) 552, 553.

system, includes among dissents also judgments which agree on the outcome favoured by the majority but whose reasoning is radically different from that of the majority.[9] These judgments are technically concurring opinions and would be defined as such in the US and in other systems where judicial opinions are given a title by their authors.

The practice of *seriatim* opinions also entails that even if all members of the panel agree, both on the outcome and on the reasons for the outcome, there may still be several full judgments in which the judges explain the decision with their own words. So the presence of more than one full judgment in an English court does not necessarily mean that there was a disagreement between the judges. In fact, composite judgments attributed to the whole Court are very rare. At the same time, single majority judgments in the name of one judge are very common.[10] Since the 17th century, majority voting has been the preferred mode of decision-making in England.[11]

This practice of '*seriatim* opinions', as the common lawyers call it, has been exercised by the highest courts only, as courts of first instance do not decide in panels. In the English court system the Judicial Committee of the Privy Council (JCPC), the Court of Appeal and the Supreme Court (previously the Appellate Committee of the House of Lords)[12] make their decisions in panels.

The JCPC hears appeals from current and former Commonwealth countries and from other overseas territories and crown dependencies, and, until 1966, it did not allow its members to publish a dissenting opinion.[13] In the past, judgments, even if the result of a majority decision, showed apparent unanimity[14] among the judges. The reason behind this is that, according to historical tradition, the Privy Council represents the monarch, and when deciding a case it expresses the opinion or recommendation of the Crown. Thus it had to speak with one voice. In fact, the Privy Council's decisions were translated into the form of an Order in Council made by the Sovereign and were formally announced as the opinion of the monarch. It would have been a paradox to allow a split of opinions. The

9 See the definition of 'dissent' by Paterson in *Final Judgment* (n 8) 12.

10 60% of cases in the first third of 2013 were single majority judgments. Such judgments are, however, almost always a collective work product of most of the judges. Paterson (n 8) 11.

11 John Alder, 'Dissents in Courts of Last Resort: Tragic Choices?' (2000) 20 *Oxford Journal of Legal Studies* 221, 233. In *Grindley v Barker* (1798) it was explicitly held that cases of public concern as opposed to purely private matters should be decided by majority vote (1 Bos and Pul 229, 238).

12 The UK Supreme Court was established by the Constitutional Reform Act 2005 and started to operate in October 2009. The expression 'highest court' will be used to refer to both the Appellate Committee and the Supreme Court.

13 The ban on dissenting opinions was established by an order of the Privy Council itself in 1627, and re-affirmed by the Order in Council of 4 February 1878 (O.C. 593), stating that 'when the business is carried according to the most voices, no publication afterwards to be made by any man how the particular voices and opinions went'.

14 Or, more precisely, univocality. The term 'unanimity' may also be used in contrast to 'univocality', which applies to a more restricted range of cases where the court is agreed not only as to the result but also to the reasons for the outcome. Paterson (n 8) 14.

Sovereign cannot speak with discordant voices.[15] Moreover, the practice of delivering unanimous judgments was reinforced by policy considerations in the heyday of colonialism, which 'dictated a single clear pronouncement for subject peoples not attuned to the institutions and conventions of their Imperial masters'.[16] In fact, the same policy considerations were not applicable in the countries of the Commonwealth, which, after gaining their independence, allowed the judges of their newly established supreme courts to express their opinions separately.[17]

The fiction that judges were simply giving advice to the Crown was however later abandoned, and dissenting opinions were allowed by a new order adopted in 1966. Since then, it is possible to write separately for the members of the JCPC.[18] But the Privy Council is still regarded to be an advisor of the monarch. So why was the practice changed? A possible explanation is that the original practice, banning dissenting opinions, ensured a greater moral weight to the decisions which were taken in cases involving peoples considered living in various stages of civilisation.[19] The change in 1966 might have been prompted by the progress of the colonies to independence, and the old paternalistic approach is not sustainable anymore. Instead, today, the importance of a uniform court practice at home and for the Commonwealth is emphasised.[20]

The Appellate Committee of the House of Lords was also a peculiar body, as its members (the Lords of Appeal in Ordinary, commonly known as Law Lords) were formally at the same time members of the upper chamber of the Parliament.[21] In practice they did not participate in the law-making activity of the

15 Karl M Zo Bell, 'Division of Opinion in the Supreme Court: A History of Judicial Disintegration' (1958–59) 44 *Cornell Law Quarterly* 186.

16 Blom-Cooper and Drewry (n 8) 82. The authors explain that the 'cloak of anonymity may have given a depersonalized objectivity and certainty to Commonwealth systems of law in their early development' (at 83).

17 With no exception. For the origins of the practice of the final appellate courts in the Commonwealth countries outside the United Kingdom see Edward McWhinney, 'Judicial Concurrences and Dissents: A Comparative View of Opinion-writing in Final Appellate Tribunals' (1953) 31 *Canadian Bar Review* 595.

18 The Judicial Committee (Dissenting Opinions) Order 1966 (SI 1966/1100) (UK). The order does not refer to concurring opinions (or assenting judgments), so it seems that only dissenting opinions are allowed. In the first five years after the reform dissenting opinions were filed in only 14 cases. For the complete list of cases see Blom-Cooper and Drewry (n 8) 111.

19 Evolutionary thinking that dominated 19th century European intellectual life also influenced legal authors, such as Henry Sumner Maine and Lewis Henry Morgan, who divided human culture history into different stages. John M Conley and William M O'Barr, 'Legal Anthropology Comes Home: A Brief History of the Ethnographic Study of Law' (1993–94) 27 *Loyola of Los Angeles Review* 41, 42–3.

20 OC Giles, 'Book Review of "Das Minderheitsvotum des überstimmten Richters" by Wolfgang Heyde' (1968) 31 *Modern Law Review* 232, 233.

21 The Appellate Committee was established by the Appellate Jurisdiction Act in 1876, but the House of Lords heard petitions for the reversal of lower court judgments since the birth of the English Parliament. Louis Blom-Cooper, Brice Dickson and Gavin Drewry (eds), *The Judicial House of Lords 1876–2009* (Oxford UP 2009) 3 ff.

Parliament, but still they were subject to the same procedural rules as the other members of the House. Thus, from a purely formalistic point of view, according to English constitutional theory, their opinions were to be regarded as speeches given in a parliamentary debate. This also meant that a single composite judgment was not possible, as the Law Lords expressed their vote and opinion individually.[22] For several centuries, these opinions were not public, as the materials of the parliamentary debates were kept secret. Consequently, also the cases decided by the Appellate Committee were discussed behind closed doors. The ban on the publication of parliamentary debate materials was lifted in the mid-19th century, and the Law Lords were allowed to express their separate opinion publicly. Since then it has been considered to be a violation of their freedom of speech not to allow that.[23] It is worth mentioning that the Law Lords were also members of the JCPC (as the Justices of the UK Supreme Court are still members of the JCPC today), so they knew the practice of deciding by majority, delivering a single opinion for the whole court.[24] There was a short period in the 18th century when, on the initiative by Lord Chief Justice Mansfield, the Appellate Committee delivered majority opinions. This practice was however abandoned after 1788 when Lord Kenyon became Chief Justice.[25]

The argument based on freedom of speech cannot be used in the same way after the detachment of the highest court from the Parliament in 2009. Justices of the current UK Supreme Court are no longer Members of Parliament. The reform, however, does not change the jurisdiction of the Court which inherited all cases and controversies handled by the Appellate Committee.[26] Even the composition remained unchanged, with the incumbent Law Lords becoming the first Justices of the Supreme Court.[27] Thus there is a clear continuity between the two organs. Consequently, what has been written about the Appellate Committee applies to the Supreme Court as well.

The adjudicating panel of the new Supreme Court is composed of an uneven number of Justices (at least three, maximum eleven),[28] who can choose between

22 At most they could limit their vote to a formal concurrence. Blom-Cooper and Drewry (n 8) 82.

23 Alan Paterson, *The Law Lords* (McMillan 1982) 98.

24 Lord Radcliffe considered it an instructive experience for the Law Lords, writing that '[t]he people who were accustomed to being in the Council got rather good at rendering one judgment that reflected the opinions of the others. There was a sort of tradition that you didn't take a strong line unless it was one which could be shared by the others'. Paterson (n 23) 98.

25 This historical fact was reported by Thomas Jefferson in his letter written to William Johnson (dated 27 October 1822) as a supportive argument for the practice of *seriatim* opinions. Quoted in Donald G Morgan, 'The Origin of Supreme Court Dissent' (1953) 10 *The William and Mary Quarterly* 353, 354.

26 The only exception are the so-called 'devolution' issues, which is a new area of jurisdiction of the Supreme Court. Before these issued were decided by the JCPC. Section 40 of the Constitutional Reform Act 2005.

27 Section 24 of the Constitutional Reform Act 2005.

28 Section 42 of the Constitutional Reform Act 2005.

writing a full judgment on their own or joining the judgment of another judge by simple concurrence. There are no guidelines restricting this choice. Rather, a certain *laissez-faire* ethos prevails on the Court,[29] meaning that it is at the complete discretion of the judge to decide to write separately or to join the judgment of a fellow, even if there is no disagreement. So, unlike in the US, we cannot always find an 'opinion of the court' expressing the view of the majority.

The classification of judgments proposed by Alan Paterson in 1982 is still applicable today. He distinguishes 'solo decisions', 'quintets' and 'concertos', taking into consideration civil cases decided by a panel of five judges. In a 'solo decision' all members of the panel express their individual opinion. It can occur in two different ways: either, one judge delivers a full judgment and the others decide to express a formal concurrence, or all five judges deliver a separate full judgment without taking into consideration the opinion of their fellows (relatively rare). The opposite of this category is constituted by the so-called 'quintets' which represent the 'acme of group decision-making'. A quintet is authored and shared by all five members of the panel who collaborate in drafting the judgment. It is obvious that this is also a rare event. The majority of the judgments are 'concertos', somewhere between a solo decision and a quintet, expressing both individualism and collaboration.[30]

A special category is comprised of criminal cases, in which it has long been considered inappropriate to deliver a dissenting opinion, on the ground that it would aggravate 'the discomfiture of the unsuccessful appellant'.[31] This was recognised by the legislature in the Criminal Appeal Act 1907, setting the procedural rules for the Court of Appeal in criminal cases, which required a leave of the presiding judge for separate judgments.[32] This restriction does not apply to the other division of the Court of Appeal, which decides civil cases. This Court usually sits in panels of three judges, so decisions composed of only one full judgment accompanied by two formal concurrences are much more common in this court than in the highest court which sits in panels of five judges.[33]

29 This term was used by Alan Paterson in *The Law Lords* (n 23) 108.

30 In 35% of the cases all Law Lords delivered their own full judgment, but in the majority of these cases they formed their opinion after a discussion with their colleagues. According to Paterson, in this case the judgment cannot be considered a 'solo decision', but a 'concerto'. Paterson (n 23) 110–11.

31 'To the criminal, punishment itself is bitter enough, without the salt of a favourable but impotent dissenting judgment being rubbed into the wound'. Blom-Cooper and Drewry (n 8) 81. Under the statute in force today, the presiding judge may authorise the publication of separate opinions in criminal appeals. Supreme Court Act 1981, s 59.

32 Section 1(5) of the Criminal Appeal Act 1907. The rule was perpetuated by the Criminal Appeal Act 1966. Criminal appeals are, however, not the only exception in England. Some special tribunals and the Justices of the Peace are not allowed to publish dissenting opinions either. In the case of the latter, the ban can be justified on the same ground as that of jury confidentiality of protecting individual justices within their local communities. Alder (n 11) 235.

33 Atiyah (n 8) 553.

2.2. The 'institutionalisation' of judicial dissent in the United States

The first 'stop' in the travel of separate judicial opinions was the United States, where they were adapted to the local court system which rationalised the English practice. As the Italian Gino Gorla observed, it is quite typical in the common law that something born spontaneously and for different historical reasons is later rationalised, 'institutionalised' and kept for new use and function.[34]

From its creation in 1789, the US Supreme Court followed the practice of the English King's Bench. Even if independence from the English Crown had been gained in 1783, the United States kept the common law as a basis for building up its own legal system. During that historical period, the English House of Lords heard petitions seeking reversal of the judgments of lower courts, but the Appellate Committee had not been officially set up yet,[35] and the Lords' opinions were not made public, as explained above. However, the other courts of the Kingdom, including the King's Bench (exercising supervisory jurisdiction over lower courts), applied the practice of *seriatim* opinions. The only difference from English practice in this first period was that the Justices of the US Supreme Court (only six at that time) delivered their opinions in inverse order of seniority.[36]

The appointment of John Marshall as Chief Justice in 1801 marked a turning point in the Court's life. Marshall was appointed by the federalist John Adams, shortly before the end of his presidential mandate.[37] In the so-called 'Revolution of 1800', the Democratic-Republican Party won control over both houses of the Congress and, with the victory of Thomas Jefferson, the presidential seat and the executive power. At that time all six Justices of the federal Supreme Court were nominees of the first two Presidents (George Washington and John Adams), both federalists. Thus after the election of Jefferson the Court was at clear odds with the other two branches of government.

In this institutional and political context, the objective of the new Chief Justice was to consolidate the prestige and authority of the Supreme Court and to bring its position to a level equal to the other two branches of government. In fact, during the first years, the Federal Supreme Court and its members did not enjoy the high respect and good name they do today. In ten years five Justices decided

34 Gorla (n 6) 1255.

35 It was done only in 1876 with the Appellate Jurisdiction Act.

36 Zo Bell (n 15) 192. Seniority refers not to age but to length of service. Seniority is often relevant in the practice of the US Supreme Court, as it usually determines the order of the Justices' performance. Robert J Janosik, 'Seniority' in Kermit L Hall (ed), *The Oxford Companion to the Supreme Court of the United States* (2nd edn, OUP 2005) 903. The first six Justices were (in order of appointment): James Wilson, John Jay (Chief Justice), John Blair and William Cushing (appointed on the same day), John Rutledge and James Iredell, all nominated by President George Washington.

37 John Marshall was appointed by the President on 20 January 1801, and he took office on 4 February. The presidential elections ended on 17 February with the victory of Thomas Jefferson, the first Republican President of the United States.

to give up their judicial career for a more prestigious and better paying job, and two candidates refused the nomination.[38]

Establishing the power of judicial review was one of the main achievements of Chief Justice Marshall, but not the only one. Another innovation connected with his name is the discontinuance of the practice of *seriatim* opinions. Even if the idea of an 'opinion of the court', representing the decision of the majority, was not his,[39] it was he who consolidated it in the Supreme Court's practice. Already in the decision *Talbot v. Seaman*,[40] the first case Marshall heard as Chief Justice, we can read the wording 'Mr. Chief Justice Marshall delivered the opinion of the court', which later became customary.[41] In the first five years of his office (1801–1805), Marshall wrote the opinion of the court in more than half of the cases (28 out of 47), while in the other half the judgment was rendered *per curiam*, i.e. collectively and unanimously.[42] In those early years he was the only one who wrote the majority opinion of the Court. During his entire tenure he authored nearly half of the 519 cases.[43] There was only one separate opinion written in this period: a concurrence by Justice Chase in 1804.[44] Later it happened sometimes that the Justices decided to return to the practice of *seriatim* opinions, but Marshall never participated in these cases (he was either absent or had recused himself).[45]

This balance was challenged in 1804 by the arrival of a new member, William Johnson, the first Justice appointed by President Thomas Jefferson. Johnson found himself working with fellow judges of opposite political orientations. He was personally linked closely to President Jefferson, and the two exchanged their ideas frequently.[46] Jefferson was a harsh critic of the Marshall Court and a

38 Even the first Chief Justice, John Jay, left the Court to become Governor of the State of New York. Morgan (n 25) 361, fn 24.

39 Before the appointment of Marshall, in the case *Bas v. Tingy*, 4 U.S. (4 Dallas) 37 (1800) Justice Chase wrote: 'The judges agreeing unanimously in their opinion, I presumed that the sense of the court would have been delivered by the president; and therefore, I have not prepared a formal argument on the occasion.'

40 *Talbot v. Seaman*, 5 U.S. (1 Cranch) 1 (1801).

41 However, he was not the first one to use this wording. Already in *Brown v. Barry* of 1797, 3 U.S. (3 Dallas) 365, then Chief Justice Elsworth wrote the opinion of the court using the same expression ('in delivering the opinion of the court').

42 With the exception of two cases in which Marshall did not participate and, therefore, the opinion of the court was authored by the most senior Justice. Percival E Jackson, *Dissent in the Supreme Court* (University of Oklahoma Press 1969) 21. A *per curiam* opinion (literally 'opinion rendered by the court') is an impersonal opinion, not attributed to the authorship to any Justice in particular, but to the court as a collective body.

43 John Marshall was Chief Justice for 34 years, between 1801 and 1835. During this period the Supreme Court decided 1106 cases. Morgan (n 25) 363, fn 32.

44 In the case *Head & Amory v. Providence Ins. Co.*, 6 U.S. (2 Cranch) 127 (1804).

45 The only exception is *Ogden v. Sanders*, 25. U.S. (12 Wheat.) 213 (1827), in which, however, he was not part of the majority delivering *seriatim* opinions. In this case he wrote a dissenting opinion. Zo Bell (n 15) 195, fn 50.

46 Thomas Jefferson's correspondence is available in a number of publications. For example, Joyce Appleby and Terence Ball (eds), *Jefferson: Political Writings* (CUP 1999), and Merrill D Peterson (ed), *Writings. Thomas Jefferson* (Library of America 1984).

fierce supporter of the practice of *seriatim* opinions. In one of his letters written to Thomas Ritchie, a well-known journalist from Virginia, he voiced a pungent criticism against the Court's working method: 'An opinion is huddled up in conclave, perhaps by a majority of one, delivered as if unanimous, and with the silent acquiescence of lazy or timid associates, by a crafty chief judge, who sophisticates the law to his mind, by the turn of his own reasoning.'[47] On another occasion he wrote:

> The practice is certainly convenient for the lazy, the modest & the incompetent. It saves them the trouble of developing their opinion methodically and even making up an opinion at all. That of seriatim argument shews whether every judge has taken the trouble of understanding the case, of investigating it minutely, and of forming an opinion for himself, instead of pinning it on another's sleeve.[48]

Johnson, appointed Justice of the federal Supreme Court at the young age of 32, was accustomed to the practice of *seriatim* opinions, as he joined the Court from the bench of the Court of Common Pleas of South Carolina, which followed that practice.[49] He wrote in a letter to Thomas Jefferson, revealing interesting and, at the same time, disconcerting facts:

> While I was on our State-bench I was accustomed to delivering seriatim Opinions in our Appellate Court, and was not a little surprised to find our Chief Justice in the Supreme Court delivering all the opinions in Cases in which he sat, even in some Instances when contrary to his own Judgment and Vote. But I remonstrated in vain; the Answer was he is willing to take the trouble and it is a Mark of Respect to him. I soon however found out the real Cause. Cushing was incompetent. Chase could not be got to think or write Paterson was a slow man and willingly declined the Trouble, and the other two (Marshall and Washington) are commonly estimated as one judge. Some Case soon occurred in which I differed from my Brethren, and I felt it a thing of Course to deliver my Opinion. But, during the rest of the Session I heard nothing but Lectures on the Indecency of Judges cutting at each other, and the Loss of Reputation which the Virginia appellate Court had sustained by pursuing such a course.[50]

47 Letter by Jefferson to Thomas Ritchie of 25 December 1820, quoted in Morgan (n 25) 358.
48 Quoted in Morgan (n 25) 355–56.
49 Donald G Morgan, 'Mr. Justice William Johnson and the Constitution' (1944) 57 *Harvard Law Review* 328, 330.
50 Letter to Jefferson, 10 December 1822, Jefferson Papers, Library of Congress, quoted in Morgan (n 49) 333–34. The reference to the Appellate Court of Virginia is not accidental. At the beginning of the 19th century there was a historical contrast between the two courts. See Jackson (n 42) 32.

Justice Johnson proved to be a clever and independent judge, and he is frequently called the 'First Dissenter' of the US Supreme Court.[51] During the thirty years of his career on the Supreme Court, he authored 169 opinions (including the ones written for the majority). Of these, 31 were dissents and 21 were concurrences. Approximately half of the 70 separate opinions delivered in this period were his.[52] Even though his campaign for re-establishing the practice of separate opinions in the name of freedom of speech was unsuccessful, he contributed considerably to the spread of separate opinions in the Supreme Court and to demolish the monopoly of the Chief Justice over the authorship of the majority opinions. In 1809, for the first time, Marshall left the task of writing for the majority to another member of the Court on three occasions.[53] In 1811, after the death of Chase, Marshall and Washington remained the sole Justices being nominated by a federalist President, and from 1812, after the appointment of Joseph Story by President James Madison, they had to work with five judges of the opposite political spectrum. It is not a coincidence that from that year Chief Justice Marshall gave up writing for the majority exclusively.[54] What is more, he even delivered dissenting opinions in a few cases.[55]

John Marshall was an eminent lawyer venerated by American legal historians.[56] His efforts were certainly not driven by the desire to be in the limelight or by an accentuated individualism.[57] He recognised early on that in order to ensure the

51 However, chronologically, the first dissenting opinion of the Marshall Court was delivered by Justice Paterson in *Simms & Wise v. Slacum*, 7 U.S. (3 Cranch) 300, in 1806. Justice Johnson was the author of the first concurring opinion, written in the case *Huidekoper's Lessee v. Douglass*, 7 U.S. (3 Cranch) 1 (1805), while his first dissent dates back to three years later, expressed in *Rose v. Himely*, 8 U.S. (4 Cranch) 241 (1808).

52 Zo Bell (n 15) 197.

53 Washington wrote the opinion of the court in *Pierce v. Turner*, 9 U.S. (5 Cranch) 154 (1809), Cushing in *Marine Insurance Company of Alexandria v. Young*, 9 U.S. (5 Cranch) 187 (1809), and Livingston in *Keene v. United States*, 9 U.S. (5 Cranch) 304 (1809). However, in the reports it is not indicated if the Chief Justice participated in these decisions. Morgan (n 25) 367.

54 In 1812 the Court decided 30 cases, and the opinion of the court was authored by the Chief Justice in only 19 of them. In the period between 1813 and 1822, he wrote on average 15 majority opinions a year, while the other Justices wrote on average 21. Morgan (n 25) 367, fn 56.

55 Between 1805 and 1833, Marshall wrote six dissenting opinions. For a summarising table of the number of separate opinions delivered in that period, see Morgan (n 25) 377.

56 The title of a biography on his life, authored by Prof. Jean Edward Smith, is indicative of Marshall's importance in American legal history: *John Marshall: Definer of a Nation* (H Holt 1998).

57 In the opinion of court delivered in *Little v. Barreme*, 6 U.S. (2 Cranch) 170 (1804), renowned as the case of the Flying Fish, Marshall admits that initially he had been in disagreement with his fellow Justices, but he was later convinced by them about the erroneousness of his position: 'I confess the first bias of my mind was very strong in favour of the opinion that though the instructions of the executive could not give a right, they might yet excuse from damages. [. . .] But I have been convinced that I was mistaken, and I have receded from this first opinion.'

Supreme Court an equal position among the branches of government it was necessary to show unity between the members of the Court. The practice of delivering opinions individually and separately, as was done in England, did not allow the Supreme Court to show such unity. The new decision-making practice made it possible for the Court to speak with one voice and to assert itself more forcefully in the US legal system, especially against the Congress and the President. Other Chief Justices, of later ages, recognised this as well. In the famous segregation case *Brown v. Board of Education*,[58] Chief Justice Earl Warren worked hard to reach unanimity, without which the enforcement of the judgment would have been even more difficult. But notwithstanding this clear advantage of speaking with one voice, giving up the practice of *seriatim* opinions met with considerable resistance, most importantly by President Jefferson, who feared that majority judgments could conceal a delegation of the decision to one single member of the Court by the other members because of their laziness or incompetence. Therefore it is interesting to look at the historical development of dissenting opinions in the US Supreme Court, and to discover how this initial suspicion turned into a positive attitude in less than a century.

Concluding, we saw that the phenomenon of dissenting opinions was born as a compromise between the practice of writing *seriatim* opinions, followed in the English legal system, and that of apparently unanimous judgments, which has been the case in continental Europe. The first was supported vigorously by President Thomas Jefferson, while Chief Justice Marshall attempted to introduce the latter (in the beginning with success). So today's practice represents a half-way solution between these two opposite positions. It allows the judges to express themselves freely, and at the same time it ensures that the court shows unity through the 'opinion of the court' shared by the majority of the judges. In this way the *ratio decidendi* to be followed as binding precedent is to be found in one opinion, and not to be deduced from more individual judgments as was often the case in the English system. It makes the job of those who have to apply and interpret the decision much easier.

This difference between the English and the American decision-making practice is also due to the principle of separation of powers, which has been at the basis of the organisation of public powers in the United States. In England, on the other hand, until recently, the court of last instance was part of the legislative organ, a committee of the upper chamber of the Parliament. The English approach changed with the Constitutional Reform Act 2005 which replaced the Judicial Committee of the House of Lords with a newly established UK Supreme Court.[59] The principal reason behind this reform was the political will of strengthening the separation of powers in the United Kingdom and, in particular, the independence of the judiciary. The principles of impartiality and of due process are enshrined in the European Convention of Human Rights, of which the UK is one of the original signatories.

58 347 U.S. 483 (1954).
59 See Section 2.1 above.

2.3. *The first 'Great Dissenters' in the history of the US Supreme Court: from Johnson to Holmes*

The possibility for the judges to express themselves freely in every case, by writing separately, contributes to the transparency of the court's work, but it also reveals the personality of its single members and brings them to the limelight. The judges become famous persons. Today they are like celebrities in the United States.[60] Their separate opinions are widely discussed and analysed not only by legal scholars, but also by journalists and specialised television programs which try to foresee the court's decision in the most important and popular cases. Predictions are made on the basis of the opinions of the single judges expressed in previous cases and the questions they ask during the oral hearings.[61] This diffuse interest in the country's highest Justices arose early on, in part due to the perceived importance of the Supreme Court, in part due to the remarkable personality of some of its members. There is no space here to present all of them, and no need either, as they have been the object of numerous scholarly accounts. I limit myself to introduce the first 'Great Dissenters' of the US Supreme Court's history: Justice Johnson (1804–34), Justice Daniel (1841–60), Justice Curtis (1851–57), Justice Holmes (1902–32) and Justice Brandeis (1916–39), who paved the way for their successors, such as Justice Scalia (1986–2016) and others.

The epithet 'First Dissenter' is applied to Justice William Johnson, the judge appointed by President Jefferson in 1804 who, as explained earlier, contributed to a large extent to the spread of separate opinions in the Supreme Court's practice. A few decades later, during the leadership of Roger Brooke Taney (1836–64), Justice Benjamin Robbins Curtis earned the title of 'Great Dissenter' thanks to one dissenting opinion that he delivered in the infamous *Dred Scott* case in 1856.[62] His dissent was sustained by the people and translated into a constitutional amendment just nine years later.[63] The Thirteenth Amendment, which provides for the abolition of slavery, would have been unthinkable at the time of *Dred Scott*. Before the Civil War, the Republican Party also supported slavery, considering it the price to pay for saving the Union.[64] When the Thirteenth Amendment was ratified, in 1865, Justice Curtis was not on the Court anymore.

60 For a more detailed discussion of the phenomenon: Craig S Lerner and Nelson Lund, 'Judicial Duty and the Supreme Court's Cult of Celebrity' (2010) 78 *George Washington Law Review* 1255.

61 A recent example of such predictions can be found in relation to the landmark case *Obergefell v. Hodges*, 576 U.S. ___ (2015) on the states' duty to recognise lawfully licensed same-sex marriages. The Guardian, among others, published a long article examining the possible position of the single Justices. Amanda Holpuch, 'The Supreme Court Arguments on Gay Marriage, Annotated for Non-Lawyers' (*The Guardian*, 29 April 2015) <www.theguardian.com/law/2015/apr/28/supreme-court-arguments-gay-marriage> accessed 18 January 2017.

62 *Dred Scott v. Sandford*, 60 U.S. (How.) 393 (1856).

63 Zo Bell (n 15) 198.

64 Donald E Lively, *Foreshadows of the Law: Supreme Court Dissents and Constitutional Development* (Praeger 1992) 31 and 37–38.

He resigned from the Court only after six years of service due to the bad blood between the judges generated by the *Dred Scott* case.[65]

However, it was Peter Vivian Daniel, another Justice who served on the Court during the same period, who came to be known as the most tenacious dissenter. He dissented in many more occasions than Justice Curtis. However, his opinions are not remembered today, as they did not contribute to the development of constitutional law. He usually wrote separately in order to defend slavery and the powers of the states.[66]

In the period following the Civil War, the most memorable dissenter was Justice John Marshall Harlan, who, in his judicial career of more than 30 years (1877–1911), wrote separately 416 times (100 concurrences and 316 dissents).[67] His most renowned and celebrated dissent was in the landmark *Plessy v. Ferguson* (1896)[68] case on racial segregation in public transportation. His opinion was defended and shared by a unanimous Supreme Court a half century later in the famous *Segregation cases*.[69] An article of the New York Times commenting on these judgments defined his dissenting opinion as 'an instance of which the voice crying in the wilderness finally becomes an expression of a people's will and in which justice overtakes and thrusts aside a timorous expediency'.[70] It was in this opinion that Justice Harlan coined the expression 'our Constitution is color-blind', which entered into American constitutional history. Even if the legendary judgment in *Brown v. Board of Education* does not make explicit reference to Harlan's dissent, as Donald E. Lively observes, '[m]odern jurisprudence now refers in a single breath to the *Brown* decision and Harlan dissent'.[71]

At the beginning of the 20th century, American constitutional history was instead dominated by the personality of Oliver Wendell Holmes, considered the best known figure ever connected to the US Supreme Court; he succeeded to Harlan's title of Great Dissenter. He actually wrote separately less frequently than most of his colleagues, but his dissenting opinions, unlike Harlan's, achieved

65 Curtis went back to his legal practice in Boston, and he was one of President Andrew Jackson's counsels in the impeachment proceedings in 1868. Richard Y Funston, 'Benjamin Robbins Curtis' in Hall (n 36) 242, 243.

66 Burton J Hendrick, *Bulwark of the Republic: A Biography of the Constitution* (rev edn, Brown 1941) 417. Justice Daniel justified his tenacity by stating that the oath of office obliges each Justice to follow his own version of constitutional truth no matter how singular it is. Maurice Kelman, 'The Forked Path of Dissent' (1985) *The Supreme Court Review* 227, 249. In a concurrence in the *License Cases*, 46 U.S. (5 How.) 504, 612 (1847) he wrote: 'I possess no sovereign prerogative by which I can put my conscience into commission. I must interpret exclusively as that conscience shall dictate.'

67 He heard a total of 7,649 cases. 107 of his dissenting opinions were joined by at least three colleagues. Zo Bell (n 15) 199.

68 *Plessy v. Ferguson*, 163 U.S. 537 (1896).

69 *Brown v. Board of Education*, 347 U.S. 483 (1954) and *Bolling v. Sharp*, 347 U.S. 497 (1954).

70 *New York Times*, 23 May 1954, § 4, p 10E, cols 1–2, quoted in Zo Bell (n 15) 201.

71 Lively (n 64) 108.

substantial recognition when they were published.[72] Holmes and Louis Dembitz Brandeis, appointed to the Court 14 years after him, formed the first 'dissenter couple' of the US Supreme Court.[73] Interestingly, after Brandeis joined the Court, Holmes dissented twice as frequently as he had before.[74] Justice Holmes was also the most fortunate dissenter of the Supreme Court. The list of his 'successes' is impressive. Several of his dissenting opinions were later vindicated. The most well-known example is his opinion according to which the federal Constitution does not incorporate any economic theory, expressed for the first time in *Lochner v. New York* (1905),[75] the case that gave its name to the famous 'Lochner Era'.[76] This dissent of Holmes was first followed tacitly (in *Bunting v. State of Oregon*),[77] then explicitly (*West Coast Hotel v. Parrish*).[78] Further examples are his dissenting opinion in *Adair v. United States*,[79] which became the law 29 years later in *National Labor Relations Board v. Jones & Laughlin Steel Corp.*,[80] and his dissent in *Baldwin v. State of Missouri*,[81] which persuaded the majority of the Justices only twelve years later in the case *State Tax Commission of Utah v. Aldrich*.[82]

72 Zo Bell (n 15) 201–2.
73 In a short article Cass R Sunstein observes that the greatest visionaries of the Court formed couples of frequent dissenters: Holmes and Brandeis at the beginning of the 20th century, Douglas and Black in the 1950s, Brennan and Marshall in the 1970s. According to Sunstein, Scalia and Thomas can be considered the successors of these great couples of dissenters. Cass R Sunstein, 'Where Are the Liberal Visionaries on the Supreme Court?' *The New Republic* (15 May 2007).
74 Zo Bell (n 15) 202, fn 89.
75 198 U.S. 45 (1905).
76 Jack M Balkin, '"Wrong the Day It Was Decided": Lochner and Constitutional Historicism' (2005) 85 *Boston University Law Review* 677.
77 243 U.S. 426 (1917). In this case Holmes was still on the Court, so it was not only his previous dissenting opinion but also himself that persuaded the majority.
78 300 U.S. 379 (1937). In the opinion of the court an explicit reference is made to Holmes's dissenting opinion delivered in *Adkins v. Children's Hospital*, 261 U.S. 525 (1923), a precedent overruled by this judgment. The first direct references to his dissent in *Lochner* were made by Justice Frankfurter in two dissenting opinions delivered in the 1940s, in the cases *Harris v. United States*, 331 U.S. 145, 157 (1947) and *Winters v. New York*, 333 U.S. 507, 527 (1948).
79 208 U.S. 161 (1908).
80 301 U.S. 1 (1937).
81 281 U.S. 586 (1930).
82 316 U.S. 174 (1942). This judgment can be considered the apogee of Holmes's influence. The opinion of the court, delivered by Justice Douglas, quotes literally several opinions authored by Holmes: his dissent in the aforementioned *Baldwin v. State of Missouri*, the majority opinion delivered by Holmes in *Blackstone v. Miller*, 188 U.S. 189 (1903), and his separate opinions written in *Farmers' Loan & Trust Co. v. State of Minnesota*, 280 U.S. 204 (1930), *Southern Pacific Co. v. Jensen*, 244 U.S. 205 (1917), and *Union Refrigerator Transit Co. v. Commonwealth of Kentucky*, 199 U.S. 194 (1905). Holmes's opinion expressed in the *Union Refrigerator* case is exemplary and illustrates his concise and witty style perfectly. This opinion consists of only one sentence: 'It seems to me that the result reached by the court probably is a desirable one, but I hardly understand how it can be deduced from the 14th Amendment; and as the Chief Justice feels the same difficulty, I think it proper to say that my doubt has not been removed.' For other examples of success of Justice Holmes see Zo Bell (n 15) 202, fn 92.

It is also worth mentioning, however, that Justice Holmes authored a few repugnant opinions as well in the field of civil rights.[83] Among these we can mention *Buck v. Bell*,[84] in which the Court refused to declare unconstitutional a statute of Virginia authorising compulsory sterilisation of the intellectually disabled for the purpose of eugenics. Holmes, writing for the majority, made an outrageous and ill-famed observation ('three generations of imbeciles are enough'), which is quoted as frequently as his more successful opinions. However, the important role he played in American constitutional development is undeniable. He contributed to the destruction of the myth of judicial certainty[85] and to the foundation of sociological jurisprudence.[86]

3. The practice of dissenting opinions in the common law tradition: the United Kingdom and the United States compared

3.1. The decision-making process: two common law supreme courts compared

There is much more written about the decision-making process of the court of last instance in the United States than in the United Kingdom. It might be, however, due to the fact that legal literature is more abundant in the US in general, as legal scholarship plays a more relevant role than in the UK.[87] The US Supreme Court, in particular since the 1940s, has received much attention by researchers and the public in general. American judges have traditionally been protagonists in the US legal system and do not refrain from public appearances and dialogue with the mass media. Moreover, the characteristics of the US court system also call for a greater amount of research. Being more complex and larger than the English court system, there is a greater variety of judicial decisions and

83 Lively (n 64) 68.

84 274 U.S. 200 (1927).

85 Philip B Kurland, 'The Supreme Court and the Attrition of State Power' (1958) 10 *Stanford Law Review* 274, 277. As the editor of a volume collecting and translating into Italian a selection of opinions and essays by Justice Holmes, Carmelo Geraci, observed: 'Holmes's way of thinking is permeated by radical skepticism that rejects any "essence" and denies any objective certainty' (my own translation). Oliver Wendell Holmes, *Opinioni dissenzienti. A cura di Carmelo Geraci* (Milano 1975) XVIII.

86 Roscoe Pound, 'Judges Holmes's Contributions to the Science of Law' (1921) 34 *Harvard Law Review* 449, which dates back to an earlier time than the cases of overruling in which the Supreme Court decided to adopt the opinion of Justice Holmes.

87 Geoffrey Samuel, in his general introduction to English common law, even entitled his concluding remarks 'Absence of a legal science'. He explains that the main reasons for this are the lack of university law faculties until the late 19th century and the old forms of action, which did not lend themselves to scientific analysis. Geoffrey Samuel, 'Common law' in Jan M Smits (ed), *Elgar Encyclopedia of Comparative Law* (2nd edn, Edward Elgar 2012) 169, 188.

of decision-making processes.[88] American studies are not limited to the federal court system, but often also include state courts.[89]

The United Kingdom's court system is smaller and less complex. Furthermore, English judges, have traditionally been more conservative and reticent. However, in the last decades personal writings and judicial notebooks of the English judges have also become available. It made it possible for English researchers to examine the internal dynamics of decision-making in the United Kingdom's final court.[90] The new Supreme Court appears to be far more accessible than the House of Lords ever was. Today oral hearings are public and broadcasted live. The increased transparency is matched by the willingness of Justices to deliver public lectures and to give interviews.[91]

A comparative perspective on the judicial decision-making process has already been presented in the previous chapter, focusing on European constitutional courts. This section will present, briefly, the decision-making process of the two most important common law supreme courts taking into consideration the same issues: the internal court structure and the role of different actors. Historically, a fundamental difference in the decision-making process between the UK and the US is that while the former followed the practice of *seriatim* opinions, the latter soon began to deliver a majority judgment, the opinion of the court, possibly but not necessarily accompanied by separate opinions. Several differences in the decision-making process between the two supreme courts are ascribable to this historical divergence, but today's practice is much less diverging than one would expect.

To begin with, in the original English practice there was no opinion-writer judge. The judge was not required to submerge his views in the composite judgment of the court. He could decide to join a colleague's judgment by delivering a so-called 'formal concurrence', but he could also write separately when he was part of the majority.[92] In the US Supreme Court, on the other hand, it became an established practice very soon that the judgment, even if written by one Justice, represented the 'opinion of the court', and not only that of the opinion-writer. However, each Justice still has the possibility to write a separate concurring opinion. If the separate opinions outnumber the majority (i.e. five or more Justices on the US Supreme Court today), it becomes difficult to argue that the judgment

88 Max Gluckman, 'Judicial Process. Comparative Aspects' (1968) 8 *International Encyclopedia of the Social Sciences* 291, 292.

89 For example, the volume edited by Cornell W Clayton and Howard Gillman, *Supreme Court Decision-making: New Institutionalist Approaches* (University of Chicago Press 1999), containing essays both on the federal Supreme Court and on state supreme courts.

90 The first two most important works are Blom-Cooper and Drewry, *The Final Appeal* (n 8), published in 1972, and Paterson (n 23), published in 1982.

91 Paterson (n 8) 3. Paterson's new book, published in 2013, is the most recent empirical study of the UK's final court which is a follow-up of his previous research carried out at the end of the 1970s and published in *The Law Lords* (n 23) in 1982. Paterson compares the practice of the Appellate Committee with that of the new Supreme Court.

92 Blom-Cooper and Drewry (n 8) 79.

really represents the opinion of the court. The problem of these so-called 'plurality opinions' will be discussed later.

In both the UK's and the US Supreme Court, Justices meet after the oral hearing to discuss the disposition of the case. This meeting, called 'conference' both in Washington and in London, is confidential. No witnesses are allowed.[93] During the conference the English Justices also jointly decide who will write the 'major opinion' or 'lead judgment'. The lead judgment includes a detailed statement of the facts, while the other judges usually limit themselves to the legal questions in their separate opinions.[94] This practice was maintained by the new Supreme Court, and there has also been an increased push for more joint or composite judgments. In the House of Lords, the assignment of these opinions was the product of collective agreement, and in just very exceptional cases the presiding judge, due to policy reasons, took this decision.[95] In general, as Paterson observes, different presiders adopted different practices, making it difficult to generalise on the process.[96] In any event, there is no formal voting at the conference in the UK's final court, and there is no written rule for the allocation of the lead judgment. Moreover, English Justices often agree on who is to deal with a particular aspect of the case, taking account of their respective workloads, expertise and interest in the case.[97]

In the US Supreme Court, on the other hand, it is for the Chief Justice to assign the opinion of the court to one of the Justices (or to herself/himself), but only if s/he is part of the majority.[98] When s/he is not, the decision on case assignment is made by the senior associate justice in the majority.[99] This rule opens the door to tactical voting by the Chief Justice who, at the conference, might join the position that seems to prevail just in order to be able to decide who will write the opinion of the court.[100] This strategy cannot be applied by the President of the UK Supreme Court.

After the conference and the allocation of who will write the 'lead judgment' (in the UK) or the 'opinion of the court' (in the US), the circulation of opinions begins,[101] and the process is the same in Washington and in London. Today,

93 In the House of Lords a clerk was present at the conference, but no minutes were taken by him. It is not the case anymore in the UK Supreme Court. Paterson (n 8) 84.

94 Paterson (n 23) 92–93.

95 Paterson (n 8) 91. This happened, for example, in the case *DPP v. Smith* (1961) AC 290 (H.L.), in which Lord Kilmuir insisted that only one opinion of the court should be produced and that it should appear under his name.

96 Paterson (n 8) 92.

97 Paterson (n 8) 91.

98 See Chapter 2, text to n 52.

99 Seniority according to length of service, not to age. See n 36.

100 Chief Justice Burger (1969–86) was accused of acting in this way on several occasions. Paterson (n 23) 93 and 239, fn 40. In the United Stated the techniques of case assignment are widely studied and analysed. See for example Thomas H Hammond, Chris W Bonneau and Reginald S Sheehan, *Strategic Behavior and Policy Choice on the U.S. Supreme Court* (Stanford UP 2005).

101 Interestingly, this drafting and circulation stage lasted a similar length of time on average in the UK and in the US until recently. In the House of Lords, it took on average six weeks

in both courts, the majority opinion is the first to be circulated, but in the UK Supreme Court this has become the rule only very recently, in 2012. Before, there was no convention as to the order in which opinions should be circulated. Thus those judges who produced their drafts swiftly could circulate them even by the end of the oral hearing.[102] At the same time, in the US Supreme Court, drafts might be exchanged informally with allies before the formal circulation. At this circulation stage, the Justice who is assigned to write for the majority receives comments and suggestions from her/his colleagues, and it is not rare that she has to modify the text in order to retain the support of the majority.[103]

A significant difference between the two supreme courts concerns the composition of the adjudicating panel. The US Supreme Court has no panels. It always decides as a full court, composed of nine judges. The new UK Supreme Court is composed of 12 Justices, but it usually decides in smaller panels of three or five members. But how are the members of the panel chosen? This question is not relevant for the US Supreme Court, as it always decides *en banc*, but it is of significant importance for understanding the practice of the UK's final court. There are two types of panels: the Appeal Committees, composed of three members, selecting the appeals that will be heard by the Court,[104] and the Appellate Committees, composed of five members, which hear and decide the appeals admitted by the Appeal Committees. While it is formally the task of the Principal Clerk of the Judicial Office to appoint the panels for these committees, over the years the senior Law Lords came to take a more prominent role in the process.[105] The system of selecting the panels, in any event, has been characterised by a high degree of discretion, both in relation to the number and the choice of the members.[106]

---

for the Law Lords to prepare the final version of their opinion. Paterson (n 23) 94. For the Justices of the US Supreme Court it takes between 35–58 days. Henry J Abraham, *The Judicial Process* (7th edn, Oxford UP 1998) 234. By the millennium, however, the circulation of opinions among the Law Lords had become a longer process exceeding three months and sometimes taking more than eight months. The average gap from hearing to handing down of the judgment dropped again to less than two months after Lord Bingham's arrival in 2000. It began to rise again when Lord Philips took over as first President of the Supreme Court, as he was more relaxed than Lord Bingham as to when judgments were produced. Paterson (n 8) 120–21.

102 Paterson (n 8) 98.

103 Henry J Abraham, in his famous work on the American judicial process, writes that he was told by Justice Brennan that 'post-conference "lineup" switches are far more common than is generally believed', and 'he estimated such switches to take place in one of every five cases'. Abraham concludes by stating that '[t]here is simply no guarantee that the conference vote on the merits of a case will really constitute the final vote'. Abraham (n 101) 236, fn 232.

104 Also called PTA committees ('permission to appeal' committees).

105 Paterson (n 8) 67–68. As to the composition of the Appellate Committees, by convention, the final say laid with the two most senior Law Lords, but in practice neither of them made any changes to the Clerk's proposals. Ibid. 71.

106 Andrew Le Sueur, 'A Report on Six Seminars About the U.K. Supreme Court' (2008) Queen Mary University of London, Legal Studies Research Paper 1/2008, 24 <http://ssrn.com/abstract=1324749> accessed 18 January 2017.

Until the 1980s, in the Appellate Committee of the House of Lords, it was for the Lord Chancellor to choose the members of the panels in each case. This task, however, was in practice delegated to his Permanent Secretary, who took account of the Law Lords' specialism.[107] At the end of each judicial term he met with the Principal Clerk of the Judicial Office (who was already in charge of selecting the members of the Appeal Committees) and the Judicial Clerk of the Privy Council in order to synchronise the composition of the panels and the dates of the hearings.[108] For organizational reasons, there was a tendency to keep the same composition for the longest time possible.

As regards the new Supreme Court, the Constitutional Reform Act and the new Rules of Court are silent on the issue.[109] The Clerk to the Judicial Office still allocates the petitions to the Appeal Committees. A small novelty today is that each Justice has the opportunity to comment on every permission to appeal a petition and to email or pass comments to a member of the relevant Appeal Committee which is dealing with the case.[110] There have been no significant changes in the selection of the hearing panels. Today these panels are selected by the Registrar, using the same criteria as in the last years of the House of Lords.[111]

The UK's final court has always been criticised for its lack of transparency. In a seminar organised in London in 2008 to discuss the constitutional reforms and the new Supreme Court to be set up, one of the Law Lords acknowledged that even they did not know exactly how panel selection was handled in practice.[112] Even if there have been several improvements since the detachment of this judicial body from the Parliament, this is still an issue.[113]

In the Supreme Court of the United States, on the other hand, the decision-making process has always received much attention by the public. It is certainly simpler to follow the work of a united body, where panel selection is not an issue at all. It happens that a Justice does not participate in the decision if s/he recuses herself/himself or falls ill,[114] but there is no other organ or officer who would

107 In cases involving Scottish law, for example, usually a Scottish Law Lord was included in the committee. Paterson (n 23) 87–88.

108 Paterson (n 23) 88.

109 The Supreme Court Rules 2009 (SI 2009/1603) (L. 17), <www.supremecourt.uk/docs/uksc_rules_2009.pdf> accessed 18 January 2017.

110 However, it is still relatively rare for the Justices to intervene concerning a PTA petition handled by a panel of which they are not a member. Paterson (n 8) 68–69.

111 Paterson (n 8) 72.

112 Le Sueur (n 106) 25.

113 As Paterson observes in the abstract of his new book: '[D]espite the oft applauded commitment of the new Court to public visibility, the book concludes that even greater transparency in the dialogue with the public may be required.' Paterson (n 8).

114 The American Justices are very cautious and willing to dispel any lingering clouds of suspicion about their impartiality. It is therefore not rare for a Justice to recuse herself/himself from the decision of a case, under the conventional rule 'when in doubt, do not sit', later incorporated in a federal statute (Title 29, s 454, USCA, and Title 28, s 455, USCA) and in Canon no 4 of the Canons of Judicial Ethics adopted by the American Bar Association. Abraham (n 101) 220.

have a say in this decision, such as the Registrar in the UK Supreme Court has. The selection of cases to be heard is also done *en banc*. According to the renowned 'rule of four', at least four Justices (so fewer than the majority) have to agree for a case to be admitted by the Supreme Court.[115] In the UK, on the other hand, the 'rule of thumb' applies, according to which a single vote in the Appeal Committee (composed of three judges) is sufficient for admission. However, the practice is that when there is disagreement, the Justices try to reach a rapprochement, and the final outcome is not always in favour of admitting the appeal.[116]

3.2. *The role of law clerks in the decision-making process*

American legal scholars and political scientists have been paying increasing attention to the role that the clerks of the Justices (the so-called 'law clerks') play in the decision-making process. Research on this subject is carried out necessarily empirically, typically through insider interviews, as there are only fragments of information published on the internal dynamics of the Supreme Court's decision-making process. Interviews are conducted with the judges and clerks at their own discretion and availability. In the second half of the 20th century, the available data on the Court's inner workings multiplied. This was thanks in part to the publication of a number of judicial memoirs. The proliferation of dissenting opinions also drew the interest of researchers into the internal dynamics of the Court. The first internal account of this kind, *The Brethren*, by Bob Woodward and Scott Armstrong, two investigative journalists of The Washington Post, published in 1979, caused a sensation.[117] It was based on information obtained from 170 anonymous law clerks and questionnaires prepared and analysed by the authors. *The Brethren* broke new ground in the literature on the US Supreme Court, and it attracted attention to the role of law clerks.

Twenty years later, in the famous *Bush v. Gore* case,[118] the Supreme Court adopted an unexpected and atypical decision, which consisted of a *per curiam* opinion accompanied by five separate opinions (one concurring and four dissenting opinions). Only two of the nine Justices did not join any of the separate opinions.[119] The case, for the obvious reason of its political importance, was widely discussed by the media and drew the attention of many scholars of the American

115 It is a customary rule, not provided by any positive law.

116 Paterson (n 8) 249.

117 Bob Woodward and Scott Armstrong, *The Brethren: Inside the Supreme Court* (Simon and Schuster 1979). Bob Woodward had become famous (together with Carl Bernstein) for his investigative reports on the Nixon administration and the Watergate scandal generated by these in 1972.

118 *Bush v. Gore*, 513 U.S. 98 (2000).

119 Justices Rehnquist, Scalia and Thomas delivered a joint concurring opinion, while dissent was expressed by Justices Stevens, Souter, Ginsburg and Breyer, each of whom joint at least one of the four dissenting opinions to various extent. All five separate opinions are shared, at least partially, by at least three Justices.

legal system. An article which appeared in *Vanity Fair* in 2004 disclosed the behind-the-curtain background of the decision and lifted a little corner of the veil on the internal dynamics of the Court in the period of the 2000 presidential elections.[120] The *Vanity Fair* article analysed the Court's decision-making process in the light of, the sometimes gossip-like, information obtained from some law clerks. The clerks' indiscreetness divided the legal community and re-opened the debate on the clerks' role and function. Edward Lazarus, a former clerk of Justice Blackmun himself, defended the indiscreet law clerks and called for more investigative research on the Supreme Court's activity.[121] According to him, the clerks are a precious source of information on the internal dynamics of the Court, and their availability to disclose this otherwise inaccessible information may contribute to greater transparency of this branch of government. He argued that the case of *Bush v. Gore* proves why the 'just read our opinions' approach of the Justices is questionable.[122]

A more recent study on Supreme Court clerks is *Sorcerers' Apprentices* by Artemus Ward and David L Weiden, published in 2006.[123] The title alludes to the famous poem by Wolfgang Goethe in which the young apprentice uses magic of his master in which he is not yet fully trained. He does not know how to break the spell and gets into trouble, which has to be solved by the old sorcerer at his return. The moral of the story: do not start something you cannot finish. The law clerks are like the sorcerer's apprentice in Goethe's poem who tries to do something which is beyond his competence and of which he lacks the necessary knowledge and experience.

While their participation in the procedure of case selection, in the so-called 'cert pool',[124] is well-known and undisputed, their opinion-writing activity is much contested and also rather unclear for the outsider. The extent to which clerks are involved in the opinion-writing process (both in relation to opinions of the court and of separate opinions) varies from judge to judge, and there is no available official data on this. We can learn something about the working methods of individual judges and their chambers from judicial memoirs

120 David Margolick, Evgenia Peretz and Michael Shnayerson, 'The Path to Florida' *Vanity Fair* (October 2004) 310.

121 Lazarus concludes: 'If law clerks do not speak, we will never know.' Edward Lazarus, 'The Supreme Court's Excessive Secrecy: Why It Isn't Merited', *FindLaw Legal News and Commentary* (30 September 2004) <http://writ.news.findlaw.com/lazarus/20040930.html> accessed 19 January 2017.

122 On this case also David Lane, '*Bush v. Gore*, Vanity Fair, and a Supreme Court Law Clerk's Duty of Confidentiality' (2005) 18 *Georgetown Journal of Legal Ethics* 863.

123 Artemus Ward and David L Weiden, *Sorcerers' Apprentices: 100 Years of Law Clerks at the United States Supreme Court* (New York UP 2006).

124 The 'cert pool' is a meeting of all law clerks working at the Supreme Court where they distribute the cases among themselves. Each law clerk is then responsible for the preparation of the so-called 'pool memo' in the assigned cases. A pool memo consists of a summary of the petition, an assessment of the case and a proposal whether to grant or deny the writ of certiorari. Michael F Sturley, 'Cert pool' in Hall (n 36) 155.

and interviews granted by law clerks to journalists and researchers. The study conducted by Ward and Weiden reveals the increasing importance of the law clerks in the Supreme Court's decision-making process. Since the Warren era (1953–1969), they have been increasingly involved in the drafting of opinions.[125] At the same time, the Court has been criticised for the less personal tone of its opinions and for the unrestrained proliferation of separate opinions. According to some, it would be ascribable to the greater involvement of law clerks in the drafting of opinions.[126] It is clear that as long as a Justice kept the opinion-writing completely for herself/himself, using her/his clerks only for collecting data and materials and for conducting case-law research, s/he would have less time to dedicate to writing separately. Given that a Justice who remains in the minority is not obliged to write separately, s/he certainly takes into consideration the time and workload factor when deciding whether to do so.

As regards the UK's final court, clerkship is a relatively new phenomenon. The practice of recruiting very bright young lawyers in the early years of qualification to help the work of appellate judges emerged first in the US Supreme Court at the end of the 19th century and thereafter spread through the common law jurisdictions (and beyond).[127] In the UK, it was introduced by Lord Bingham in 2001, after he became senior Law Lord.[128] In the English system, clerks are called 'judicial assistants'.[129] Not all Justices of the Supreme Court have their own clerk, as in the US Supreme Court. At the beginning, only four judicial assistants were recruited, as there was physically no space for more of them in the House. One was assigned to each of the four senior Law Lords as their lead judge, and the remaining Law Lords took a share of what was left by the seniors. When the Supreme Court was set up and the Justices moved into another building, the number of judicial assistants was increased to eight, still a lower number than that of the judges.[130] Therefore, there are no 'chambers' on the UK's final court, like in the US Supreme Court, where each Justice has four clerks.[131] Judicial assistants

125 This major involvement is partially due to the similar practice of distributing the cases among the Justices, introduced by Chief Justice Warren. Before Warren, the cases had been allocated according to the single judges' swiftness. Thus after the introduction of the new practice the slower judges had to deal with a greater number of cases, and began to delegate more work to their clerks. Ward and Weiden (n 123) 204.

126 Ward and Weiden (n 123) 231.

127 Paterson (n 8) 247. In the Supreme Court it started in 1882 and received legislative sanction in 1919.

128 Ibid. The figure of clerk already existed in the magistrates' court though. They are professional lawyers (usually solicitors or, less often, barristers) who assist the lay judges and advise them on legal questions. This is, however, a clearly different job of that of a law clerk in an appellate court. Brian Fraser Harrison, *The Work of a Magistrate* (Shaw & Sons 1964) 115, and Terence Ingman, *The English Legal Process* (10th edn, OUP 2004) 49–50.

129 As already mentioned, I use the term 'law clerk' consistently throughout the book in relation to all examined courts. See Chapter 2, n 101.

130 Paterson (n 8) 247.

131 The Chief Justice has five. These chambers are composed of the Justice and her/his clerks, and they work as team, almost like a law firm. The term 'chamber' refers also to the place where

form a team, have their offices on the same floor, and are bound together by a communal spirit. The recruitment process was coordinated by Justice Lord Hope until his retirement in 2013, but the other Justices had a say in it too and expressed their preferences.[132] However, interestingly, no attempt seems to be made to link candidates and Justices in terms of philosophical outlook, like in the United States.[133]

The primary stated function of the UK Supreme Court's clerks is similar to the American 'cert pool' practice. They divide up the petitions between them and write a memorandum of the key points in the case, which is circulated to all Justices.[134] English clerks, unlike their US counterparts, attend the discussion of the petition in the Appeal Committee.[135] They do not participate in the conference of the Appellate Committee though.

When the position was established in 2001, English judicial assistants were definitely not supposed to be involved in the writing of the first drafts of judgments. They still do not write first drafts themselves, but their input is increasing. Some Justices discuss their drafts with their assistant and ask them to comment on it and to be as critical as possible of it.[136] According to Paterson, the role of the judicial assistant is evolving and probably will continue to evolve. It could go in the same direction as in the US Supreme Court 70 years ago, where the involvement of clerks in the writing of the drafts was an unintended consequence of a reform in the 1940s. Then Chief Justice Vinson tried to equalise workloads on the Court, but it led to some Justices asking their clerks to be responsible for the first draft of their opinions. However, today in the UK Supreme Court there is still a robust consensus among the Justices that the assistants' role should not encompass the writing of judgments.[137]

3.3. *Separate opinions and the doctrine of binding precedent: the problematic issue of plurality opinions*

A special issue for common law jurisdictions is the relationship between dissenting opinions and the value of precedents. This relationship is of lesser relevance, though not completely insignificant, in civil law legal systems. The doctrine of binding precedent, or principle of *stare decisis*, which is one of the pillars of the

---

the offices of the Justice and her/his clerks are located in the Supreme Court Building. Maxwell Bloomfield, 'Chambers' in Hall (n 36) 157.

132 For example, Lord Bingham's assistants were often graduates with a First in an Arts subject, Lord Rodger appreciated candidates with a background in civil law, and Lord Hope himself often chose a Scottish solicitor. Paterson (n 8) 248.

133 Ibid.

134 The memos are circulated to all Justices, although only those on the relevant Appeal Committee are expected to read them. Paterson (n 8) 69.

135 Increasingly, some of the Justices have been asking the assistant to review the applications for leave in order to assist the Justice in preparing for PTA panel and to provide their opinion on whether the application should be granted. Paterson (n 8) 249.

136 The extent of this involvement varies quite much between Justices. Paterson (n 8) 252.

137 Paterson (n 8) 255–56.

common law tradition, is not formally advocated in continental Europe, but civil law courts also consider their own precedents as imperative.[138]

There are at least two questions that arise in relation to the precedential value of judicial opinions. First, what precedential value can a separate opinion have? Second, does a judgment accompanied by a dissenting opinion have the same precedential value as a unanimous decision? In particular, what if the reasons underlying a decision are not supported by the majority of the judges? The answer to the first question is the easier one: separate opinions do not have any precedential value. They are not binding for anybody. It does not mean, however, that they cannot have an impact or even be adopted fully in a future case. They certainly may have a persuasive effect, even if not a binding one. In the United States, in particular, certain dissenting opinions have become part of the canons of constitutional law.[139]

The proliferation of dissenting opinions, especially in the US, has emphasised the second question. Its side-effect, the phenomenon of the so-called 'plurality opinions', puts a serious challenge on a legal system built on the rule of precedent.[140] We call 'plurality opinion' a judgment that lacks a clear majority. That is why sometimes they are also called 'no-clear-majority' decisions or decisions of relative majority. A plurality opinion is shared by the majority only as regards the outcome of the case, but not the reasoning. This means that more than half of the judges deliver a separate opinion (or join one). Therefore, in these cases, the only certainty for those who have to follow the judgment as precedent is the outcome of the case. In US legal scholarship, according to the classical theory, an opinion of the court which is not clearly shared by the majority in its entirety is not a binding precedent, and its authority is limited to the outcome of the case.[141] The outcome consists of the statement concerning which party wins the case.[142]

The continuously increasing number of plurality opinions, however, made it impelling to find a reasonable solution to this problem.[143] The US Supreme

138 Merryman (n 4) 46–47. See also Chapter 5, Section 5.

139 These so-called 'canonical' dissents were mainly authored by Justices Holmes, Brandeis and Harlan. Jack M Balkin and Sanford Levinson, 'The Canons of Constitutional Law' (1998) 111 *Harvard Law Review* 964, 1008. G Edward White, 'The Canonization of Holmes and Brandeis: Epistemology and Judicial Reputations' (1995) 70 *New York University Law Review* 576.

140 A note published in the *Harvard Law Review* explains this phenomenon with the fact that the Supreme Court has been increasingly engaging in substantive reasoning – 'a form of reasoning which is heavily value laden and relies on an arbitrary choice of values from sources external to the Constitution'. Substantive reasoning arose as a reaction to legal formalism during the Lochner era. In constitutional law it has been called 'noninterpretivist' or purposive reasoning. Note, 'Plurality Decisions and Judicial Decisionmaking' (1981) 94 *Harvard Law Review* 1127, 1140–41.

141 Linda Novak, 'The Precedential Value of Supreme Court Plurality Decisions' (1980) 80 *Columbia Law Review* 756, 758, fn 11. Linda Novak refers to a handbook of Henry Campbell Black, founder of Black's Law Dictionary, published in 1912 and to a study of Professor Eugene Wambaugh of 1894.

142 Not in a constitutional court, where the outcome of the case is the answer to the question of constitutionality, i.e. whether the reviewed law violated the constitution.

143 In the history of the US Supreme Court, until 1979, a third of all plurality opinions (45 of 146) were delivered in the last 24 years. Novak (n 141) 756, fn 2.

Court faced the problem for the first time in the 1970s in *Gregg v. Georgia*,[144] when it had to decide whether to follow a plurality opinion as precedent. The plurality opinion in question had been delivered in *Furman v. Georgia*,[145] a famous case concerning death penalty, decided four years earlier. In that case, the opinion of court did not bear the name of any Justice, but had been delivered *per curiam*, i.e. anonymously.[146] Rather atypically, all nine Justices had written separately.[147] In *Gregg v. Georgia* the Court adopted the so-called 'narrowest grounds approach',[148] which was later confirmed and applied in *Marks v. United States.*[149] This approach looks for the concurring opinion that represented the 'narrowest grounds' for the decision and applies that as a precedent. The Court, however, did not define the concept of 'narrowest grounds'. It emerges from the cases in which the approach has been used and has various understandings. Usually the Court follows the concurring opinion which is the most clearly tailored to the specific fact situation and thus applicable to the fewest cases, or the one based on statutory grounds rather than on constitutional grounds. In other occasions, the Court chose to follow the concurring opinion which departed the least from the *status quo* as the narrowest one.[150]

3.4. *Dissent rates and judicial style in the US and the UK Supreme Courts*

A comparison of statistical data on dissent rates reveals a significant difference between the highest courts of the US and the UK. In the period 1990–2007, there were one or more separate opinions in 62% of the cases in the US Supreme Court,[151] peaking at 78% in 1952 and 1972.[152] In the UK the average dissent rate between 1966 and 1999 was 9.3%.[153] The dissenting percentage of Lord Denning, one of the 'Great Dissenters' of the English judiciary, was 19%, while the other Law Lords' dissent rates have been considerably lower.[154]

144 428 U.S. 153 (1976).
145 408 U.S. 238 (1972).
146 For a definition of *per curiam* opinions see n 42 above.
147 A concurring opinion was written separately by each of the five Justices in the majority, and there were also four dissenting opinions (three of them shared by all four dissenting Justices).
148 In the opinion of the Court we can read: 'Since five Justices wrote separately in support of the judgments in *Furman*, the holding of the Court may be viewed as that position taken by those Members who concurred in the judgments on the narrowest grounds.' *Gregg v. Georgia*, 428 U.S. 153, 169, fn 15 (1976).
149 430 U.S. 188 (1977).
150 Novak (n 141) 763–64.
151 Lee Epstein, William M Landes and Richard A Posner, 'Why (and When) Judges Dissent: A Theoretical and Empirical Analysis' (2011) 3 *Journal of Legal Analysis* 101, 103.
152 Alder (n 11) 238, fn 87.
153 Ibid.
154 Alder (n 11) 243, fn 124.

There is also less romantic rhetoric around dissenting opinions in the UK than in the US. John Alder suggests that this might be influenced by the fact that the legislative process in the US is less responsive to change than in the UK.[155] The style of the English Justices is different from that of their American colleagues mainly due to their different conception of the law. Their more formalist-positivist approach may lie behind the lower dissent rate as well.[156] While English judges have traditionally applied the doctrine of binding precedent more strictly, and preferred the literal rule over more creative canons of statutory interpretation as a sign of respect for the sovereignty of the Parliament, the attitude of American judges has been more flexible.[157]

There are also other significant differences between these two common law supreme courts. Unlike in the US Supreme Court, it is rare that judicial opinions in the UK's highest court directly engage with each other.[158] The phenomenon of the so-called 'canonical dissents' is also uniquely American, unknown in the UK or other common law jurisdictions.[159] Some English dissenting opinions, especially in the 1960s and 1970s, did have an impact on legal development, as they expressed the conflict taking place within the House of Lords between the more formalist and the more progressive Law Lords, but they were not redeemed in later cases, as happened to some classic dissents of Justice Harlan or Justice Holmes in the US.[160] However, even in the US the canonisation of dissenting opinions has taken place gradually. It is either the result of a long public deliberation process or a dissent is first supported by legal doctrine and is vindicated by the court.[161]

Concluding, it seems that while legal tradition certainly plays a role in the judicial process, there are significant differences within the common law tradition as regards the practice of judicial dissent. These differences are likely to be the biggest between the two supreme courts I examined in this chapter, and for at least two reasons. First, the US Supreme Court has the power of striking down statutory law. Second, its members are appointed through a very political process. These two features of the US Supreme Court contributed to its dividedness to a great extent.[162] Thus one has to be careful when making generalised comparative statements involving the common law tradition and take these differences into account.

155 Alder (n 11) 241.
156 Alessandra Di Martino, *Le opinioni dissenzienti dei giudici costituzionali. Uno studio comparativo* (Jovene 2016) 197.
157 For a general comparison between English and American judge's legal thinking, see Konrad Zweigert and Hein Kötz, *An Introduction to Comparative Law* (Weir tr, 3rd edn, Oxford UP 1998) 259 ff.
158 Alder (n 11) 243.
159 Di Martino (n 156) 461 ff.
160 See Section 2.3 above.
161 Di Martino (n 156) 464.
162 On these points also Frederic Reynold, *Disagreement and Dissent in Judicial Decision-making* (Wildy, Simmons & Hill 2013) 125 ff.

4 Judicial dissent in the civil law tradition

1. Judicial decision-making in the civil law tradition: founded on secrecy?

It is a well-known fact, which immediately catches the eye of the reader, that judicial decisions delivered by common law judges differ considerably from decisions of ordinary judges in civil law systems. The main difference derives from the basic approach of these two legal traditions to the judicial profession. In addition, the prevalent manner of formulating judicial decisions in the respective legal systems not only affects the actual judgments, but also the decision-making process. The extremely abstract style of French judgments is a natural consequence of the traditional legal view of the French that disapproves judicial activism, labelling it as *gouvernement des juges*,[1] restricting the judges' role in the lawmaking process.[2] German judgments are also impersonal, but unlike the French, they include a more detailed statement of the case explaining the factual background and the legal questions. However, these are still less ample than the ones we find in common law judgments.[3]

In continental Europe, under the traditionally dominant influence of the French and German legal cultures, judgments are delivered in the name of the people, the republic or the monarch. They are seemingly unanimous decisions. In these systems there is no possibility for the judge to dissent publicly from her/his colleagues. The court must show unity. We are inclined to see the judge as 'only the mouth of the law that pronounces the words of the law, inanimate beings that are not able to modify either its force or its rigour', to use Montesquieu's words.[4] The personal nature of common law judgments, on the other hand, opens the door to separate opinions. 'A [common law] judge takes responsibility for what

1 The French expression was coined by Édouard Lambert in *Le gouvernement des juges et la lutte contre la législation sociale aux États-Unis* (Giard 1921).

2 Antonio Gambaro, 'Lo stile della sentenza francese' in Letizia Vacca (ed), *Lo stile delle sentenze e l'utilizzazione dei precedenti* (Giappichelli 2000) 121.

3 Arthur Von Mehren, 'The Judicial Process: A Comparative Analysis' (1956) 5 *American Journal of Comparative Law* 197, 208.

4 Charles de Montesquieu, *The Spirit of the Laws* (first published 1748, Cambridge UP 1989) 163. See also Chapter 2, Section 3.

he thinks and writes, and this responsibility is openly attributed to him by the judgments and the published Reports' – the English Patrick Atiyah writes.[5] In the United States, the judgments' personal nature is mitigated by the practice of delivering an 'opinion of the court' in every case. However, as we have seen in the previous chapter, votes are public and the members of a judicial panel always have the right to write separately. This high degree of transparency of the judicial decision-making process in the common law tradition has always been seen as essential for the judiciary's legitimacy.[6] Not so on the continent, where the dominant view is that judges are mere instruments of the law.

This difference in mind-set is demonstrated by the legal language as well. In a civil law legal system, it is not appropriate to talk about *opinion* of the court. In continental European languages 'opinion' or its equivalent is not used with reference to judgments.[7] Judgments are considered to be decisions applying the relevant law to a concrete factual situation, not opinions. Conversely, in the common law tradition, and especially in the United States, not only do individual judges have opinions, but so does the court as a whole. The 'opinion of the court' (expression coined by the US Supreme Court at the beginning of the 19th century), however, does not coincide with the judgment entirely. A judgment is composed of the decision, which is the outcome of the case, and the opinion, which sets forth the reasons. This distinction between the two parts of the judgment is highly relevant in a legal tradition that recognises the binding force of precedents. It is the decision which makes the precedent, while the opinion 'has no authority as a precedent beyond the point or points actually and necessarily decided'.[8]

Several scholars and other jurists who argue against introducing dissenting opinions in the judgments of continental European countries claim that publishing the individual opinion of all members of a judicial panel would be a practice foreign to the civil law tradition.[9] In fact, in continental Europe, and especially in Western Europe, it is still relatively rare that a legal system allows its ordinary judges to make their disagreement public. But in the last half-century there has been a clear trend to allow a special category of judges, constitutional judges, to write separately and, in some countries, to extend it even to ordinary judges.

As a matter of fact, constitutional courts are relatively new institutions. The first court of this kind was devised by Hans Kelsen and set up in Austria and

5 Patrick S Atiyah, 'Judgments in England' in *La sentenza in Europa. Metodo, tecnica e stile* (Cedam 1988) 140.

6 Mitchel de S-O-L'E Lasser, *Judicial Deliberations: A Comparative Analysis of Judicial Transparency and Legitimacy* (Oxford UP 2004) 1.

7 *Opinione* or *parere* in Italian, *Menung* in German, *mening* in Swedish, *opinion* in French, *opinión* in Spanish, *vélemény* in Hungarian, just to mention a few examples.

8 Henry Campbell Black, *Handbook on the Law of Judicial Precedents: Or, the Science of Case Law* (West Publishing Company 1912) 38. Henry Campbell Black was the founder of *Black's Law Dictionary*, the most widely used law dictionary in the United States.

9 For example, Gustavo Zagrebelsky, 'La Corte costituzionale italiana' in Pasquale Pasquino and Barbara Randazzo (eds), *Come decidono le corti costituzionali (e altre Corti)* [How Constitutional Courts Make Decisions] (Giuffrè 2009) 59.

Czechoslovakia after the First World War. Constitutional courts, specialised in constitutional review of legislation, spread all over Europe as a reaction to the devastating experience of totalitarian regimes after the Second World War in the West and the breakdown of socialist regimes in the East. The publication of judicial dissent has not spread to the same extent, but it is considered to be part of the 'package' of German constitutional justice which has had an especially strong impact on the common European constitutional tradition, if such a common tradition exists.[10] This strong impact seems to be confirmed by the spread of dissenting opinions in European constitutional justice. The German Federal Constitutional Court, unlike the French Constitutional Council and the Italian Constitutional Court, as this chapter will explain, introduced dissenting opinions soon after its establishment, and it was taken as the main model at the setting up of several other constitutional courts, such as the Spanish, the Portuguese, the Polish and the Hungarian ones.

Arguments based on the legal tradition are used by the other side as well. Some who support the publication of dissenting opinions argue by referring to the few 'enclaves' of civil law in common law countries, such as the State of Louisiana in the United States and the Province of Quebec in Canada, which permit the publication of dissent.[11] This argument, however, since it could also be used to the contrary, is not truly convincing. One can also argue that the fact that these legal systems allow the publication of dissent only demonstrates that they do not fully belong to the civil law tradition. Rather they are mixed legal systems, representing a hybrid between civil law and common law.

In any event, arguments based on legal tradition are hardly ever convincing in relation to judicial decision-making.[12] Not only because reality does not always meet theory, but also because there are several historical examples of exception to the secrecy rule even in continental Europe. In the Spanish legal tradition the origins of judicial dissent date back to the 15th century, to an Ordinance of Medina issued by Ferdinand and Isabella the Catholic in 1489.[13] The Ordinance allowed judges to write separately, even though their opinions were not published together with the judgment, but registered in a secret book. In case of appeal they were shared with the parties and the superior court. However, until the 18th century, in three territories of the Iberian Peninsula judges had the duty to give

10 Franz C Mayer, 'Constitutional Comparativism in Action. The Example of General Principles of EU Law and How They Are Made – A German Perspective' (2013) 11 *International Journal of Constitutional Law* 1003.

11 Luisa Paola Oneto, 'Le opinioni dissenzienti dei giudici della Corte costituzionale tedesca' in *Annali della Facoltà di Scienze Politiche di Genova* (1976–77) 1093. Kurt H Nadelmann, with reference to the Province of Quebec, explains this curiosity with the fact that even this territory was part of the British Commonwealth. See Kurt H Nadelmann, 'The Judicial Dissent: Publication v. Secrecy' (1959) 8 *American Journal of Comparative Law* 415, 418.

12 That is also the opinion shared by Nuno Garoupa and Tom Ginsburg who have carried out extensive research on the judicial decision-making process. They argue that the traditional common law-civil law divide is not convincing, because it does not capture the current configuration of judicial organisation. Nuno Garoupa and Tom Ginsburg, *Judicial Reputation: A Comparative Theory* (University of Chicago Press 2015) 8.

13 Chapter XIV of the Ordenanzas de Medina, in *Novíssima Recompilación de las leyes de España*, Tomo II (Boletín Oficial del Estado 1976) 350–51.

reasons for their vote, and the parties could read these opinions.[14] The practice of separate opinions reserved for the appeal procedure (called *votos reservados* in Spanish) was codified by the Spanish legislature in the 19th century[15] and upheld until 1985. Since 1985 all Spanish judges, including ordinary and constitutional judges, can express their dissent publicly in a separate opinion attached to the judgment.[16] Consequently, there is no more need for the *votos reservados*. They have been replaced by public separate opinions, the *votos particulares*.

On the Italian Peninsula, before the unification of the country and the adoption of the French model of judicial decision-making, some local laws were inspired by the Spanish legal tradition. Dissenting opinions were delivered, but kept confidential, in the Kingdom of Naples, the Este States and Tuscany.[17] All these local laws, however, introduced variations on the Spanish model. In the Kingdom of Naples, the Rules of Judicial Authorities of 1828 established that the parties could not ask for a copy of these opinions without the consent of the Minister of Justice.[18] The possibility of writing separately served the purpose of reconciling the principle of unity of the court with the judges' individual will, and not the interests of the parties.[19] In the Este States judges could express their dissent publicly after the delivery of the judgment since the 18th century.[20] Finally, in Tuscan civil procedure, after 1771, the dissenter judge could explain the reasons for his disagreement in writing at the foot of the judgment.[21] Thus it seems that concealing judicial dissent had not been part of the tradition on the entire Italian peninsula, but in several Italian states it was imported following French influence after Napoleon's rise.

Finally, dissenting opinions were published also in a few Germanic territories. In the State of Baden, for example, it was allowed until the unification of the German Empire in 1871. Single judgments became the rule in the Empire under the

14 The Crown of Aragon, the Kingdom of Valencia and the Principality of Catalonia introduced the duty to give reasons for judgments in the higher courts at the beginning of the 16th century in order to reduce the number of futile appeals and accelerate the judicial process. Alessandra Di Martino, *Le opinioni dissenzienti dei giudici costituzionali. Uno studio comparativo* (Jovene 2016) 24.

15 Ley de Enjuiciamiento Civil of 3 February 1881 and Ley de Enjuiciamiento Criminal of 14 September 1882. The reserved separate opinions were accessible only to the Supreme Court and to the parties of the case, and only if the appeal was found admissible. Javier Salas, 'Il rinnovamento del linguaggio nella giurisprudenza del Tribunale costituzionale' (1988) 8(1) *Quaderni costituzionali* 226, 232.

16 Lorenzo Luatti, *Profili costituzionali del voto particolare. L'esperienza del tribunale costituzionale spagnolo* (Giuffrè 1995) 163–69.

17 Vittorio Denti, 'Per il ritorno al "voto di scissura" nelle decisioni giudiziarie' in Costantino Mortati (ed), *Le opinioni dissenzienti dei giudici costituzionali ed internazionali* (Giuffré 1964) 1, 3–6, and Gino Gorla, 'Le opinioni non "segrete" dei giudici dissenzienti nelle tradizioni dell'Italia preunitaria' (1982) 105(5) Il Foro italiano 97. For a more comprehensive overview see Di Martino (n 14) 25–30, 38–40 and 50–54.

18 Regolamento per la disciplina delle Autorità Giudiziarie of 15 November 1828, art 348.

19 Denti (n 17) 4.

20 Denti (n 17) 4–5.

21 Regolamento di procedura civile per i Tribunali del Granducato di Toscana, art 481. Denti (n 17) 5.

dominant influence of Prussia,[22] with the only exception of the State of Württemberg, where publishing the minutes of the deliberation, including the result of the vote and individual opinions, remained the rule until the Second World War. There, the roots of public voting actually date back to the Middle Ages. According to Germanic customs, court proceedings were public and judges voted publicly.[23]

Thus, there are examples of disclosing judicial dissent in continental European legal history. Nonetheless, legal tradition does count. In the common law tradition separate opinions were a natural consequence, a side-effect of the orality of court procedures. Not in civil law, where the possibility to express dissent has been rather conceived as a guarantee for the judges themselves, for their dignity and moral responsibility[24] and as an instrument of hierarchical control over lower courts.[25]

Table 4.1 Dissenting opinions in Western and East-Central European civil law systems[26]

Legal system	*Dissenting opinions allowed in ordinary courts*	*Dissenting opinions allowed in the constitutional court*
Austria	x	x
Belgium	x	x
Bulgaria	√	√
Cyprus	√ C	√
Czech Republic	√ (only in administrative courts)	√
Estonia	√ C	√ (Constitutional Chamber of the Supreme Court)
France	x	x
Germany	x	√
Greece	√ C	√ (Special Highest Court)
Hungary	x	√
Italy	x	x
Latvia	x	√
Lithuania	√	√
Luxembourg	x	x
Netherlands	x	Ø
Poland	√	√
Portugal	√ C	√
Romania	√	√
Slovenia	x	√
Slovakia	√ (in appeal cases, but not used in practice)	√
Spain	√	√

22 The Reichstag committee which decided to extend this rule to the whole Empire approved it by a majority of only one vote. Wolfgang Heyde, *Das Minderheitsvotum des überstimmten Richters* (Verlag Ernst und Werner Gieseking 1966) 83–94.

23 Oneto (n 11) 1087, citing, among others, PJA von Feuerbach, *Betrachtungen über die Öffentlichkeit und Mündlichkeit in der Gerechtigkeitspflege*, vol I (Siegen 1821) 51–52. Also Di Martino (n 14) 54.

24 Denti (n 17) 6.

25 See Section 2.2 in this chapter.

26 The table is drawn up partly on the basis of the information provided in a study commissioned by the European Parliament: Directorate-General for Internal Policies, *Dissenting*

In any event, these examples of dissenting opinions in continental Europe still do not make the rule. The majority of ordinary judges are not allowed to disclose their disagreement. At the same time most of the constitutional judges are. The following table presents the current situation in European civil law systems.

2. Dissenting opinions in three Western European legal systems

2.1. *Dissenting opinions in the German Federal Constitutional Court*

2.1.1. *The history of dissenting opinions in German constitutional justice*

The first modern legislature in Europe to allow the disclosure of judicial dissent was the German – more precisely West German – Parliament in 1970. The issue of dissenting opinions had been, however, widely debated much earlier both in the legislature and in legal scholarship. The first proposal to allow judges whose views remained in minority to express their disagreement in the judgment emerged already during the preparatory work of the *Gerichtsverfassungsgesetz*, the fundamental law on the judiciary, in the 1880s. On that occasion, it was rejected on the ground that the possibility to show the lack of unity within the panel could increase disputatiousness. There were fears that it would jeopardise good relations between the judges, fostering their vanity, without helping legal development. The Germans believed that 'the development of law and of legal science [would] be fostered by careful reflection in libraries, but not through violent discussions following expressions of polemically motivated dissenting opinions'.[27]

The issue came up again after the Second World War with regard to a judgment delivered by the Constitutional Court of Bremen (one of the *Länder* of the federation) in a case of high public and political importance. The decision upheld the constitutionality of a state law, which provided that Communist Party members

---

Opinions in the Supreme Courts of the Member States (PE 462.470, November 2012) <www.europarl.europa.eu/committees/en/supporting-analyses-search.html> accessed 19 January 2017. The check marks mean yes and the 'x' mean no. 'C' indicates that ordinary courts also perform constitutional review. 'Ø' indicates that there is no constitutional court in that legal system. Scandinavian countries, which for some form a special group in the civil law tradition, are not included in this table and will not be discussed in this chapter, for the reasons set forth in the Introduction.

27 Carl Hahn (ed), *Die gesammten Materialien zu dem Gerichtsverfassungs-Gesetz* (2nd edn, 1883), Bericht der Kommission, 72, quoted and translated in von Mehren (n 3) 208, fn 42. The parliamentary committee's report concluded that a 'court's principal function is to decide the individual case justly and to uphold the authority of the laws, not to provoke scientific discussions over legal questions'.

would lose their seat in the State Parliament.[28] The judgment also contained two separate dissenting opinions, each one comprised of three judges. They disagreed with the majority on two different points, but considering that the Court was composed of only seven members, this means that only one judge supported the decision in its entirety. The case brought back to the spotlight the question of judicial dissent.[29] Those scholars who suggested that dissenting opinions of the common law tradition were worthy of serious consideration also argued that some of the more appalling judgments of the Nazi period had been undoubtedly facilitated by the fact that the judges participating in it 'could rely on the shelter of the anonymity of judicial activities'.[30]

In 1951, at the setting up of a new constitutional court, some members of the Bundestag supported the idea of introducing dissenting opinions on the ground that it could foster the development of this new field of law. That proposal was rejected, but for a different reason. Contrary to the debate on dissenting opinions in ordinary courts, where the German legislature was concerned for the good relations between judges, this time it recognised the possible benefits of disclosing dissent in the specific field of constitutional law. However, it considered that German society was not ready for it yet. It was thought that the trust in justice, especially in constitutional justice, was not yet sufficiently consolidated. A constitutional court would have to deal with litigation involving political issues, and dissenting opinions could trigger public reactions dangerous to the court's legitimacy.[31]

Dissenting opinions were finally introduced in German constitutional justice by legislative reform in 1970, two decades after the setting up of the Bundesverfassungsgericht. However, this reform had been preceded by a few important steps taken by the Court itself. The Court had taken up office in September 1951, and by December 1952 made the result of the voting in a case (20 judges in favour and two against the decision) known to the public. Ten days after the decision, one of the two judges who remained in minority, Willi Geiger, published a dissenting opinion in a law review.[32] The case was of primary importance for the German legal system: the constitutional review of the European Defense Community Treaties.[33] However, the disagreement between the members of the Court did not concern

28 BremStGH, Decision of 5 January 1957 (St 2/1956). A summary in German is available in Staatsgerichtshof der Freien Hansestadt Bremen, 'Entscheidungen des Staatsgerichsthofs Zusammenfassungen der Entscheidungen der Jahre 1950 bis 1989', 24 <www.staatsgerichtshof.bremen.de/sixcms/media.php/13/StGH-ENTSCH-ZUSAMMENF50-89.pdf> accessed 18 January 2017. The state law in question was adopted after an earlier judgment of the Federal Constitutional Court (Bundesverfassungsgericht) had outlawed the Communist Party.

29 EJ Cohn, 'Dissenting Opinions in German Law' (1957) 6 *International Comparative Law Quarterly* 540.

30 Cohn (n 29) 541.

31 Von Mehren (n 3) 209, fn 42.

32 Documented in *Der Kampf um den Wehrbeitrag* (Institut für Staatslehre und Politik 1953), vol 2, II, 882.

33 Decision of 8 December 1952, BVerfGE 2, 79. The review had been requested by the Bundespräsident.

the central issue of the case (the compatibility of the treaties with the Basic Law), but the effects of the decision. According to the Court, even its advisory opinions, such as the one delivered in this case upon request of the Federal President, have binding force and precedential value in future cases involving the same issue. Judge Geiger argued that these decisions should not have binding force since the parties had not been heard during the procedure.[34] For him the binding effect of advisory opinions was not a question of interpretation but of law-making, so the Constitutional Court did not have the power to fill in this gap in procedural law. Partially as a result of this controversy over the effect of advisory opinions, this competence of the Bundesverfassungsgericht was abolished in 1956.[35]

The Court changed its practice gradually: the next step towards a more transparent procedure was taken in 1966, when, in a case decided by the First Senate, two opposing opinions were published, without however revealing which position was shared by which judges.[36] Neither of the two opinions gained the majority in the panel, so according to the law no violation of the constitution could be declared.[37] The Court disclosed the split between its members and included both positions in its judgment in order to demonstrate that the complaint could not be sustained. Just one year later, in another case, the plenary session decided to permit the panels to publish the result of the voting whenever they deemed it appropriate; thus no longer restricting it to tie votes.[38] Since April 1967 it has become regular practice for the Second Senate to publish the result of the voting, and since then each and every decision delivered by the Senate contains the number of votes for and against, but not the names of the judges in the majority and the minority.[39]

In December 1970, the Bundestag unanimously modified the Law on the Federal Constitutional Court (BVerfGG) on a proposal presented by the social-democratic government a year earlier.[40] The new rule made it possible for the Court to publish both separate opinions (*Sondervotum* in German)[41] and the number of votes for each opinion (without identifying which judges subscribed

34 Jörg Luther, 'L'esperienza del voto dissenziente nei paesi di lingua tedesca' (1994) *Politica del diritto* 241, 244.

35 Luther (n 34) 244.

36 Decision of 5 August 1966, BVerfGE 20, 162. The case was initiated by the weekly magazine 'Der Spiegel', which in an article published on 18 October 1962 had criticised the military strategy of the German Defence Minister Strauss, who supported the production of nuclear weapons in West Germany. The chief editors of the magazine were later arrested by the secret police for having disclosed state secrets. 'Der Spiegel' filed a constitutional complaint against the measures of search and attachment. Oneto (n 11) 1090.

37 Art 15(2) of the Law on the Federal Constitutional Court.

38 Luther (n 34) 246. Decision of 16 February 1967.

39 If the case involves more questions of constitutionality, the proportion of votes is indicated for each question separately. Oneto (n 11) 1091.

40 Fourth amendment to the Law on the Federal Constitutional Court (BVerfGG) of 2 December 1970, in *Bundesgesetzblatt*, I, 1765. The BVerfGG entered into force on 25 December 1970.

41 *Sondervotum* is a term used in doctrine, but the dissenting opinions themselves are named *abweichende Meinung*.

to which opinions).[42] This reform was preceded by legal research which compares the practice of dissenting opinions in other systems, including the US.[43] The introduction of dissenting opinions was accompanied by the change from renewable terms to single, non-renewable 12-year terms. Since German constitutional judges are appointed by the legislature,[44] there was concern that if they could be re-appointed they might feel less free to express dissenting opinions.[45] The Court modified its Rules of Procedure to conform to the reform in January 1971,[46] but the first dissenting opinion had been delivered in a case already a few weeks earlier by Judges Geller, Rupp and Schlabrendorf.[47]

Even though comparatist scholars usually focus on the Federal Constitutional Court when studying Germany, it is not to be forgotten that the *Länder* (the federated states) also have their own constitutional courts. The German system of constitutional justice has been meant to fit within the legal and political framework of a federal state. As a matter of fact, when the Constitutional Court of the State of Bavaria allowed the publication of dissent in 1948, the Federal Constitutional Court was still to be born. In Bavaria, however, separate opinions are published anonymously.[48] Signed dissenting opinions are published only by the Constitutional Court of Hamburg (since 1982) and the Federal Constitutional Court. In the other states the publication of separate opinions is neither allowed nor prohibited by the legislature. German legal scholarship is of the opinion that it could be introduced by the courts themselves if there is no explicit obligation of secrecy in the law.[49]

2.1.2. The practice of dissenting opinions in the Bundesverfassungsgericht

As regards the quantity of dissenting opinions in the practice of the Bundesverfassungsgericht, they are quite rare compared to the Unites States. Since German constitutional judges were allowed to write separately, it has happened in only 158 cases in 44 years (up to 2015).[50] In light of the fact that the two

42 BVerfGG, art 30(2).
43 Konrad Zweigert and Hein Kötz, *An Introduction to Comparative Law* (3rd edn, Oxford UP 1998) 16.
44 Eight judges are elected by the Bundestag and eight by the Bundesrat. Thus the German system of appointment is an example of the parliamentary model. With variations, but it was followed by Poland and Hungary for their constitutional courts. Katalin Kelemen, 'Appointment of constitutional judges in a comparative perspective – with a proposal for a new model for Hungary' (2013) 54 *Acta Juridica Hungarica* 5, 15–17.
45 Vicki C Jackson and Mark Tushnet, *Comparative Constitutional Law* (Foundation Press 1999) 525.
46 Decision of the plenary session of 27 January 1971, in Bundesgesetzblatt, I, 99. Other modifications to the rules concerning dissenting opinions were adopted on 2 September 1975, in Bundesgesetzblatt, I, 2521.
47 Decision of 4 January 1971, BVerfGE 30, I, 33.
48 Rules of Court of 23 May 1968, arts 7a and 8, in Bay GV Bl., 125.
49 Luther (n 34) 243.
50 Data from the Annual Statistics 2014 of the Bundesverfassungsgericht, 12, <www.bundesverfassungsgericht.de/DE/Verfahren/Jahresstatistiken/2015/statistik_2015_node.html> accessed 15 January 2017.

Senates delivered a total of 2,172 decisions in the same period, it is a quite low number (7.27%). Moreover, it seems that there is even a decreasing tendency. 62% of these cases date back to 1993 or earlier, so only 38% were delivered in the last 20 years.[51] Considering that the publication of dissent has been allowed for more than 40 years, there is a clear disproportion. Recently there have been only one to three cases each year in which the judgment included a separate opinion.[52]

Even if Germany was the first in Europe to allow its constitutional judges to express their dissent publicly, we can see that the use of dissenting opinions is still modest in comparison to the common law tradition. There is a culture of consensus in the Court, which means that the judges cast their vote at the end of the deliberative process only if it they are unable to reach an agreement on the decision.[53] German scholars look with a certain disdain at the numerous plurality opinions in the American practice, which they find hard to reconcile with clear rules of law.[54] Indeed, the German practice can be understood as placed within the context of the civil law tradition. Separate opinions are allowed, but there are other elements in the decision-making practice which clearly distinguish the German experience from the Anglo-American one. For example, German judgments are not signed by their author. The judge who writes in the name of the majority remains anonymous. Also, all members of the panel who participated in the case have to sign the judgment, including the dissenters. This strengthens the idea of an impersonal decision delivered in the name of the law rather than expressing an opinion.

It also seems that in the Bundesverfassungsgericht a dissenter may, if s/he was the rapporteur of the case, write for the majority. As the judgments are signed by all judges, we cannot know who the author is, but various accounts tell us that in certain cases it has been a dissenting judge.[55] For the Germans, it seems, the possibility to write separately is a sufficient guarantee of the judges' freedom of conscience. This low-key approach to the judges' freedom of conscience can be also seen in Austria. Publication of dissenting opinions is not allowed there, but

51 Between 1971 and 1993, there was at least one separate opinion in 96 cases. Luther (n 34) 250–51. For a summarising chart of the number of separate opinions and cases with separate opinions from 1971 to 2001 see Christoph Hönnige, 'Impliziter Verfassungswandel durch das Bundesverfassungsgericht in gesellschaftlichen und politischen Fragen' (Gemeinsame Tagung DVPW, ÖGPW und SVPW, 21–23 November 2008) 10.

52 With the exception of 2008, when there were seven such cases. The Annual Statistics have been available on the website of the Court since 2006. They only publish the total number of separate opinions from 1971 until the given year, but by examining all the annual reports one can calculate the number of judgments with separate opinions in a given year.

53 Di Martino (n 14) 367.

54 Donald P Kommers, 'The Federal Constitutional Court: The Guardian of German Democracy' (2006) 603 *Annals of the American Academy of Political and Social Science* 111, 123. Nevertheless, there are a few examples of plurality opinions in German constitutional case-law as well. For example, the case BVerfGE 32, 199, of 15 November 1971. For a comment see Luther (n 34) 249.

55 Luther (n 34) 248 and Dieter Grimm, 'The German Constitutional Court' in Pasquino and Randazzo (n 9) 41, 50.

a dissenting rapporteur judge is not obliged to write the judgment.[56] The Austrian rule also aims to save the dissenter's conscience. Still, the main goal of the judgment is to give a clear answer to the legal questions at hand, and not that of displaying to the public how the decision was reached.

German constitutional judges prefer to write separately if they consider the case of particular public or political interest. In fact, separate opinions were filed, for example, in cases concerning abortion,[57] registered civil partnerships,[58] the electoral system,[59] nationalisation of private property in East Germany,[60] the use of Islamic veil,[61] and so on.[62] Moreover, an empirical study carried out by Christoph Hönnige, a German political scientist, also found that constitutional judges are policy-seekers just as the Justices of the US Supreme Court.[63] Hönnige measured the relation of distance between the constitutional court and the political opposition in Germany and France, analysing the results of cases of abstract review. He could have a look at the dissenting opinions in the German court and bring the analysis to the micro-level there, finding support for the hypothesis that constitutional judges have political preferences when adjudicating constitutional questions. In 77% of the cases with separate opinions examined by Hönnige the dissenting opinion was delivered by a judge nominated by the losing political party. At the same time, in the examined cases, no judge ever dissented if the party which had nominated him won the case.[64] A classic example is offered by the first abortion case, in which the German judges voted in line with their nominating party's preferences.[65]

In rare, but significant cases a dissenting opinion contributed to a change in the Court's orientation. Some important examples are the famous *Solange* cases on the relationship between EU law and the German Basic Law[66] and the cases

56 Art 35 of the Rules of the Court.

57 Judgment of the First Senate of 28 October 1998, 1 BvR 2306/96, 1 BvR 2314/96, 1 BvR 1108/97, 1 BvR 1109/97, 1 BvR 1110/97.

58 Precautionary measure of the First Senate of 18 July 2001, 1 BvQ 23/01, 1 BvQ 26/01.

59 Judgment of the Second Senate of 8 December 2004, 2 BvE 3/02.

60 Judgment of the Second Senate of 26 October 2004, 2 BvR 955/00, 2 BvR 1038/01.

61 Judgment of the Second Senate of 24 September 2003, 2 BvR 1436/02.

62 For a list of the cases with separate opinions from 1994 to 2009 see Maria Theresa Rörig, 'L'opinione dissenziente nella prassi del Bundesverfassungsgericht (1994–2009)' (Seminario di studio, Roma, 22 June 2009), 5–7 <www.cortecostituzionale.it/documenti/convegni_seminari/CC_SS_opinione_dissenziente_12012010.pdf> accessed 18 January 2017.

63 Christoph Hönnige, 'The Electoral Connection: How the Pivotal Judge Affects Oppositional Success at European Constitutional Courts' (2009) 32 *West European Politics* 963.

64 Hönnige (n 63) 979. In the remaining 23% of cases dissent was expressed jointly by more judges, including also one or more judges nominated by the winning party.

65 The majority of the judges had been nominated by the centre-conservative parties (CDU/CSU), and dismissed the challenged social-liberal law as unconstitutional. The two dissenters, instead, had been nominated by the social-democratic party (SPD). For a comment see Felix Lange, 'American Liberalism and Germany's Rejection of the National-Socialist Past – The 1973 *Roe v. Wade* Decision and the 1975 German *Abortion I Case* in Historical Perspective' (2011) 12 *German Law Journal* 2033.

66 BVerfGE 37, 271 of 29 May 1974 and BVerfGE 73, 339 of 22 October 1986.

on the financing of political parties.[67] This contribution has been usually mediated by legal doctrine through scholars' commentaries to the judgments taking up the dissenter's arguments. Some commentators talk about an alliance between dissenting opinions and legal doctrine in German constitutional justice.[68] This alliance and the low dissent rates seem to support the former minister of justice, Brigitte Zypries's defence of the Bundesverfassungsgericht against criticism that it interferes with the legislative and executive branches excessively. She argued that the Court 'has always judiciously dealt with its authority', and it is 'held in high esteem by citizens and political actors alike' notwithstanding the occasional separate opinions published by individual judges.[69]

2.2. *Dissenting opinions in the Spanish legal tradition*

2.2.1. *Votos reservados and votos particulares: the history of judicial dissent in Spain*

Dissenting opinions, though allowed in constitutional justice only since 1979, do not represent an absolute novelty in the Spanish legal system. In Spain, judicial dissent has its special roots. The secret *voto reservado* introduced in the 15th century and upheld until 1985 was a forerunner of the public *voto particular*. They co-existed from 1979 to 1985, when only the Spanish Constitutional Court (Tribunal Constitucional) could publish separate opinions. In this period, ordinary judges could write only a *voto reservado* which was not published with the judgment. When the disclosure of dissent was allowed for ordinary courts as well in 1985, the *voto reservado* was abolished. The latter's *raison d'être* had been in any event quite different. In the Ordinance of Medina, as in the 19th century codes of procedure, the recording of the dissenting votes had the purpose of separating the responsibility of the dissenter judges from that of the rest of the adjudicating panel when it came to appeal. Therefore, it was mainly a means of hierarchical control over the judges of lower courts. At the same time, however, the reserved separate opinion could be useful for the losing party too, since s/he could avail herself/himself of the arguments offered by the dissenter before the superior court.[70]

It should not be forgotten that, besides the experience of the aforementioned three kingdoms of the Iberian Peninsula,[71] in Spanish legal history there had also been a brief episode of publication of dissenting opinions at the end of the 19th century, even if limited to administrative justice. The *Ley de lo Contencioso-Administrativo* of 13 September 1888 provided for the publication of dissenting opinions, for the same reason as the law establishing the Tribunal Constitucional

67 BVerfGE 73, 40 of 14 July 1986 and BVerfGE 85, 264 of 9 April 1992.
68 Luther (n 34) 255.
69 Brigitte Zypries, 'The Basic Law at 60 – Politics and the Federal Constitutional Court' (2010) 11 *German Law Journal* 87, 95–96.
70 Luatti (n 16) 166–67.
71 See Section 1 above.

did so 90 years later: in order to make the reasons of the dissenter public. The 1888 provision, however, lived a short life. Just six years later, in 1894, the Spanish legislature decided to abolish it and to return to the system of reserved opinions in administrative justice as well. This step backward was justified by a negative experience of those six years. The publication of dissenting opinions was considered to have contributed to a loss of authority of the judgments and a loss of prestige of the administrative courts.[72]

Moreover, there is a historical precedent in the field of constitutional justice as well. The Tribunal de Garantías Constitucionales (a forerunner of today's Tribunal Constitucional) in its short period of activity (between 1933 and 1936) during the Second Republic could publish dissenting opinions.[73] And indeed, it did publish several of them. Actually, Spanish constitutional judges of the Second Republic had a real aptitude for dissent. According to many commentators of that period this is explained by the excessively politicised character of the Tribunal and the *espíritu partidista* (partisan spirit) of its members.[74] The inappropriate composition and the overabundant number of its members (26 judges) were two factors that together exposed the Tribunal to the logic of groups and political partisanship.[75] Moreover, during the Second Republic in Spain, as elsewhere in Europe between the First and Second World Wars, the situation was too divisive for a consensus on constitutional interpretation to emerge.[76]

A proper Kelsenian constitutional court was established in Spain only in 1978, after the fall of Franco's totalitarian regime. But even if the Spanish legislature was inspired by the Kelsenian model, it chose to follow the more recent examples of European constitutional courts which departed from Kelsen's ideas in many respects. By the end of the 1970s, these new constitutional courts, namely the German Bundesverfassungsgericht and the Italian Corte costituzionale, had already demonstrated that they were successful guarantors of the constitutional order.[77] For this reason, to say it with the words of Roman Herzog, the Spanish Tribunal Constitucional, together with its Portuguese counterpart, may be considered to be the daughter of Karlsruhe (while the Hungarian and Polish constitutional courts would be her granddaughters).[78] Indeed, Spanish constitutional judges are allowed to publish their dissent, as their German colleagues, but unlike

72 Luatti (n 16) 168–69.

73 Art 41(3), Ley Orgánica del Tribunal de Garantías Constitucionales of 14 June 1933.

74 Jose Luis Cascajo Castro, 'La figura del voto particular en la jurisdiccion constitucional española' (1986) 17 *Revista española de derecho constitucional* 171, 172.

75 Luatti (n 16) 175–79.

76 Víctor Ferreres Comella, *Constitutional Courts and Democratic Values: A European Perspective* (Yale UP 2009) 30–31.

77 Roberto Romboli and Rolando Tarchi, 'La giustizia costituzionale in Spagna' in Jörg Luther, Roberto Romboli and Rolando Tarchi (eds), *Esperienze di giustizia costituzionale*, Vol 2 (Giappichelli 2000) 285, 289.

78 Roland Herzog is a former President of the Bundesverfassungsgericht. Quoted in László Sólyom, 'The Role of Constitutional Courts in the Transition to Democracy – With Special Reference to Hungary' (2003) 18 *International Sociology* 133, 153, fn 4.

in Germany, they have been allowed to do so from the very beginning. Even if MP Peces-Barba, when arguing for the introduction of dissenting opinions in the Spanish Parliament, invoked the American experience,[79] the fact that at that time the Bundesverfassungsgericht already allowed separate opinions might have also influenced this choice. There was a large consensus among the constitution-makers regarding the introduction of dissenting opinions.

So, unlike in Germany, in Spain the rules concerning dissenting opinions have been provided by law from the outset. And there is more. Spain is one of the few countries in Europe (besides Albania and Greece), where dissenting opinions are mentioned explicitly in the Constitution.[80] In these legal systems the publication of dissent is part of the principle of publicity of judgments, but the Greek Constitution goes further in the application of this principle than the Spanish one. While in Spain writing separately is an option for a judge, in Greece dissent has to be made public.[81] In the practice of the Greek Special Highest Court, which can be considered a sort of constitutional court,[82] the dissenting opinions are written down not by the dissenters themselves, but by the judge who writes the majority decision (the opinion-writer), and the dissenters remain anonymous.[83] Spanish dissenting opinions, on the other hand, are signed by their author, who may also decide not to write separately even s/he voted against the decision.

The Spanish Constitution simply states that dissenting opinions, if any, should be published in the Official State Gazette (*Boletín Oficial del Estado*) together with the judgment. Further rules are provided by the Organic Law on the Constitutional Court.[84] This Law clarifies that a separate opinion (*voto particular su opinión discrepante*) may concern either the decision or the reasoning. Thus there is a statutory distinction between dissenting and concurring opinions.

79 MP Peces-Barba argued that the introduction of dissenting opinions would have been a guarantee for all citizens and a guarantee of transparency. *Diario de Sesiones del Congreso de los Diputados* de 19 de junio de 1978, pág. 1724, quoted in Eduardo García de Enterria, 'La posición jurídica del Tribunal Constitucional en el sistema español: Posibilidades y perspectivas' (2014) 100 *Revista Española de Derecho Constitucional* 39, 128, fn 256.

80 Art 164 of the Spanish Constitution, Art 132 of the Albanian Constitution, and Art 93(3) of the Greek Constitution.

81 Art 93(3) provides that the 'publication of the dissenting opinion shall be compulsory' (translation by the Hellenic Parliament).

82 The Special Highest Court settles, among others, conflicts between courts of different jurisdiction and controversies on the constitutionality of statutes (art 100(1) d)-e)) of the Greek Constitution). Greece has a mixed centralised-decentralised model of judicial review, while its court system resembles the civil law tradition. See more in detail Epaminondas Spiliotopoulos, 'Judicial review of legislative acts in Greece' (1983) 56 *Temple Law Quarterly* 463, and, more recently, Akritas Kaidatzis, 'Greece's Third Way in Prof. Tushnet's Distinction Between Strong-Form and Weak-Form Judicial Review, and What We May Learn from It' (2014) 13 *Jus Politicum* <https://ssrn.com/abstract=2548024> accessed 23 February 2017.

83 Saulle Panizza, *L'introduzione dell'opinione dissenziente nel sistema di giustizia costituzionale* (Giappichelli 1998) 116.

84 Art 90(2), Ley orgánica 2/1979, de 3 de Octubre, del Tribunal Constitucional.

In 1985, after a positive experience with the practice of including dissenting opinions in the Tribunal Constitucional, the possibility to write *votos particulares* was extended to ordinary judges as well. While constitutional judges are authorised directly by the Constitution, the other Spanish judges are allowed to write separately by the Organic Law on the Judiciary.[85] Thus, today the Spanish legal system allows all judges to publish dissenting and concurring opinions. And, as Giancarlo Rolla, the author of a monograph on Spanish constitutional justice, observed, the introduction of dissenting opinions does not seem to have had a 'traumatic impact' on the Spanish legal system.[86] This is confirmed by a more recent reform which made it possible for the judges of the Tribunal Constitucional to attach a separate opinion also to an order (*auto*) or declaration (*declaracion*) of the Court, not only to a judgment (*sentencia*).[87]

2.2.2. *The practice of dissenting opinions in the Tribunal Constitucional*

As regards the frequency of dissent in the Tribunal Constitucional, we find that today it is considerably greater than in the Bundesverfassungsgericht. Writing separately is not the rule, but it cannot be considered exceptional either.[88] While Spanish constitutional judges write separately less often than common law judges, they do so twice as many times as their German colleagues. Furthermore, there has been an opposite trend than in Germany. While the Bundesverfassungsgericht publishes considerably fewer separate opinions today than in the 1980s and earlier, the number of *votos particolares* written by Spanish constitutional judges has increased progressively. In the first three years, when the Tribunal Constitucional had to establish the bases of its case-law, the rate was relatively high: around 16%.[89] But later, from 1984, it stabilised at around 6.8%.[90] The trend started to change in 1993, when the dissent rate went up to 13.65%, probably due to the appointment of four new judges in July 1992.[91] The frequency of

85 Art 260(1), Ley orgánica 6/1985, de 1 de Julio, del Poder Judicial.

86 Giancarlo Rolla, *Indirizzo politico e Tribunale costituzionale in Spagna* (Jovene 1986) 150.

87 Ley orgánica 6/2007 of 24 May 2007 which modifies art 90(2) of the Constitutional Tribunal Act.

88 Luatti (n 16) 195.

89 Gregorio Cámara Villar, *Votos particulares y Derechos fundamentales en la práctica del Tribunal Constitucional español (1981–1991)* (Secretaría General del Ministerio de Justicia 1993) 372.

90 Thus in the first 14 years of its functioning there was at least one published separate opinion in 8.6% of the cases (the Court decided 245 cases in that period). For a more detailed account of statistics concerning the first 14 years, see Luatti (n 16) 194–227.

91 Luis Javier Mieres Mieres, 'Votos particulares y Derechos fundamentales en la práctica del Tribunal Constitucional español (1981–1991)' (1995) 15 *Revista Española de Derecho Constitucional* 349, 359. Carmen Guerrero Picó indicates 10% for the same year (39 cases with separate opinions of 388 cases in total). In any event, her data also shows a clear increasing tendency from 1993. Carmen Guerrero Picó, 'L'opinione dissenziente nella prassi del *Tribunal Constitucional* spagnolo (1994–2009)' (Seminario di studio, Roma, 22 June 2009) 16 <www.cortecostituzionale.it/documenti/convegni_seminari/CC_SS_opinione_dissenziente_12012010.pdf> accessed 18 January 2017.

dissent reached its peak in 2004, when there was at least one separate opinion in every fifth case.[92] Since then it stabilised at around 16%. It is still a very low rate compared to the US Supreme Court's 62%,[93] but modest when compared to other European constitutional courts. Spanish constitutional judges seem to be comfortable with writing separately. According to a former president of the Court, Pedro Cruz Villalón, dissenting opinions are accepted in Spain as a completely normal phenomenon, and the public opinion was not shocked by seeing the judges' personalities behind certain decisions.[94]

If we look at the type of cases that trigger dissent, we see that most of the separate opinions are delivered in *amparo* cases.[95] The *recurso de amparo* is an individual appeal for protection through which a person may challenge violations of certain constitutional rights caused by action or inaction of public powers.[96] Therefore, at first glance it might appear that questions of individual constitutional rights cause more disagreement among Spanish constitutional judges than other constitutional questions, such as conflict of competences between public powers or constitutional review of legislation. However, one cannot reach that conclusion since a good portion of the cases decided by the Tribunal Constitucional are in fact *amparo* cases.[97]

The voting behaviour of Spanish constitutional judges has been the object of empirical study by legal and political scientists.[98] One such study, carried out by Chris Hanretty, compared the Spanish Tribunal Constitucional with its Portuguese counterpart.[99] He applied ideal point estimation techniques developed in the American context, modelling each judge's vote in a particular case as function of her/his ideal point plus characteristics of the case.[100] His data came from the 400 published non-unanimous decisions of the Spanish court from

92 Guerrero Picó (n 91) 16.

93 See Chapter 3, Section 3.4.

94 Pedro Cruz Villalón, 'El Tribunal Constitucional Espanol' in Pasquino and Randazzo (n 9) 85, 93–94.

95 63.93% of the cases with separate opinions between 2000 and 2009 (257 out of 402 cases). Guerrero Picó (n 91) 18.

96 Arts 53(2) and 161 of the Spanish Constitution. More specifically, the *amparo* can be exercised to challenge administrative acts, judicial decisions and legislative enactments, with the exclusion of statutes. Art 41 of the Constitutional Tribunal Act. Also, Gianluca Gentili, 'A Comparison of European Systems of Direct Access to Constitutional Judges: Exploring Advantages for the Italian Constitutional Court' (2012) 4 *Italian Journal of Public Law* 159, 169–72.

97 The exact percentages vary from year to year. See the official statistics <www.tribunalconstitucional.es/en/memorias/Paginas/Cuadros-estadisticos.aspx> accessed 27 February 2017.

98 One of the first studies of this kind was: Pilar de Castillo Vera, 'Notas para el estudio del comportamiento judicial. El caso del Tribunal Constitucional' (1987) 20 *Revista Española de Derecho Constitucional* 177.

99 Chris Hanretty, 'Dissent in Iberia: The ideal points of justices on the Spanish and Portuguese Constitutional Tribunals' (2012) 51 *European Journal of Political Research* 671.

100 Hanretty (n 99) 675–76. Judges' ideal points are those points in some *n*-dimensional political space that they prefer to all other points in the space. Ibid. 672.

2000–2009.[101] Hanretty examined the relationship between the judges' voting behaviour and their nominating party's political preferences just like Hönnige did in relation to German and French constitutional judges,[102] even if with a different technique. Hanretty found that, with a few exceptions,[103] Spanish constitutional judges' votes tend to reflect the political preferences of the nominating party. He also found that the Spanish media describes judges' orientations in terms of left and right, dividing them into progressive and conservative blocs, quite accurately, except for judges whose ideal points are extreme. These judges have been described by the media as moderate, while the data analysis shows that it is not true.[104]

Another research carried out by scholars of law and economics showed that even though party alignment plays an important role in explaining the behaviour of Spanish constitutional judges, there are certain institutional features that create incentives for independence from party politics. Nino Garoupa, Fernando Gomez-Pomar and Veronica Grembi looked at all constitutional review cases initiated by political actors from 1980 to 2006. Of the examined decisions, 64.65% were unanimous, that is without any separate opinion.[105] The individual votes were divided into those which found something to be constitutional (40%) versus those which found something to be unconstitutional (60%). The analysis showed that a vote against constitutionality is only slightly more likely when the petitioner and the judge are of the same party (considering the judge's party to be the one that nominated her/him, as in Hanretty's study).[106] In addition, Garoupa and his colleagues showed that other considerations temper a judges' advancement of individual ideological goals. Political influence in the voting behaviour of Spanish constitutional judges is maximal when national party interests are directly involved.[107] In the other cases they could be willing to sacrifice mere ideological goals to satisfy alternative goals, such as strengthening the legitimacy of the Court and increasing its prestige in front of other courts.[108] Moreover, Spanish

101 According to Hanretty, a unanimous opinion provides no new information about judges' ideal points because it can always be perfectly explained either by saying that the case lay outside the set of judges' ideal points, or that the case did not discriminate. Hanretty (n 99) 679.

102 See Section 2.1.2, text to nn 63 ff.

103 Thus, a number of consensus nominees occupy extreme positions (Judges Rodríguez-Zapata Pérez and de Mendizábal Allende), and Judge Jiménez de Parga is an outliner amongst judges nominated by the socialist party (PSOE). Hanretty (n 99) 684.

104 In particular Judges Aragon Reyes and Gonzalez Campos, whose ideal points are more to the left than described by the media. Hanretty (n 99) 685.

105 192 out of 297 decisions. Nuno Garoupa, Fernando Gomez-Pomar and Veronica Grembi, 'Judging under Political Pressure: An Empirical Analysis of Constitutional Review Voting in the Spanish Constitutional Court' (2011) 29 *Journal of Law, Economics, and Organization* 513, 521.

106 Ibid. 522. Even the two career judges appointed to the Court by the Judicial Council (*Consejo General del Poder Judicial*) are members of largely politicised judicial associations. Ibid. 519.

107 Garoupa, Gomez-Pomar and Grembi (n 105) 530.

108 According to the authors, excessive political or ideological division reduces the prestige of the Constitutional Court, and therefore diminishes the influence of constitutional judges over other judicial ranks and, ultimately, the legal system overall. Garoupa, Gomez-Pomar and Grembi (n 105) 521.

constitutional judges are less likely to vote according to party interests in the presence of strong regional or nationalist interests.[109]

2.3. Attempts at introducing dissenting opinions in Italian constitutional justice

If one reads Italian constitutional doctrine, it seems quite surprising that Italy is one of the few European countries that does not allow its judges to disclose their dissent. Italian legal scholarship, especially constitutional law scholarship, has been traditionally in favour of the publication of separate opinions.[110] As one of the founding fathers of the Italian Constitution, Piero Calamandrei, once wrote: 'The secrecy of the court chamber is the institutional consecration of conformism'.[111] His severe criticism of the Italian courts' practice dates back to the 1930s, decades before the birth of the Italian Constitutional Court. In his characteristic witty and ironic style, Calamandrei wrote:

> The judge can think for himself in secret as long as no one finds out. The judgment is therefore like a cliché closing diplomats' secret meetings: even if we are on the eve of a war, 'a perfect agreement has been reached with the full satisfaction of all participants'. This secrecy may be appreciated by the judge who is fond of a quiet life and prefers to alleviate his personal responsibility by hiding behind collegiality; but on the long run it affects his character as a drug. It is a classic example of state unanimity, which saves the appearances at the cost of conscience.[112]

Calamandrei's words are reminiscent of Thomas Jefferson's, who, more than a century earlier, criticised the practice of delivering a single judgment introduced by Chief Justice Marshall. Jefferson argued that it was convenient for the lazy, the modest and the incompetent judges.[113] Calamandrei's opinion has been shared by several other Italian scholars since then. Among others, the comparatist Mauro Cappelletti, who wrote in 1962 that dissenting opinions 'may be considered a sign of democracy and freedom, and a way of making the system of collegiality fruitful and lively'. He argued that the Italian system of collegiality, with no possibility of publishing dissenting opinions, had often become 'a pure (but cumbersome and expensive) formality'.[114]

109 Ibid. 516.

110 Panizza (n 83) 176.

111 In the original Italian: 'La segretezza della camera di consiglio è la consacrazione istituzionale del conformismo.' (my own translation) Piero Calamandrei, *Elogio dei giudici scritto da un avvocato* (first published 1935, Ponte alle Grazie 1989) 274.

112 Ibid. (my own translation)

113 See Chapter 3, Section 2.2.

114 Mauro Cappelletti, 'Ideologie nel diritto processuale' (1962), in *Rivista trimestrale di diritto e procedura civile* 193, 215.

Moreover, as explained at the beginning of this chapter, dissenting opinions are not completely unknown in Italian legal history.[115] In fact, the question has been on the table from the outset. Shortly after it started to operate, the Corte costituzionale itself took up the issue of dissenting opinions when drafting its Rules in 1956.[116] It seems that on that occasion one of the constitutional judges, Mario Bracci, strongly supported the introduction of dissenting opinions, but he was not able to convince his more traditionalist colleagues.[117] Nor could anyone convince the Italian legislature. The possibility of introducing dissenting opinions at the Constitutional Court has aroused interest among constitutional law scholars from time to time,[118] but so far it has been a fruitless debate.

The constitutional scholar and judge Costantino Mortati initiated and organised a discussion on dissenting opinions in the 1960s. It resulted in the publication of a volume composed of six essays by Italian and foreign authors, aiming to present the history of the institution and its use in different legal systems.[119] In the Preface Mortati wrote:

> After more than eight years from the setting up of the Court . . . one result is certainly achieved . . .: the public opinion is today favourably disposed towards how the Court fulfils its safeguarding role and the efficacy of its work in spreading faith in the constitution and the supreme principles enshrined in it aiming to guide and limit the public powers; a faith that had been foreign to the spirit of the people.[120]

Mortati's words remind one of the German debate that took place in the 1960s.[121] A newly established constitutional court may be ready for the publication of dissent after a certain period of time, when popular trust in constitutional justice is already consolidated. In Italy, however, even though this trust was achieved and the Corte costituzionale gained authority in the country just as its German counterpart, Mortati's proposal to introduce dissenting opinions by amending the Court Rules fell on deaf ears.[122]

115 Section 1, text to n 17 ff.

116 Norme integrative per i giudizi davanti alla Corte costituzionale, adopted on 16 March 1956, published in the *Gazzetta Ufficiale* of 24 March 1956, no 71.

117 Paolo Barile's comment to V Andrioli, 'Motivazione collegiale e dissensi dei giudici di minoranza' (1963) *Democrazia e diritto* 508, 515.

118 Luatti (n 16) 22. It is worth mentioning that the topic aroused interest in French legal doctrine too. See the monograph by Wanda Mastor, *Les opinions séparées des juges constitutionnels* (Presses Universitaires d'Aix-Marseille 2005).

119 Namely three essays by Italian scholars (Vittorio Denti, Giuliano Amato and Angelo Piero Sereni) and the Italian translation of three foreign contributions (Kurt H Nadelmann, Karl M Zo Bell and William D Douglas). Mortati (n 17).

120 Costantino Mortati, *Prefazione*, in Mortati (n 17) III, VI–VII. (My own translation.)

121 See Section 2.1.1.

122 *Relazione illustrativa della proposta di emendamenti dell'art 18 Norme integrative* (Quaderno n 13 dell'Ufficio studi della Corte costituzionale, 1965), which proposed the introduction of an art 18-bis on separate opinions.

A decade after the publication of Mortati's volume, in 1973, a series of newspaper articles written by legal scholars discussed the issue of secrecy of deliberation in the Constitutional Court on the occasion of a bill presented at the Parliament providing for the publication of dissent.[123] The bill was later withdrawn before it could be numbered and handed out to the deputies.[124] At the end of the same decade, Stefano Rodotà, professor of private law and left-wing politician, drew attention to the problem of the Constitutional Court's excessively concise style of reasoning, which according to him would entail uncertainty about the significance of the single judgments. He pointed out that this problem had given the Parliament a hard time on several occasions when it had to legislate on matters previously decided by the Constitutional Court. Rodotà explained that the issue of dissenting opinions had come in the limelight again for this reason. It had become clear that a rationality check of the Constitutional Court's work was needed, and the political reactions to the Court's single decisions did not fulfil this function.[125] Rodotà himself, as member of the Parliament, presented a legislative proposal to introduce the institution of dissenting opinions in 1981, and the issue was brought up again in the Italian Parliament two years later, when the 'Bozzi Committee' discussed institutional reforms.[126]

It is worth mentioning that all these – fruitless – proposals to introduce dissenting opinions, with the only exception of Costantino Mortati's 'campaign', emerged outside the Court.[127] Most Italian constitutional judges have been traditionally hostile or reluctant to the publication of dissent.[128] This hostility was expressed explicitly by some of them. In February 1981, an interview with then President of the Court Leonetto Amadei published in the newspaper *Corriere della Sera*, caused a sensation. He said:

> It would take great courage for a judge who comes from a political party to declare that he supports a position that is not shared by his party. . . . It

123 Stefano Rodotà, 'Corte costituzionale. Abolire il segreto sul voto dei giudici' *Il Giorno* (31 March 1973), Enzo Cheli, 'Render noti i motivi del dissenso in giudizio' *Corriere della sera* (8 April 1973), and Aldo Sandulli, 'Voto segreto o palese dei giudici costituzionali' *Corriere della sera* (8 May 1973), all cited in Luatti (n 16) 25, n 39.

124 Constitutional bill of 9 July 1973 concerning the modification of art 135 of the Constitution and provisions on the Constitutional Court, presented by the deputies De Martino, Bertoldi, Ferri M, Achilli, Della Briotta, Salvatore. Art 4 of the bill provided that: 'The dissenting opinions and reasonings of constitutional judges, signed by their author, are published in attachment to the Constitutional Court's judgments and orders'. Giustino D'Orazio, 'Corte costituzionale. Cronaca (1968–1974)' (1974) Giurisprudenza costituzionale 2838 (my own translation).

125 Stefano Rodotà, 'L'opinione dissenziente dei giudici costituzionali' (1979) *Politica del diritto* 637, 638.

126 On Rodotà's bill and the Bozzi Commission's debates see Luatti (n 16) 25–26.

127 Costantino Mortati, who is considered to be one of the founding fathers of the Italian Constitution, was also a member of the Corte costituzionale from 1960 to 1972.

128 Salvatore Carlo Panza and Antonio Reposo, 'Le "dissenting opinions" ancora alla ribalta' (1981) *Quaderni costituzionali* 595, 597.

> might happen once, but if it happens two or three times during his term of office, the party could tell him: get out of the way.[129]

Six years later, an amendment to the Rules of Court introduced an important novelty from the point of view of the publicity of the Court's decision-making process.[130] Until that moment, the rule had been that judgments and orders had to be signed by all judges participating in the decision, like in several other constitutional courts. The only little crack in the Court's secrecy was represented by the practice of indicating the name of the rapporteur judge (*relatore*) in the heading of the decision.[131] In 1987, the rule became that the decisions must be signed only by the President of the Court and the opinion-writer (*redattore*). The latter is nominated by the former after the vote, and s/he is not necessarily the same judge who acted as rapporteur in the case.[132] As a rule, the rapporteur drafts the judgment even if s/he remains in minority with her/his view. This means that s/he abandons the drafting of the judgment only in exceptional cases.[133] Initially, the difference between rapporteur and opinion-writer could be deduced from a comparison between the heading and the conclusive part of the decision: the rapporteur judge was indicated in the heading, while the opinion-writer put his signature at the bottom of the decision. This divergence could catch the eye of a very careful reader only.

This second little crack in the Court's secrecy was slightly widened by a new practice started in 2003, which increased the visibility of the cases of discrepancy between rapporteur and opinion-writer. That year, for the first time, President Gustavo Zagrebelsky pointed out in his annual report that there was one case in which the opinion-writer was a different person from the rapporteur judge.[134] It then became a usual practice for all the following Presidents, interrupted in 2014, to specify in their annual report the number of times that a rapporteur judge passed the case to a colleague. A further small step was taken by the Court in 2006, when for the first time the discrepancy between rapporteur and

129 *Corriere della Sera*, 10 February 1981, quoted in Antonio Baldassarre, 'L'"opinione dissenziente" e l'intervista di Amadei' (1981) *Democrazia e diritto* 238, 239 (my own translation).

130 Art 18(5) of the Supplementary Rules (*Norme integrative*) for the Procedure before the Constitutional Court, Decision of 16 March 1956 of the Corte Costituzionale (*Gazzetta Ufficiale*, 24 March, no 71, special edn), modified by Decision of 7 July 1987 of the Corte costituzionale (*Gazzetta Ufficiale*, 9 July 1987, no 158).

131 Since 1957, the second year of functioning of the Court.

132 Alessandro Pizzorusso, 'Dal "relatore" al "redattore" delle sentenze della Corte costituzionale' (1988) Il Foro italiano, I, cols 2–3. See also Chapter 2, Section 2.2.

133 Saulle Panizza, 'Composizione, organizzazione e funzionamento della Corte costituzionale' in Roberto Romboli (ed), *Aggiornamenti in tema di processo costituzionale (2002–2004)* (Giappichelli 2005) 25.

134 Presidente Gustavo Zagrebelsky, *La giustizia costituzionale nel 2003* (Palazzo della Consulta, Rome, 2 April 2004) 5 <www.cortecostituzionale.it/ActionPagina_276.do> accessed 18 January 2017. The case in question was no 116/2003 (*Gazzetta Ufficiale* 16 April 2003, no 15).

opinion-writer was explicitly mentioned in the heading of a judgment, in this way increasing its visibility.[135]

From the annual reports, it emerges that between 2003 and 2012 there were only 22 cases in which the rapporteur judge relinquished the task of writing, and we do not even know in which cases this decision was actually prompted by a disagreement. This means two cases per year on average.[136] It is a very low number considering that the Court decided on average 400 cases a year in the same period. As President Valerio Onida explained in his 2004 annual report, it is a deep-rooted trend at the Italian Constitutional Court that the rapporteur judge is also the author of the judgment.[137]

Of course, the number of cases of discrepancy between the rapporteur and the opinion-writer does not reveal much about the rate of dissent in the Constitutional Court's work. It reveals only a possible disagreement of one of the members of the Court: the judge acting as rapporteur in the given case. These are, however, undoubtedly interesting cases of dissent, since they might signal an especially strongly accentuated difference of opinion within the Court. It might not be a coincidence that President Zagrebelsky decided to point out the one case of discrepancy that occurred that year in his annual report. It was a case that had received considerable media attention and, at the same time, represented 'the conclusion of a difficult path' in the Court's case-law concerning conflicts of powers, as one commentator put it.[138] Thus it seems that after a long line of cases this decision settled a long debate in the legal community and, as the discrepancy between rapporteur and opinion-writer demonstrates, within the Court.

These small cracks in the secrecy of the Constitutional Court's decision-making process were therefore opened by the Court itself, by the way of its publication practice, and not by the Italian legislature, which has never intervened in this matter. Besides changing its publication practice, the Constitutional Court organised seminars first in 1993,[139] and a second time in 2009,[140] to discuss the issue of dissenting opinions, which shows an – at least episodic – interest on behalf of the Court. The

135 Judgment no 393/2006 of 23 October 2006.

136 The last annual reports do not mention the number of cases of discrepancy between rapporteur and opinion-writer anymore, but this does not mean that there are no more such cases. Indeed, there were two cases in 2013, two in 2014 and five in 2015.

137 This statement of President Onida was actually repeated by all presidential reports in the following years until the 2012 annual report. Presidente Valerio Onida, *La giustizia costituzionale nel 2004* (Palazzo della Consulta, Rome, 20 January 2005) <www.cortecostituzionale.it/ActionPagina_264.do> accessed 18 January 2017.

138 Filippo Benelli, 'Una battaglia non decide la guerra (Nota in dissenso con la sentenza n. 116 del 2003 della Corte costituzionale)' (2003) Forum di Quaderni Costituzionali <www.forumcostituzionale.it/wordpress/wp-content/uploads/pre_2006/536.pdf> accessed 18 January 2017.

139 The contributions to this seminar were published in a volume: Adele Anzon (ed), *L'opinione dissenziente. Atti del seminario svoltosi in Roma nei giorni 5–6 novembre 1993, Palazzo della Consulta* (Giuffrè 1995).

140 The contributions to this second seminar are published on the Court's website: <www.cortecostituzionale.it/convegniSeminari.do> accessed 18 January 2017.

Italian Constitutional Court, however, has never taken such decisive steps as its German counterpart. It has never revealed either two different opinions or the result of the voting in a case. In 2002, the President of the Court proposed the introduction of a rule allowing the publication of dissenting opinions in the Rules of Court, but it was dismissed by an overwhelming majority of the judges (13:2 decision). This crushing failure can probably be explained by two facts. First, the President proposed to introduce anonymous dissenting opinions, which could have been seen as a problematic practice by the judges. Second, the Rules of Court might have been considered an inadequate source of law for such an important reform.[141]

Judge Sabino Cassese, whose term of office terminated in 2014, was among the few Italian constitutional judges who supported the introduction of dissenting opinions and expressed this in public on several occasions. According to his own account, the last time the Court discussed this possibility, four judges were supportive.[142] Also Gaetano Silvestri, at the time President of the Constitutional Court, expressed himself favourably to the publication of dissent. He said that the public should be informed about the different opinions that emerge within the Court in a given case so that the debate can continue in society.[143] Both Sabino Cassese and Gaetano Silvestri explained that the Court always seeks the broadest consensus possible in every case. Even if unanimity is often difficult to achieve, the Court rarely decides by simple majority (which would mean eight judges out of 15 in favour of the decision), and voting as such is used in *extrema ratio*.[144] The judges usually make serious efforts to obtain larger support for the majoritarian position, which also makes case conferences considerably longer. A drawback of this practice is that the decision is often the result of a compromise. There is an attempt to make the minority views fit in the decision, which causes flaws in the linearity and consistency of the reasoning.[145] As Judge Silvestri put it, dissenting opinions would 'purify' the reasoning, because the dissenters would have their own space for expressing their views.[146] Another former president of the Court, Gustavo Zagrebelsky, instead admittedly changed his mind on the matter. As a legal scholar, before being appointed to the Constitutional Court, he had been in favour of publishing dissenting opinions. Then, after having practical experience on the Court and being persuaded of the value of collegiality, he changed his mind.[147]

141 The proposal on which the judges voted had been drafted five years earlier, in 1997. Di Martino (n 14) 365.

142 *Cosa significa fare il giudice costituzionale?*, public conversation between Marta Cartabia, Sabino Cassese and Joseph Weiler (Rimini, 25 August 2015) <www.meetingrimini.org/default.asp?id=904&item=6364> accessed 18 January 2017.

143 Diletta Tega, 'La Corte costituzionale vista da vicino Intervista di Diletta Tega a Gaetano Silvestri' (2014) 3 *Quaderni costituzionali* 757.

144 Di Martino (n 14) 367.

145 Paola De Luca, 'Che fine ha fatto l'introduzione dell'opinione dissenziente?' (2014) 11 *Forum di Quaderni Costituzionali* <www.forumcostituzionale.it/wordpress/wp-content/uploads/2014/12/deluca.pdf> accessed 18 January 2017.

146 Tega (n 143) 758.

147 Gustavo Zagrebelsky, *Principi e voti. La Corte costituzionale e la politica* (Einaudi 2005), cited in Di Martino (n 14) 365–66.

The introduction of dissenting opinions is currently not on the table for discussion either in the Italian Constitutional Court or in the Italian Parliament. It seems that there is limited support within the Court, but still far from even a simple majority. Italian legal scholars continue to be supportive and interested in the idea,[148] but a reform can be made only by the legislature or the Court itself. The different proposals that have emerged since the establishment of the Constitutional Court have had differing views on which normative instrument would be the most appropriate one for the introduction of dissenting opinions. Costantino Mortati had suggested to modify the Rules of Court, while bills presented in the 1970s and 1980s aimed to amend the law on the Constitutional Court or to regulate dissenting opinions in a constitutional law.[149] The currently prevalent view seems to support the statutory level.[150]

There are four reasons that help to explain the Italian Constitutional Court's high level of secrecy. First, the Court's competences are limited compared with other European constitutional courts. It does not hear constitutional complaints and cannot be accessed directly by individuals. Italian constitutional judges perceive themselves as guardians of the constitutionality of laws, judging laws rather than persons. Second, one-third of the members of the Court come from the ordinary judiciary. They are in particular not prepared for writing separate opinions, and do not support their introduction. Third, as Gustavo Zagrebelsky, a former member and president of the Court, argues, the Italian constitutional judges' efforts to reach consensus on each constitutional question would be in conformity with the nature of the Italian Constitution – a pluralist constitution, in which different principles co-exist and have to be harmonised with each other. Thus, the spirit of the Italian Constitution would be betrayed by a constitutional court that does not aim at the largest consensus possible.[151] Finally, in the context of current political turmoil, the publication of dissenting opinions could lead to factiousness and delegitimisation of the Court. In the last two decades, the Italian political landscape changed considerably. After several decades of a very fragmented multi-party system, from the 1990s Italian politics began to be characterised by bipolar tendencies in which two coalitions alternated in government, and the 2000s saw the rise of an anti-party movement which now constitutes a 'third pole'.[152] In this context of aggravated tensions between the political forces, many, like Zagrebelsky, argue that the publication of dissenting opinions might not be a good idea. They would expose the Court to public pressure and make

148 See the recent book by Alessandra Di Martino (n 14).

149 De Luca (n 145) 5.

150 Tega (n 143) 758.

151 Zagrebelsky writes: 'la nostra Costituzione (. . .) ha dentro tante anime e, nella decisione del caso concreto, queste tante anime devono trovare un punto di incontro'. (In English: There are many souls in our Constitution and, in the decision of the concrete case, these many souls must find common ground.) Gustavo Zagrebelsky, 'La Corte costituzionale italiana' in Pasquino and Randazzo (n 9) 59, 79. On the other hand, one could arrive at the opposite conclusion: pluralism is better protected by a plurality of opinions and, consequently, the publication of separate opinions.

152 Di Martino (n 14) 503.

room for the personal aspirations of its members.[153] There is no lack of contrary opinions among Italian scholars,[154] but the judges currently sitting on the Court prefer not to publish separate opinions, believing that unanimity and confidentiality constitute a 'protective net' against the accusations of political partisanship which were common among politicians in the 2000s during the centre-right government.[155]

3. Judicial dissent in the European courts

While this book focuses on national constitutional courts, two international courts operating in Europe also deserve attention. International courts may play a fundamental role in the legal systems of the countries covered by their jurisdiction, as there is often an intense dialogue between them and national courts. This is especially true in Europe, where the European Court of Human Rights (ECtHR) adjudicates on the compliance with the European Convention of Human Rights ratified by the Council of Europe's 47 member states, and the Court of Justice of the European Union (CJEU) has jurisdiction over the 28 member states of the European Union (EU). It has also been argued that the jurisprudence of these two courts empowers ordinary judges of the member states in ways that undermine the centrality of constitutional courts in reviewing national legislation.[156] In fact, as Víctor Ferreres Comella aptly pointed out, constitutional courts have lost their general monopoly over legislation, which today may also be scrutinised by international courts on the basis of international standards. They retain this monopoly only under the national constitution.[157]

Both the ECtHR and the CJEU exercise constitutional functions,[158] and as such they have a direct impact on national constitutional justice. The ECtHR is

153 According to these skeptical voices, the situation is aggravated by the poor quality of public debate in Italy in recent times, which implies that the political forces and the mass media tend to trivialise the constitutional debate and misrepresent the role of the Constitutional Court as the guardian of the Constitution. Di Martino (n 14) 366–67.

154 Alessandra Di Martino in her recent book argues that dissenting opinions would not delegitimise the Court, but rather the opposite. They would make it clear that the divergence of opinion between constitutional judges usually does not coincide with the political-ideological cleavage, and would prevent more harmful speculations. Di Martino (n 14) 505 ff.

155 Patrizia Pederzoli, *La Corte costituzionale* (Il Mulino 2008) 159. Judge Marta Cartabia expressed similar concerns in our interview (Rome, Italy, 16 September 2016). About these attacks see Di Martino (n 14) 505.

156 In particular, the CJEU laid the foundations for a decentralised system of judicial review in the landmark *Simmenthal* case, when it asserted that a national court is under a duty to give full effect to the provisions of EU law, if necessary refusing to apply any conflicting provision of national legislation (*Amministrazione delle Finanze dello Stato v Simmenthal SpA*, Case 106/77, para 24). Ferreres Comella (n 76) 122.

157 Ferreres Comella (n 76) 126.

158 As Hjalte Rasmussen Louise Nan Rasmussen pointed out, both functionally perform constitutional review *en masse* and are reputed for their activist rewriting and reconstructions of the laws they were meant to protect and guard. See Hjalte Rasmussen and Louise Nan

a human rights adjudicator, and as such its constitutional relevance is undebatable. The CJEU, on the other hand, has been depicted as 'the most powerful and influential supranational court in world history', which 'effectively constitutionalized the European treaty system'.[159] In particular, there are at least four factors that have made it possible: the CJEU rules on the validity of secondary EU law;[160] it acts as an arbiter in conflicts between EU institutions; it gives interpretations on the conformity of national law with EU law;[161] and it can be accessed directly by citizens.[162]

International courts have at least two characteristic features that one should keep in mind when comparing their practice of dissenting opinions with that of national courts. First, they apply a body of law that consists of treaties, principles and general rules mainly developed through case-law. This important feature, according to some scholars,[163] makes dissenting opinions especially useful, even necessary, in the field of international law. If the law is developed mainly by judges, the argument goes, every opinion expressed contributes to this development. From this point of view the body of law applied by the ECtHR and the CJEU is comparable to constitutional law, since it consists of principles and general rules which are further developed through case-law. The second peculiarity of international courts to be taken into consideration is their composition. They are comprised of one judge from each of the member states. Their members come from different jurisdictions and, consequently, have different legal cultural backgrounds. The relevance of the heterogeneous composition for the practice of judicial opinions, as we will see, is manifold.

The discussion of the practice of the two European courts will be followed by a comparative excursus on the International Court of Justice (ICJ), which constituted the main model for the structure of the ECtHR and offers a valuable point

Rasmussen, 'Comment on Katalin Kelemen – Activist EU Court "Feeds" on the Existing Ban on Dissenting Opinions: Lifting the Ban is Likely to Improve the Quality of EU Judgments' (2013) 14 *German Law Journal* 1373, 1374.

159 Alec Stone Sweet, *Governing With Judges: Constitutional Politics in Europe* (Oxford UP 2000) 153.

160 This power is, however, limited, as the CJEU cannot rule on the validity of acts adopted in the field of common foreign and security policy (CFSP). See art 24(1) of the Treaty on the Functioning of the European Union (TFEU). There are only two exceptions: the CJEU can monitor compliance with the dividing line between CFSP and non-CFSP matters (laid down in art 40 TEU) and review the legality of the external restrictive measures (laid down in art 275(2) TFEU).

161 Even though the CJEU cannot annul a national law, its decision creates an obligation of the member state not to apply it. Ferreres Comella argues that the *Simmenthal* decision (n 156) 'Americanised' the practice of judicial review of legislation in the EU member states. Ferreres Comella (n 76) 125–26.

162 Under the conditions laid down in art 263(4) TFEU. For a discussion about the CJEU's constitutional functions see Ingolf Pernice, Juliane Kokott and Cheryl Saunders (eds), *The Future of the European Judicial System in a Comparative Perspective* (Nomos 2005).

163 For example, JG Merrills, *The Development of International Law by the European Court of Human Rights* (2nd edn, Manchester UP 1993) 38–42.

of reference for comparison. As the following sections will reveal, the practice of these three courts differ considerably. Indeed, they only have one thing in common: they have to give reasons for their decisions.

3.1. Dissenting opinions in Strasbourg: the practice of the European Court of Human Rights

The European Court of Human Rights (ECtHR) was established in 1959 within the ambit of the Council of Europe, on the basis of the European Convention of Human Rights (ECHR).[164] The founding states of the Council of Europe represented different European legal traditions; they included civil law, common law and Nordic countries.[165] The latter two already had a well-established practice of separate opinions at the time. This in part explains why the ECHR authorised the judges to write separately from the very beginning.[166] Another part of the explanation is that the ECtHR was modelled after the ICJ,[167] discussed later, which also allowed for the publication of dissent.

The ECtHR consists of 47 judges; one from each member state of the Council of Europe.[168] Each member state nominates three candidate judges, and the Parliamentary Assembly selects one of the three by majority vote.[169] So, each judicial panel will necessarily be multinational.[170]

Consequently, while the voting patterns of judges in the national courts are usually analysed to place the judges along a liberal-conservative continuum, studies on the voting behaviour of international judges most often focus on national bias. This follows for studies that focus on dissenting opinions within the ECtHR, which usually analyse the frequency of dissent in cases in which the Court found against the individual judge's home state.[171] Such an analysis can be based on a

164 Art 19 ECHR.

165 Namely Belgium, Denmark, France, Ireland, Italy, Luxembourg, the Netherlands, Norway, Sweden and the United Kingdom. Greece and Turkey joined three months later, in August 1949. Iceland and Germany joined in 1950, and Austria in 1956. Thus, at the moment of the creation of the ECtHR, the Council of Europe had 15 members.

166 Art 51(2) ECHR provided: 'If the judgement does not represent, in whole or in part, the unanimous opinion of the judges, any judge shall be entitled to deliver a separate opinion.' The same provision is now contained in art 45(2).

167 Robin CA White and Iris Boussiakou, 'Separate Opinions in the European Court of Human Rights' (2009) 9 *Human Rights Law Review* 37, 39, fn 8.

168 Art 20 ECHR.

169 Art 22 ECHR. In 2010, an Advisory Panel of Experts on Candidates for Election as Judge to the European Court of Human Rights, composed of seven members, was established by the Committee of Ministers (Resolution CM/Res(2010)26 of 10 November 2010), which shall advise the member states whether their candidates meet the criteria stipulated in the ECHR.

170 Even if there is the possibility that a member state nominates a foreigner, it happened only once so far, and this appointment increased, rather than diminished heterogeneity, as in this case a non-European judge was chosen (the Canadian Ronald St John MacDonald nominated by Liechtenstein in 1980).

171 For example, three studies by Fred J Bruinsma: 'Rules of Law From Westport to Wladiwostok. Separate Opinions in the European Court of Human Rights' (1997) 15 *Netherlands*

large set of data since, as a rule, every court panel composed to hear against a state must include *ex officio* the judge nominated by that state. If that judge is unable to sit, an *ad hoc* member is chosen by the President of the Court from a list submitted by the member state concerned.[172]

A quantitative analysis of the frequency of dissent revealed an interesting difference in the voting pattern of *ex officio* and *ad hoc* judges; it found that the latter have a considerably higher national bias than the former.[173] This may be explained by the fact that often *ad hoc* judges are potential future candidates to the Court. Thus, voting against one's home state might place one's nomination at risk. In addition, the *ad hoc* judge is nominated when the state-party is already familiar with the content of the complaint, which may play a role in the choice.[174] A further explanation is that *ad hoc* judges are less exposed to 'collegial' group pressure than *ex officio* judges, since they sit on the bench only for that particular case. Consequently, they do not feel much solidarity with the other members of the adjudicating panel.[175] The higher frequency of dissent also demonstrates that the *ad hoc* judges have an insignificant influence on the outcome of the case, as their views often remain in minority.[176] While national bias is an important issue, as it affects judicial independence, it is also argued that the primary role of the *ad hoc* judge is to reassure the appointing state that its position has been fully taken into account in the formulation of the judgment.[177] Bruinsma and De Blois claim that the role of the *ad hoc* judge is similar to the role of separate opinions: they

---

Quarterly of Human Rights 175 (with Matthijs De Blois); 'Judicial Identities in the European Court of Human Rights' in A Van Hoek, A Hol, O Jansen, P Rijpkema and R Widdershoven (eds), *Multilevel Governance in Enforcement and Adjudication* (Intersentia 2006) 203; and 'The Room at the Top: Separate Opinions in the Grand Chambers of the ECHR (1998–2006)' (2008) Ancilla Iuris 32. Also Martin Kuijer, 'Voting Behaviour and National Bias in the European Court of Human Rights and the International Court of Justice' (1997) 10 *Leiden Journal of International Law* 49.

172 Art 26(4) ECHR and Rule 29 of the new Rules of Court adopted on 19 September 2016. The *ex officio* judge may be unable to sit if a conflict of interest prevents her/him from ruling on the case. An *ad hoc* judge may also be appointed until the appointment of a new *ex officio* judge when the former one resigns or retires. Council of Europe, Parliamentary Assembly, Committee on Legal Affairs and Human Rights, *Ad hoc Judges at the European Court of Human Rights: An Overview*, Information Report (Doc 12827, 23 January 2012), para 9. In order to avoid delays in the appointment of an *ad hoc* judge, now Rule 29(2) provides that if the member state does not submit a list within 30 days, the President shall choose among the *ex officio* judges.

173 Between 1970 and 1994, in ten of 23 cases the *ad hoc* judges dissented from the condemning majority. Kuijer (n 171) 60. Between 1991 and 1995, eight of the twelve times the *ad hoc* judges delivered a separate (dissenting or concurring) opinion, and seven times in eleven cases the *ad hoc* judge dissented from a finding of violation by the majority. Bruinsma and De Blois (n 171) 182. Another study also found that *ad hoc* judges dissent twice as often as their elected fellows, while they write the same amount of concurring opinions. Bruinsma, 'Judicial Identities' (n 171) 237.

174 Kuijer (n 171) 52–53.

175 Bruinsma. 'The Room at the Top' (n 171) 37.

176 Bruinsma and De Blois (n 171) 183.

177 Terry D Gill, *Litigation Strategy at the International Court* (Martinus Nijhoff 1989) 101.

may not be significant to the outcome of the case, but they are significant with respect to the legitimation of the court.[178]

The significant difference in the national bias of *ex officio* and *ad hoc* judges shows that the former have established their independence from national governments. Nonetheless, the possibility to publish dissenting opinions is an important tool to maintain constitutional pluralism in Europe on which the system of European human rights has been built. Bruinsma and De Blois illustrate the role of separate opinions in the ECtHR with an elegant metaphor: 'The European Court furnishes the house of Europe with its majority judgments. Separate opinions are symbols, not instruments. They make legal traditions – in the sense of different interpretations of the rule of law – feel at home in the house of Europe.'[179] Indeed, the separate opinions of Strasbourg judges are often limited to explaining or supplementing the judgment; this is especially so for the separate opinions written by the judges nominated by the party-state, since they know their own national legal system better than their fellow judges.

The use of separate opinions in the ECtHR has been the object of analysis in a number of studies in the fields of legal and political science.[180] Besides the individual judges' national bias, separate opinions enabled researchers to examine, among other things, the 'coalitions' formed between members of the Court in relation to specific legal issues,[181] the relevance of the judges' previous career path, and the peculiarities in the behaviour of judges nominated by the new member states.[182] There have also been attempts to estimate the judicial ideology of ECtHR judges along an activism-restraint dimension.[183] This has been done by looking at their interpretation of the doctrine of margin of appreciation. The belief that this margin should be broad is usually labelled as judicial self-restraint, while the conviction that states have less room to invoke national interests is labelled as judicial activism. In the specific context of the ECtHR, an activist judge is more likely to rule in favour of the applicant, and thus against

178 Bruinsma and De Blois (n 171) 183.

179 Ibid. 186.

180 Including a monograph published in French: Florence Rivière, *Les opinions séparées des juges à la Cour Européenne des Droits de l'Homme* (Bruylant 2004).

181 For example, Bruinsma, 'Judicial Identities' (n 171) 228–29, examining the two 'coalitions' formed concerning the interpretation of Art 6 of the ECHR (right to a fair trial).

182 Bruinsma and De Blois (n 171) 185–86, and Jean-François Flauss, 'Les juges des pays d'Europe centrale et oriéntale à la Cour Européenne des droits de l'homme: vues de l'extérieur' in *Mélanges en hommage à Louis Edmond Pettiti* (Bruyland 1998) 344. Voeten, for example, found that judges from former socialist countries were harsher on other former socialist countries than they were on countries without a socialist heritage. This would demonstrate that judges are policy seekers, as they appear motivated by rectifying a particular set of injustices. Erik Voeten, 'The Impartiality of International Judges: Evidence From the European Court of Human Rights' (2008) 102 *American Political Science Review* 417, 430–31.

183 Bruinsma and De Blois (n 171) 183–85, and, more recently, Erik Voeten, 'The Politics of International Judicial Appointments: Evidence From the European Court of Human Rights' (2006) SSRN <https://ssrn.com/abstract=939062> accessed 18 January 2017, and White and Boussiakou (n 167) 41–44.

a government.[184] While there seems to be no correlation between the degree of activism of the judge and the level of domestic human rights protection,[185] researchers have found that governments use judicial appointments to signal their human rights commitments to interested parties, especially the European Union. Governments more favourably disposed towards European integration are more likely to appoint activist judges.[186] Voeten suggested that the EU has been the driving force behind the increased activism of the ECtHR, even if there is still no formal relationship between them.[187] Moreover, there is a correlation between a judge's previous career path and her/his judicial ideology. It seems that academics become the most activist judges, while judges appointed from the domestic ordinary courts are more inclined to self-restraint.[188]

3.2. *The absence of dissenting opinions in Luxembourg: the practice of the Court of Justice of the European Union*

The experience of the Court of Justice of the European Union is to be taken into consideration and involved in the discussion for at least two reasons. First, the Court of Luxembourg has become one of the most important courts in Europe with a continuously expanding jurisdiction, today deciding numerous cases of constitutional relevance. Second, it is being criticised for its high degree of secrecy and for the absence of dissenting opinions. According to many, this secrecy is to be blamed for the poor quality of the CJEU's reasoning in many judgments.[189]

The reasons for the non-publication of separate opinions are historical. The Court of Luxembourg was established in the 1950s as the court of the European Coal and Steel Community, and soon became the court of all three European Communities. The founding members of the Communities, all civil law countries, aimed at setting up a strong and prestigious court which could consolidate its authority before the member states.[190] The newly established system of

184 Voeten (n 183) 8–9.

185 So, it is not true that governments that offer better protections for individual rights would generally appoint more activist judges. Ibid. 30.

186 Ibid. 33–34. Aspiring EU members appoint more activist judges than other non-members.

187 Ibid. 39. The accession of the EU to the ECHR is an ongoing project, commanded by art 6 TEU, recently arrested by the negative opinion of the CJEU on the draft agreement concluded by the Commission and the Council of Europe (Opinion 2/13 of 18 December 2014).

188 Bruinsma found that former practitioners, such as trial judges and lawyers, are used to thinking in terms of case peculiarities, whereas former academics and administrators are used to thinking as lawyer statesmen, i.e. in terms of the general interest and policy considerations. Bruinsma, 'Judicial Identities' (n 171) 230. A striking example for the activist approach of former academics is the concurring opinion of Judges Pinto de Albuquerque and Dedov in the recent case *Baka v Hungary* App no 20261/12 (ECtHR, 23 June 2016), where they state that the ECHR has a direct supra-constitutional effect, as it represents the European *ius constitutionale commune*, and the ECtHR acts as a 'European Constitutional Court'.

189 Rasmussen (n 158).

190 Angelo Piero Sereni, 'Le opinioni separate dei giudici dei tribunali internazionali' in Mortati (n 17) 144.

Community law was considered to be vulnerable at the time, since the CJEU was not designed to act as a court of revision over national courts. The mechanism of the preliminary reference procedure was introduced instead, which left the application of the CJEU's rulings to the domestic courts.

While the ECtHR was modelled after the ICJ, the principal model for the CJEU was the *Conseil d'Etat*, the French supreme administrative court. Both the procedure and the style of the judgments resemble the French tradition.[191] In fact, when the first common law countries (the United Kingdom and Ireland) entered the European Communities in the first half of the 1970s, a procedural system based on the civil law tradition turned out to be challenging for the judges nominated by these two states, as they were not familiar with the continental European way of making judicial decisions.[192] However, the accession of the UK and Ireland was unable to alter the negative attitude assumed to the notion of dissenting opinions.[193] The issue has been discussed a couple of times since then,[194] but a sufficient political consensus in the EU institutions to change the *status quo* has not been reached yet.

Even though it is not possible for the judges in Luxembourg to write separately, there is a special institution which is considered to make up for this limitation in part: the Advocate General's opinion. The Advocates General (AGs) are professional lawyers who assist the judges in the making of their decisions. There are currently 11 Advocates General at the Court, and they work individually on the cases assigned to them. Their job is to advise the Court on how to decide the given case.[195] They file their non-binding opinion before the judges make their decision, and before the rapporteur judge prepares her/his first draft. The functions of the AG were also modeled after the French system, in particular the figure of the *commissaire du gouvernement* which had been established at the Conseil d'Etat in the 19th century. And it was precisely the French delegation that proposed the introduction of this figure for the European Court. The motivation behind this proposal was that it could contribute to the development of case-law and legal doctrine.[196] The AGs have the same status as the judges: for

191 Actually, at the time of the Court's establishment none of the member states allowed the publication in dissent. Dissenting opinions were introduced in German constitutional justice more than a decade later. See Section 2.1.1 above.

192 Valerio Grementieri and Cornelius J Golden, wrote at that time: 'The Common Law judge may find it difficult to reconcile himself to this prohibition; consequently, this occasion may present a good opportunity to eliminate it as an impediment to the development of Community jurisprudence' in 'The United Kingdom and the European Court of Justice: An Encounter between Common and Civil Law Traditions' (1973) 21 *American Journal of Comparative Law* 664, 669.

193 Julia Laffranque, 'Dissenting Opinion in the European Court of Justice' (2004) 9 *Juridica International* 14, 16.

194 For example, the Resolution on the Intergovernmental Conferences in the context of the European Parliament's strategy for the European Union, OJ No C 324 1990, 219, 231.

195 Art 252(2) of the Treaty on the Functioning of the European Union (TFEU).

196 Laffranque (n 193) 15. Also Michal Bobek, 'A Fourth in the Court: Why Are There Advocates-General in the Court of Justice?' (2011–12) 14 *Cambridge Yearbook of European Legal Studies* 529.

the purposes of appointment, qualification, removal, and term of office, they are subject to the same rules and procedures as the judges[197] But they are not judges. The AG advising the Court in a given case is not a member of the judicial panel that hears the case. They participate neither in the discussion nor in the decision of the case.[198]

Consequently, even if an AG's opinion may propose a different solution or a different reasoning, it is not the result of a discussion with the judges but of an autonomous reflection. This reflection takes into careful consideration the previous decisions of the Court and AG opinions, but it either benefits from or is constrained by the debate that takes place in the decision-making panel. It has been suggested that rather than providing an explanation of or a dissenting opinion from the judgment in the individual case, an AG may be explaining or disagreeing on the more systemic level, in relation to the direction a certain line of case-law might be taking.[199] The AGs certainly offer a critical perspective on the Court's case-law and ensure an ongoing critical interaction within the Court,[200] and for this reason their contribution to the development of EU law and to the transparency of the Court has been appreciated by several scholars.[201] As AGs are not part of the 'team', they enjoy a greater liberty to express their views. Therefore the style of their opinions is different from that of the judgments. Unlike the judge writing for the majority, the Advocate General usually uses a more informal and personal tone, explicitly makes use of legal doctrine and comparative law, and offers relatively non-deductive forms of reasoning.[202]

The opinions of the AGs are more frequently followed by the Court than not since AGs rely on case-law and, like the Court, often engage in purposive reasoning.[203] It is not easy to determine the exact numbers, as the Court may agree with the Advocate General to a greater and lesser extent or may reach the same

197 Art 253 TFEU.

198 There are some remarkable differences from the original French model. The *commissaire* of the French government, until the ECtHR found that it violated art 6(1) of the Convention (*Kress v. France*, App no 39594/98, 7 June 2001), did participate in the discussion (but not in the voting), and delivered her/his opinion after reading the first draft of the rapporteur judge. Moreover, the opinion of the *commissaire du gouvernement*, until a few years ago, were not published, as their principal aim has been to contribute to an internal discussion, and not to enhance the transparency of the deliberative process. Di Martino (n 14) 421.

199 Bobek (n 196) 551.

200 Bobek (n 196) 560. Besides canvassing the major doctrinal positions, the AGs routinely summarise the arguments put forward by the multiple parties to the case. Thus they juxtapose conflicting partisan arguments and make it clear that the existing legal materials can be interpreted in different ways. Lasser (n 6) 134–35.

201 Bobek (n 196) 559, Di Martino (n 14) 424.

202 Lasser talks about a 'discursive bifurcation' within the CJEU. Lasser (n 6) 103ff.

203 Lasser concludes that the CJEU and its AGs resort to a fundamentally similar conceptual framework. This is in clear contrast with the French practice that served as a model for the CJEU, where the AG opinions are not published, therefore the interpretive controversy is not made public. Lasser (n 6) 236–38. Even if the AG's opinion is published together with the judgment, they arouse the interest of a narrower audience only, namely that of legal scholars. Journalists rarely cover the AG opinion when they report on CJEU judgments. Di Martino (n 14) 428–29.

conclusions on different grounds, and it is not always obvious which parts of the AG's reasoning are endorsed.[204] Some suggested that the judgments are made contrary to the AG's opinion in only 15% of the cases.[205] Considering also that today, due to workload concern, AGs are no longer appointed in every case,[206] the AG opinions cannot make up fully for the lack of dissenting opinions.

But is it desirable to allow the judges of the CJEU to make their dissent public? This question has been a matter of debate in legal scholarship and within the EU institutions.[207] To begin with, it is important to remember that the judges' term (of six years) is renewable. Dissenting opinions may jeopardise judicial independence if the judges are re-eligible. There is a danger that judges who desire to be re-appointed would attempt to please their governments by expressing favourable positions in their separate opinions.[208] Even if the written rule is that the members of the CJEU shall be appointed by common accord of the member state governments,[209] in practice the candidates nominated by the national governments are always approved by the other member states. The establishment of a panel of experts in 2010 to assess the candidates constituted an encouraging first step in providing some safeguards to the appointment process, but the panel's working methods are not transparent and its opinion is not binding.[210] In a few member states appointments still remain exclusively controlled by the executive.[211] Thus the double legitimisation from the home state and the European Union remains largely formal, which has been indicated as a democratic deficit of the European Union.[212] Consequently, a reform allowing the publication of dissent should be accompanied by the elimination of re-eligibility.[213]

204 Takis Tridimas, 'The Role of the Advocate General in the Development of Community Law: Some Reflections' (1997) 34 *Common Market Law Review* 1349, 1363.

205 Laffranque (n 193) 19.

206 According to the Court's new Statute, the Court 'may decide, after hearing the Advocate General, that the case shall be determined without a submission from the Advocate General' (art 20(5)).

207 In 2012, the European Parliament's Committee on Legal Affairs commissioned a study on the practice of dissenting opinions in the member states to the Directorate-General for Internal Policies, which however did not bring to any legislative proposal or internal reform. Directorate-General for Internal Policies (n 26). For a scholarly article calling for the introduction of separate opinions at the CJEU see Vlad F Perju, 'Reason and Authority in the European Court of Justice' (2009) 49 *Virginia Journal of International Law* 307.

208 Grementieri and Golden argue that it would be likely to happen given the enormous economic and political effects that the CJEU's decision can have for member states' internal affairs. Grementieri and Golden (n 192) 670.

209 Art 253(1) TFEU.

210 Camilla Cordelli, 'Judicial appointments to the Court of Justice of the European Union' (2013) 54 *Acta Juridica Hungarica* 24, 31.

211 Namely in Greece, Italy and Spain. See Tomáš Dumbrovský, Bilyana Petkova and Marijn Van Der Sluis, 'Judicial Appointments: The Article 255 TFEU Advisory Panel and Selection Procedures in the Member States' (2014) 51 *Common Market Law Review* 455, 467.

212 Laffranque (n 193) 16.

213 Joseph Weiler considers the renewability of the term of CJEU judges an 'elementary anomaly' and 'a continuous affront to the integrity of the European legal system', which once

The lack of transparency of the CJEU is, therefore, double: it characterises both the judicial appointments and the Court's decision-making process. In fact, the lack of separate opinions makes the appointing governments more prudent in choosing the candidates that they believe will act in their interest, since they will not be able to monitor their voting preferences. Consequently, former government officials are overrepresented at the Court.[214] Due to opacity of both the appointment and the decision-making processes, it is difficult for an external observer to evaluate the independence and impartiality of the individual judges or to analyse their judicial behaviour. Nonetheless, there have been attempts to discover the Court's internal dynamics by conducting interviews with its staff (judges and their clerks) and analysing its judgments. One recent study of this kind found that the quality of CJEU judges varies significantly, due to the politicised appointments, and consequently some judges are dominated by their clerks (called *référendaires* at the CJEU).[215] While many judges serve relatively short tenures at the Court, clerks may serve for several years and they are often 'inherited' by another judge upon the departure of the original judge they work for. The same study also found that there has been a clear dominance of the French judicial culture on the Court,[216] which certainly contributes to the reluctance to change the practice of secrecy. Another study carried out by political scientists aimed to evaluate whether, and to what extent, the threat of non-compliance and legislative override shapes judicial rulings, and found that the preferences of member-state governments have a systematic and substantively important impact on CJEU decisions.[217] Thus, even in the absence of separate opinions, it is possible to demonstrate that political constraints substantially affect the CJEU's decision-making.[218]

---

corrected would open the conditions for separate opinions. JHH Weiler, 'Epilogue: The Judicial Après Nice' in Gráinne de Búrca and JHH Weiler (eds), *The European Court of Justice* (Oxford UP 2001) 215, 225–26.

214 Since the establishment of the Court in 1952, 67% of the judges have had backgrounds in the government. See Angela Huyue Zhang, 'The Faceless Court' (2015) King's College London Law School Research Paper No 2015–45, 11 <https://ssrn.com/abstract=2640861> accessed 19 January 2017.

215 Zhang (n 214) 18.

216 First, judges that come from countries belonging to the French legal circle have served the longest, and during the first two decades, when the foundations of EU law were laid down, almost all the judges and Advocates General (with the exception of those nominated by Germany) were trained in the French legal tradition, to which the Benelux states and Italy also belong. Second, as proficiency in French is a requirement for law clerks, and French as a second language is losing its popularity in Europe, native French speakers enjoy an inherent advantage. Zhang (n 214) 34 ff.

217 Clifford J Carrubba, Matthew Gabel and Charles Hankla, 'Judicial Behavior Under Political Constraints: Evidence From the European Court of Justice' (2008) 102 *American Political Science Review* 435.

218 For other similar studies see, for example, Alec Stone Sweet and Thomas L Burnell, 'Constructing a Supranational Constitution: Dispute Resolution and Governance in the European Community' (1998) 92 *American Political Science Review* 63, and Marie-Pierre F Granger, 'When Governments Go to Luxembourg . . .: The Influence of Governments on the Court of Justice' (2004) 29 *European Law Review* 3.

The ban on publishing dissent has been criticised by several scholars,[219] especially since the number of judges sitting on the Court increased to 28 and the Lisbon Treaty introduced the principle of transparency.[220] This criticism goes hand in hand with another serious objection to the CJEU: the poor quality of its reasoning. It is reasonable to assume that the growing number of judges sitting on the Court, and the judges' increased diversity, have made it more difficult for them to reach consensus. The need for finding an operational majority in every case in all likelihood brought to look for satisfactory solutions that accommodate diverging views.[221]

The problem of increased number of judges sitting on the Court was addressed by the Nice Treaty, which created a Grand Chamber within the CJEU, composed of 13 members nominated for a period of three years, necessarily including the Court's president and the presidents of the three five-member chambers.[222] As a result of the reform, now there is a 'Grand Four' composed of four judges who sit in all important cases and have more influence on the Court's jurisprudence than the remaining 24 judges.[223] According to Hjalte Rasmussen, the judges' highly differentiated access to influence could be compensated, at least in part, by giving the non-elite judges a voice and allowing them to write separately.[224] He also argued that the permanent members of the Grand Chamber were chosen from among the most federalist judges.[225] This theory has the potential to explain the CJEU's surprising hostility towards the last draft agreement on the EU's accession to the ECHR.[226] In all likelihood the judges (sitting in full court) were not able to reach a compromise, and the majority wrote the opinion.

219 For example, Laffranque (n 193), Perju (n 207), Rasmussen (n 158), Weiler (n 213), and Alberto Alemanno and Oana Stefan, 'Openness at the Court of Justice of the European Union: Toppling a Taboo' (2014) 51 *Common Market Law Review* 97, 132. The Austrian judge of the General Court also published an article weighing the pros and cons of the publication of dissent. His conclusions, however, are not clear-cut. Josef Azizi, 'Unveiling the EU Court's Internal Decision-Making Process: A Case for Dissenting Opinions?' (2011) 12 *ERA Forum* 49.

220 Art 11(2) TEU now provides that 'the institutions shall maintain an open, transparent and regular dialogue with representative associations and civil society'.

221 Hjalte Rasmussen went even further in his criticism, presuming that these difficulties in finding an operational majority let the Court to further tighten its control over information flows, thereby cementing knowledge monopolisation, and to strip the plenary session of the real power of decision, with the establishment of a 13-member grand chamber (introduced by the Nice Treaty in 2004). Rasmussen (n 158) 1381.

222 Art 16(2) of the Statute of the CJEU.

223 Hjalte Rasmussen, 'Present and Future European Judicial Problems After Enlargement and the Post-2005 Ideological Revolt' (2007) 44 *Common Market Law Review* 1661, 1671. In another essay he argues that the 'second class' rotating members of the Grand Chamber have been left behind, while looking as if they had voted for the judgment. Rasmussen (n 158) 1385.

224 Rasmussen (n 223) 1679.

225 Rasmussen (n 158) 1382.

226 Opinion 2/13 of 18 December 2014.

This majority seems to have been dominated by the most federalist members.[227] Indeed, research found that not all judges are pro-integrationists, but their preferences lie on a continuum between Europhilia to Euroscepticism.[228]

There might also be a link between the ban on dissenting opinions and the CJEU's activism, which, according to Rasmussen, feeds on the lack of separate opinions. He argued that 'a ban on dissents must be dear to policy-happy members of collegiate benches, because it grants them a golden opportunity to yield to their instincts or vices, while the apparent unanimity of their court's output shields them . . . from any possible identification and answerability'.[229] But while a ban on dissents makes sense as a means of protecting a court's authority in its infant years,[230] it would become unjustifiable, and even harmful several decades later, as – according to many – it contributed to the poor quality of the reasoning in its judgments.[231] If we set aside the critique of the quality of the CJEU's reasoning, the same argument put forward by Rasmussen might also be used against the publication of separate opinions. From a pro-integrationist perspective, EU law has not reached a consolidation stage yet. The EU still aspires to 'an ever closer union among the peoples of Europe', as clearly stated in the Preamble to the TEU. It does not seem, in fact, likely that the ban on separate opinions will be lifted in the near future, as the EU institutions, in particular the CJEU itself, have no interest in such a reform.

3.3. *Excursus – dissenting opinions in The Hague: the practice of the International Court of Justice*

Even if its jurisdiction is not restricted to Europe, the practice of the International Court of Justice (ICJ) deserves attention, as it served as a model for the ECtHR. Looking at judicial dissent at the ICJ allows us to discover the historical roots of dissenting opinions in international adjudication, and it also provides a good ground for a more articulate comparative reflection.

The use of dissenting opinions in this court is historically linked to the peculiarities of international arbitration. Among the first international courts we find the commission set up by the so-called Jay Treaty, an agreement between Great Britain and the United States,[232] whose members did not cease to represent and

227 Katalin Kelemen, 'Opinion 2/13 of the CJEU: Whose Opinion?' (*Diritti Comparati*, 4 June 2015) <http://www.diritticomparati.it/opinion-213-of-the-cjeu-whose-opinion/> accessed 19 January 2017.

228 The research in question used the CJEU's system of chambers as a window on the impact of the individual judges. Michael Malecki, 'Do ECJ Judges All Speak With the Same Voice? Evidence of Divergent Preferences From the Judgments of Chambers' (2012) 19 *Journal of European Public Policy* 59.

229 Rasmussen (n 158) 1382.

230 Ibid. 1380.

231 Ibid. 1385.

232 Treaty of Amity, Commerce, and Navigation, Between His Britannic Majesty and the United States of America, signed on 19 November 1794, commonly known as Jay Treaty after the principal negotiator on behalf of the United States, John Jay, then Chief Justice of the Federal Supreme Court.

defend the interests of the state that appointed them. The dissenters wrote a separate opinion putting forward the arguments sustaining the point of view of the state they represented. The members of the commission came from two common law countries, but their dissenting opinions served a different purpose than those delivered by judges of the domestic courts. They aimed at expressing their author's loyalty towards his state and, therefore, their partiality.[233]

The matter of publicity of dissent was then discussed at the first Hague Peace Conference in 1899 when the Permanent Court of Arbitration was set up. The Convention approved by the Conference expressly allowed the arbitrators who remain in minority to record their dissent when signing.[234] They were, however, not allowed to explain the reasons for their dissent in a separate opinion. In 1907, at the second Hague Peace Conference, this provision was removed, and the presence of dissent was not to be mentioned in the awards anymore. Less than two decades later, when the Permanent Court of International Justice (PCIJ) was set up in 1922, the problem was discussed once again by the Advisory Committee of Jurists, which favoured allowing the mere indication of dissent not accompanied by an explanation of the reasons for dissent. The Council of the League of Nations, however, changed this and decided to allow the publication of reasoned separate opinions.[235] In December 1927, the Court began to make known the result of the voting but not the names of the dissenters.[236]

During the Second World War, a committee of experts appointed to prepare for the establishment of a new court recommended to maintain the system of separate opinions.[237] The committee stated that the absence of dissenting judgments would be false and misleading, while their presence has a very considerable political and psychological value for the losing party, as they show that its arguments have been given full weight. The committee also recognised the usefulness of dissenting opinions for the development of international law, and their role as a commentary on the decisions of the Court. For these reasons the committee went even further and suggested that it should be obligatory for the dissenters to write their reasons separately.[238] The ICJ, which replaced the

233 Sereni (n 190) 129.

234 Art 52(2) of the 1899 Convention for the Pacific Settlement of International Disputes. Hersch Lauterpacht argued that a bare dissent, unaccompanied by reasons, is of no greater value than a decision without reasons; it presumes to substitute the authority of the individual judge for the strength of the argument underlying the dissent. Hersch Lauterpacht, *The Development of International Law by the International Court* (Cambridge UP 1982) 67–68.

235 Edvard Hambro, 'Dissenting and Individual Opinions in the International Court of Justice' (1956/57) *Zeitschrift für ausländisches öffentliches Recht und Völkerrecht* 229, 235.

236 For a detailed historical account see Ijaz Hussain, *Dissenting and Separate Opinions at the World Court* (Martinus Nijhoff 1984).

237 The Informal Inter-Allied Committee on the Future of the Permanent Court of International Justice, chaired by Sir William Malkin and composed of 12 members. HM Stationary Office, Miscellaneous No 2 (1944) Cmd. 6531, 23/24, cited in Hambro (n 235) 241.

238 Hambro (n 235) 242.

PCIJ in 1945, inherited the latter's legal framework and continued its practice. New Rules of Procedure were adopted only in 1978. Since then, the judgments also indicate the names of the judges constituting the majority.[239] Thus, it is now possible to identify all dissenters, including those who decided not to write separately.

Internal diversity has actually been part of the ICJ's DNA, as the judges necessarily come from different states and, consequently, different legal cultures. Even if the Court has only 15 judges, art 9 of the Statute of the ICJ provides that the Court as a whole shall represent the main forms of civilisation and the principal legal systems of the world, and art 3(1) prohibits that two judges share the same nationality. The application of this rule is, however, difficult. In practice the system of election ensures that the composition reflects voting strength and political alliances in the Security Council and General Assembly.[240] Even so, the ICJ has been designed to bring together different legal cultures, so it would contradict the main objective of these provisions if the Court's decisions could not give expression to this diversity.[241] Moreover, given the Court's consensual jurisdiction[242] and the fact that only governments may refer disputes to it, not individuals,[243] the heterogeneity of its composition and the possibility to publish dissent are fundamental to the Court's legitimacy.

The experience of the first decade immediately showed that the Court is more divided when the law is uncertain or when the issue is too much tainted with political controversy.[244] In 1956, Edvard Hambro wrote that the frequent dissents within the Court are but a reflex of the unsettled state of international law in a period of transition. The dissents are a symptom, not a cause, he argued.[245] In particular, in the 1950s and 1960s a split emerged between judges with regard to the role of the Court in the interpretation of sources of international law. Positivist judges, who were in majority, sustained that no source has legal character without the consent of the states, while other judges believed that principles of international law can be inferred from the essential nature of the state.[246] This conflict was solved by the landmark *Namibia* opinion in 1971, in which the

239 Art 95(2) of the Rules of Procedure, <http://www.icj-cij.org/documents/index.php?p1=4&p2=3&p3=0> accessed 19 January 2017.

240 James Crawford, *Brownlie's Principles of Public International Law* (8th edn, Oxford UP 2012) 723. The system of election is regulated by arts 2–14 of the ICJ's Statute.

241 Ram Prakash Anand, 'The Role of Individual and Dissenting Opinions in International Adjudication' (1965) 14 *International and Comparative Law Quarterly* 788, 806.

242 All states involved in the dispute have to have given their consent either by means of a compromissory clause in a treaty or by means of a special agreement between the parties. (Art 36 of the Statute of the ICJ.) The consensual basis of the Court's jurisdiction, however, does not mean that a state can easily withdraw its consent. In fact, the Court frequently rejects objections to its jurisdiction from unwilling respondents as ill-founded. JG Merrills, *International Dispute Settlement* (5th edn, Cambridge UP 2011) 117.

243 Art 34(1) of the Statute.

244 Hambro (n 235) 245.

245 Ibid. 248.

246 Hussain (n 236) 73.

latter approach prevailed.[247] The internal divisiveness was especially accentuated before the fall of the Iron Curtain, when a few judges were nominated by socialist countries. Kazimierz Grzybowski sustained that these judges actually formed a separate group inside the Court because of their special background and education, and interpreted international law rules differently, as demonstrated by their dissenting opinions.[248] Statistics show that dissents have become even more frequent later.[249]

The ICJ has often been criticised for the excessive length of separate opinions. On the other hand, it has also been argued that a remedy for such an excessive use cannot be found by the lawmaker, but only through self-restraint of the judges themselves.[250] The voting patterns of ICJ judges have been analysed in order to test their national bias, as art 31 of the Court's Statute ensures that a party to a case has an effective right to representation by a national judge.[251] Posner and de Figueiredo studied 76 judgments on substantive questions and showed that while judges vote in favour of a state about 50% of the time when they have no relationship with it, that figure rises to 85–90% when it is the judge's home state.[252] The high degree of national bias demonstrates that the ICJ maintained much of the conciliatory function of the first international arbitration courts.

3.4. Comparative remarks

It has been shown that separate opinions are delivered by judges of the ICJ and the ECtHR, while dissenters on the CJEU have to remain silent. As showed in the previous sections, this difference can be explained with history. The origins of the three international courts differ considerably, and the presence or lack of separate opinions is to be found in different circumstances. In particular, in the case of the ICJ, the introduction of dissenting opinions can be traced back to the practice of the first mixed commission of international arbitration, the

247 Legal Consequences for States of the Continued Presence of South Africa in Namibia (South West Africa) notwithstanding Security Council Resolution 276 (1970), Advisory Opinion of 21 June 1971. In the following years, however, the ICJ returned to a positivist approach, even though a more moderate one, without taking rigid formalist positions. Hussain (n 236) 207.

248 Kazimierz Grzybowski, 'Socialist Judges in the International Court of Justice' (1964) 3 *Duke Law Journal* 536.

249 A summarising table on the use of separate opinions at the ICJ in the 1980s see Arthur Watts, 'The International Court of Justice: Efficiency of Procedures and Working Methods – Report of the Study Group with additional comments' in Derek W Bowett, James Crawford and Arthur Watts (eds), *The International Court of Justice: Process, Practice and Procedure* (British Institute of International and Comparative Law 1997) 27, 78.

250 Watts (n 249) 61–62.

251 Similarly to the ECtHR, if there is no *ex officio* judge of the party-state's nationality, an *ad hoc* judge can be nominated, who may be of some other nationality.

252 Eric A Posner and Miguel FP de Figueiredo, 'Is the International Court of Justice Biased?' (2005) 34 *Journal of Legal Studies* 599, 601.

members of which were not impartial judges but persons chosen by the parties to defend the position of the appointing state and to reach an agreement. Thus, these commissions, composed of an even number of members, had a conciliatory function.[253] The ECtHR followed the example of the ICJ and had a more heterogeneous composition from the beginning than the CJEU, as the first judges represented three different legal traditions (civil law, common law and Nordic legal traditions). In the case of the CJEU, the lack of separate opinions is mainly ascribable to the fact that none of the founding member states of the European Communities allowed for the publication of dissent at the time of the setting up of the Court.[254] Moreover, it was also a conscious choice of the founders not to compromise the coherence and clarity of the newborn Community law by delivering conflicting opinions.

While the ICJ and the ECtHR are two international courts deciding cases on the basis of international treaties under public international law, the CJEU has distinguished itself from other international legal orders by establishing the principle of direct effect of European Union law.[255] The three principal sources of classic international law (treaties, customary law and general principles)[256] have a structure different from sources enacted by legislative organs. International law is a less coherent and systematic body of law than a state legal system. Therefore international judges cannot be simply the 'mouth of the law', but they are required to find the law by interpreting the treaties, determining international customary law and applying general principles. It is a necessarily more creative activity. Consequently, case-law plays a fundamental role in the development of international law. EU law, on the other hand, has assumed an intermediate position between classic international law and domestic law. EU institutions act as legislative organs and adopt acts that are directly applicable in the domestic legal system of the member states, regardless whether those states are monist or dualist in their approach to international law.[257]

It is also relevant to consider the way judges are appointed to these three courts. As presented above, the CJEU's appointment procedure lacks democratic

253 In some cases, however, an umpire also participated in the decision which was taken by an uneven number of members. In these cases the commission had a decision-making function, not a conciliatory one. Sereni (n 190) 129.

254 Even the two German states, Baden and Württemberg, in which courts had published separate opinions, had already given up this practice when the CJEU was created. The six founding members still do not allow their ordinary judges to write separately today. See Section 1 above.

255 In the landmark *Van Gend en Loos* case (Case 26/62, Judgment of 5 February 1963) the CJEU famously stated that the Community constituted a 'new legal order of international law'.

256 Art 38 of the Statute of the ICJ has commonly been considered as the provision enumerating the sources of international law. Besides these three sources, it also indicates 'judicial decisions and teachings of the most highly qualified publicists of the various nations, as subsidiary means for the determination of rules of law'.

257 Robert Schütze, *European Constitutional Law* (2nd edn, Cambridge UP 2016) 77–79.

legitimacy and transparency, while the judges of the other two courts are elected by the principal decision-making body of the international organisation they represent.[258] There is, however, an important difference between the ECtHR and the ICJ in this respect: while all member states of the Council of Europe can nominate one judge to the ECtHR, it is obviously not possible for the Court of the United Nations which currently represents 193 states. This difference is, however, less pressing if we consider two factors. First, the ECtHR rarely decides in full court, but sits in chambers in most cases, so not all states are represented in the individual cases. Second, both courts guarantee 'national representation', and include an *ad hoc* judge in the adjudicating panel if there is no permanent member nominated by the state concerned in the case or she is unable to participate in order to ensure that the position of this state is taken into account by the court. Consequently, the party-state is always represented by a judge in the individual cases. It is not the case in the CJEU, which is in fact consistent with the idea of a faceless court that speaks with one voice. If separate opinions will be allowed in the CJEU, the issue of 'national representation' should be taken into careful consideration.

While in the ICJ the frequent use of an *ad hoc* judge is a logical consequence of the low number (15) of *ex officio* members with respect to the high number of member states of the Unites Nations, in the ECtHR the percentage of cases in which *ad hoc* judges are involved is considerably lower.[259] A comparison between the voting patterns of the judges sitting on these two courts is made possible by the publication of separate opinions. From a comparison of statistics it emerges clearly that judges of the ICJ (including *ad hoc* judges) have a stronger national bias than judges of the ECtHR. The former voted in favour of the nominating state in about 90% of the cases,[260] while the latter did so only in 13% of the cases. This striking difference may be explained by certain features of the ICJ. First, given the consensual basis of its jurisdiction, for a government to refer a dispute to the ICJ is like an act of faith, and the presence of the *ad hoc* judge provides an important link between the state party and the Court.[261] Second, the difference between represented legal systems is greater than at the ECtHR. Moreover, as Martin Kuijer observed, a certain 'Strasbourg culture' has developed at the ECtHR, and the protection of European human rights is not a struggle of different national influences, but has its own

258 Governments nominate judges both to the ECtHR and to the ICJ. In the case of the ICJ, the candidate needs an absolute majority from both the Security Council and the General Assembly (art 10 of the Statute of the ICJ). Their nomination is a highly political process. Crawford (n 240) 723. ECtHR judges are elected by the Parliamentary Assembly of the Council of Europe (art 22 ECHR). Generally the government's preferred candidate is elected. Voeten (n 183) 10.

259 Only 77 *ad hoc* judges were appointed between 2007 and 2010, participating in the delivery of 516 judgments. In the same period the ECtHR decided 6,170 cases in total, which means that an *ad hoc* judge was participated in 8.4% of the cases. Committee on Legal Affairs and Human Rights (n 172) para 15.

260 Posner and de Figueiredo (n 252) 615.

261 Merrills (n 242) 136.

judicial momentum.[262] Unlike, the ECtHR and the CJEU, whose jurisprudence has been built around a purpose (the protection of human rights for the former and the creation of an ever closer union for the latter), the ICJ remains a classic international court with consensual jurisdiction that resolves disputes between states, without a direct impact on individuals' rights and obligations.

As we could see, an important feature common to all international courts is the variety of the nationalities of its members. This variety has at least two important consequences: first, the different legal knowledge and mind-set of the judges ascribable to the different legal traditions their home legal systems represent; second, linguistic diversity within the court, as judges have different native languages. In particular, the fact that the working language of the court is not the native language of most of its members may discourage non-native speaking judges from writing separately.[263] Interestingly, however, linguistic difficulties do not seem to be an impediment for ICJ judges. At the same, the ICJ also decides a considerably lower number of cases than the other two courts. Thus, judges have more time to spend on writing opinions.

The practice of an international court may also be influenced by the changing composition of the international organisation it represents. Both the Council of Europe and the European Union admitted many new member states in the last few decades. In particular, the performance of judges nominated by formerly socialist countries on the ECtHR has attracted scholarly attention. Research found that these judges write separately less often than their Western European colleagues. Bruinsma argued that the lower dissent rate might be ascribable to the insufficient language skills of judges appointed by the formerly socialist countries.[264] It is, however, to be underlined that insufficient language skills are not absolute, but rather limited to the two working languages of the Court, French and English. It is not surprising, as German and Russian were the most common second languages in the socialist bloc.[265] A similar research cannot be carried out in relation to the CJEU, as the lack of separate opinions excludes the possibility of any quantitative analysis. Such a high linguistic variety does not characterise any national court, even if there are countries in Europe with more than one official language. But in a national context it is much less problematic to require fluency in the other official language of the country, than to require the knowledge of French which is not a common second language in Europe anymore.[266]

262 This would be demonstrated by the fact that in 39% of the cases (until 1997) the judgment was rendered unanimously. Kuijer (n 171) 66.

263 Laffranque (n 193) 19.

264 Bruinsma, 'Judicial Identities' (n 171) 236.

265 French is not widely spoken in the Nordic countries either. Zhang (n 214) 20.

266 French, even if still the second most common second language in Europe, is considerably behind English, and its popularity is decreasing. Only 12% of Europeans speak French as foreign language. See European Commission, *Europeans and Their Languages Report* (Special Eurobarometer 386, 2012) 19.

Concluding, even if the ECtHR and the CJEU are not constitutional courts in the strict sense, they are to be involved in a discussion on constitutional courts, due to the several constitutional functions they have and the strong mutual influence and interaction between them and national courts. They are both heavily influenced by, and to a certain extent are the product of, the civil law tradition. Their inclusion is reasonable and desirable, and it enriches the comparative perspective. Moreover, as constitutional courts, they are relatively new institutions that had to justify their *raison d'être* in the period immediately following their creation. In fact, in that context the publication of dissenting opinions could be viewed as dangerous to the court's legitimacy and authority. This argument was used in relation to the CJEU. From the comparison it also emerges that legal tradition is a determining factor. The civil law tradition, and especially the French legal tradition, still struggles with the publication of judicial dissent. This is shown by the fact that the CJEU, which is dominated by the French legal culture in many ways, prohibits it, while the more pluralist ECtHR and those national constitutional courts that are not in the French legal orbit allow for it.

4. Judicial dissent in East-Central European constitutional courts

4.1. *A new generation of constitutional courts: why treat them separately?*

Constitutional courts of formerly socialist countries of Eastern Europe have commonly been considered a new generation. And that is for a good reason: they were born in the same period, within one decade, and in similar historical circumstances.[267] They all had to face and handle a transition from a socialist regime to the rule of law and democracy. Though they shared similar problems, the solutions they chose were often remarkably different. Therefore, it is not possible to talk about an 'Eastern European model' of constitutional courts. All formerly socialist countries but three used the Kelsenian model as a basis, with the exception of Bulgaria, Estonia and Romania, and those that did then enriched it with many new elements and competences unknown to the original model.

The most important common feature of this new generation of constitutional courts is the role they played in the democratic transition. One should be aware of the peculiarities of a transitional context. A careful student of post-socialist legal transformation, Ruti Teitel, argued that the usual doubts about the legitimacy of judicial lawmaking do not hold in transitional periods. According to her, 'theories of adjudication associated with understandings of the rule of law

267 Two notable exceptions, however, are the Polish Constitutional Tribunal and the constitutional courts of former Yugoslavia, established already under the socialist regime. For a history of constitutional courts of formerly socialist countries see Herman Schwartz, *The Struggle for Constitutional Justice in Post-Communist Europe* (University of Chicago Press 2000).

in ordinary times are inapposite to transitional periods'.[268] This then calls for a separate treatment of this new generation. On the other hand, the transitional period does not last forever, even if in certain Eastern European countries it ended earlier than in others. Wojciech Sadurski argued that as the post-socialist states became more mature and stable, the objections against judicial law-making, which are pertinent elsewhere in the democratic world, apply with equal force to Eastern Europe, especially to those East-Central European states that fully resemble mature democracies.[269]

4.2. Law in the books: the rules concerning judicial dissent

Today, all formerly socialist countries allow their constitutional courts to publish separate opinions. Five of them allow it even in ordinary courts (Bulgaria, Estonia, Lithuania, Romania, and Slovakia) and one in administrative courts (the Czech Republic). In other formerly socialist countries, as in Poland and Hungary, ordinary judges may write separately, but those written opinions are not published. Instead they are attached to the case dossier in a sealed envelope.[270] In Hungarian civil procedure, younger judges cast their vote before the older judges, and the presiding judge is the last one to cast her/his vote. A judge who remains in the minority has the right to attach her/his separate written opinion to the case dossier, but it may only be accessed by the superior court in an appeal procedure, a disciplinary proceeding or a uniformity procedure,[271] and by the persons entitled to initiate these proceedings.[272] In criminal procedure, the parties (the prosecutor and the defendant) do not have access to the separate opinions in case of appeal.

268 Ruti Teitel, 'Transitional Jurisprudence: The Role of Law in Political Transformation' (1997) 106 *Yale Law Journal* 2009, 2034.

269 Wojciech Sadurski, 'Introduction' in Wojciech Sadurski (ed), *Constitutional Justice, East and West* (2nd edn, Kluwer Law International 2002) 1, 14.

270 Polish doctrine calls these opinions *votum separatum*. Consultative Council of European Judges, 'Questionnaire for 2008 CCJE Opinion Concerning the Quality of Judicial Decisions: Reply Submitted by the Delegation of Poland' (March 2008) <https://wcd.coe.int/ViewDoc.jsp?id=1263345&Site=COE> accessed 19 January 2017. The term '*votum separatum*' has also been used by constitutional judges. See, for example, the dissenting opinion of Judge Zbigniew Cieślak to Decision no K 9/11 of 20 July 2011 <https://trybunal.gov.pl/fileadmin/content/omowienia/K_09_11_EN.pdf> accessed 19 January 2017.

271 It is for the Supreme Court (Kúria) to ensure the uniform application of the law. A uniformity procedure may be initiated by the president of the Supreme Court, the presidents of the Supreme Court's chambers, the presidents of the courts of appeal and the prosecutor general. Arts 32–33 of Act no CLXI of 2011 on the organisation and administration of courts.

272 Art 214(2) of the Code of civil procedure. The current text of this provision is in force since 2001. There have been three modifications (in 1957, 1995 and 2001), all concerning the list of persons entitled to access the separate opinions. The list changed according to the reforms of the system of appeals. Parties of the disciplinary proceedings have only been entitled to access separate opinions since the last modification, which entered into force on 1 January 2002.

Only the superior and disciplinary courts do.[273] Originally the prosecutor had access to the minutes of the deliberation and the dissenting opinions, if any, but in 2007 the Constitutional Court found this unconstitutional as a violation of the right to fair trial. According to the Constitutional Court, it violated the principle of equality of arms, because the defendant was not given the same possibility.[274]

A provision on separate opinions was already included in the original version of the Hungarian Code of civil procedure, adopted in 1952, during the harshest period of Stalinist dictatorship, and the same rule was introduced in the Soviet Union in 1961.[275] This openness towards judicial dissent was, however, only apparent, and the rule was hardly ever applied.[276] Socialist judges were, in practice, no more than the 'mouth of the law', and – as it is understandable in a totalitarian regime dominated by a culture of conformity – they tended to avoid calling the public's attention to themselves by writing separately. Such a provision rather aimed at giving the false impression of a progressive regime. Indeed, some Western scholars, as the Italian Vittorio Denti, argued during the 1960s that this rule would demonstrate that socialist legal systems have a similar attitude towards the judicial function as the common law tradition, which recognises a more creative role of the judge, in opposition to the rigid attitude of the civil law tradition.[277] As a matter of fact, the opposite was true. The dominating concept of law during the socialist era was a positivist and state-centred one, which advocated that judges have no law-making power. As Zdeněk Kühn observed, communist dictatorship necessarily generated an authoritarian understanding of law, with resulting authoritarian judicial discourse, in which the pluralism of opinions was absent.[278]

In Eastern Europe, separate opinions have been made known to the wider public only after the democratic transition, and this possibility has been mostly limited to constitutional courts. As we have seen, it had been argued in Western Europe and the United States in earlier times that separate opinions may

273 Art 255(2) of the Code of criminal procedure (Act no XIX of 1998). Deliberation minutes are prepared only in case of lack of unanimity. In any event, the dissenter is not obliged to write separately. It is only a possibility. If a dissenting opinion is prepared, its existence (but neither its content, nor its author) is indicated in the minutes of the trial. Arts 255(1) and 256(5).

274 Decision no 11/2007 (III.7.) AB of 6 March 2007.

275 Art 57(5) of the Principles of Civil Procedure of the Soviet Union, approved by the Supreme Soviet on 8 December 1961, in Bulletin du Centre d'Étude des pays de l'Est (Bruxelles 1962), cited in Vittorio Denti, 'Per il ritorno al "voto di scissura" nelle decisioni giudiziarie' in Mortati (n 17) 1, 10, fn 31.

276 I am thankful to Andrius Valuta, doctoral researcher at Vilnius University, Lithuania, for this remark and for discussing this issue with me.

277 According to him, the reasons behind this attitude, however, were different. Socialist law aimed to protect the interests of the workers, while in common law it is an essential part of the legal tradition. Denti (n 17) 10, fn 32.

278 Zdeněk Kühn, 'The Authoritarian Legal Culture at Work: The Passivity of Parties and the Interpretational Statements of Supreme Courts' (2006) 2 *Croatian Yearbook of European Law and Policy* 19.

contribute to the development of case-law and legal doctrine.[279] Similarly, Julia Laffranque, an Estonian legal scholar who dedicated her doctoral dissertation to the topic of dissenting opinions, observed in relation to her country:

> [A dissenting opinion] is an instructive commentary which is especially important for a legal culture that is not yet fully developed, as is the case in Estonia where sometimes a clear and precise provision of a law is lacking, or established interpretation and legal theories in certain issues have still not emerged. The dissenting opinion prepares the ground for changing the court practice.[280]

This observation can be extended to the whole region of East-Central Europe that experienced democratic transition in the same period, and it could also serve as a justification for the introduction of dissenting opinions in these countries. There is, however, little evidence that this would be the main reason behind it. We can hypothesise that formerly socialist countries allowed the publication of dissent because most of them took the experience of the German Federal Constitutional Court into consideration as their main model.

The Romanian Constitutional Court provides an interesting example of a court that was not designed on the German model, but adopted the practice of publishing dissents. Indeed, the original framework, designed on the French and Italian systems, did not provide for publishing dissents. Romanian constitutional judges, however, started to write separately early on, in 1993,[281] since it was not prohibited by the law. In addition, the Code of civil procedure already provided this possibility to their colleagues deciding civil cases.[282] Constitutional judges published both dissenting and concurring opinions, even in cases decided by a chamber and not in full court.[283] This practice was later acknowledged and codified by the legislature.[284] This Court's early adoption of publishing dissents,

279 Donald E Lively, *Foreshadows of the Law: Supreme Court Dissents and Constitutional Development* (Praeger 1992) and Section 2.1.1 in this chapter.

280 Julia Laffranque, 'Dissenting Opinion and Judicial Independence' (2003) 8 *Juridica International* 162, 172.

281 In case no 38/1993 of 7 July 1993, a 3:2 decision, the President of the Court Gionea and Judge Muraru wrote a long joint dissenting opinion (*opinie separată*), available in Romanian at <www.ccr.ro/files/products/D038_93.pdf> accessed 19 January 2017. Shortly after, the plenary session of the Court delivered a decision to which three judges attached a joint dissenting opinion (Judges Ciobanu, Constantinescu and Iorgovan). Decision no 1 of the Plenary Session of 7 September 1993.

282 Art 258 of the Code of Civil Procedure. This code was in force until 2013.

283 For example, the concurring opinion (*opinie concurentă*) of Judges Cochinescu and Doldur delivered in case no 86/2003 of 27 February 2003.

284 Act no 47/1992 on the Constitutional Court was modified and renumbered by Act no 232/2004 of 3 June 2004. The new art 59(3) provides: 'Judges who have given a negative vote may formulate a separate opinion. With regard to the reasoning of the decision, it is also possible to write a concurring opinion. The separate (dissenting) and, as the case may be, concurring opinion shall be published in the *Official Gazette* of Romania, Part I, together with the decision.'

notwithstanding legislative silence on point, suggests that it recognised their value in developing case-law and doctrine.

Even in countries where constitutional judges are allowed to write separately, there are some instances in which secret deliberation is prescribed by the law, thus the disclosure of dissent is prohibited. In Bulgaria, for example, the secrecy of deliberation concerns two kinds of cases: decisions on lifting a judge's immunity or establishing his actual incapacity to perform his duties,[285] and decisions on impeachment by the National Assembly against the President or the Vice President.[286] The Slovak Constitutional Court renders its decision by secret vote in any case that involves its decision to allow or not allow the criminal prosecution and pre-trial detention of one of its members, of any other judge or of the General Prosecutor, or to convene disciplinary proceedings regarding the Chief Justice, the Deputy Chief Justice of the Slovak Republic and the General Prosecutor.[287] These two examples might be sufficient to notice that secrecy is provided for in cases in which the decision concerns the criminal or disciplinary responsibility of a Justice or other high official of the state, and not for cases of constitutional review. It seems that in the former cases the publication of dissent is considered to be inappropriate.

Admittedly, some states withhold publishing dissents in ordinary criminal appeal cases out of concern for the accused. For example, England and Estonia. In the English criminal appeals, it has been long regarded as imperative that 'the discomfiture of the unsuccessful appellant should not be aggravated by an overt division of opinion among the judges'.[288] In a similar way in Estonia, where the Code of Criminal Procedure allows judges to have their dissent recorded in the file of the case, but it is not disclosed to the parties.[289] By contrast, the withholding of appeals in high-profile cases in constitutional courts appears to be out of a different concern: these cases have also political implications. The overt expression of disagreement in the court could lead to friction between the judiciary and the other two branches of power.

Observing the rules of East-Central European countries we can see that dissenting opinions, where they exist, are (a non-binding) part of the judgment. Proof of this assertion is the fact that separate opinions, with the sole exception of Latvia, are published together with the majority opinion. There is a curious situation in Slovenia, where dissenting opinions are not published in the *Official Gazette*, but on the website of the Court, in the Digest and in a special law journal. The explanation is simple: it is too expensive, since the Court must pay for publication in the *Official Gazette*.[290] Also in the Czech Republic, dissents and

285 Art 148(2) of the Bulgarian Constitution.

286 Art 149(1.8) of the Bulgarian Constitution and art 32(4) of the Rules of the Constitutional Court.

287 Art 136(2)–(3) of the Slovak Constitution and art 32(3) of the Act on the organisation of and the proceedings before the Constitutional Court of 20 January 1993.

288 See Chapter 3, text to n 31.

289 Art 266 of the Code of Criminal Procedure, Riigi Teataja (State Gazette) I 1995, 6/8, 69; 2000, 56, 369. Also Laffranque (n 280) 166.

290 I thank Arne Mavčič for this observation.

concurrences are published in the Court's own reporter but not in the Collection of Laws, where there is only a note at the bottom of the judgment about the existence of a separate opinion.[291]

4.2.1. The Baltic story: three degrees of openness

Examining the rules concerning dissenting opinions in the three Baltic states leads us to an interesting conclusion: until 2008, these three legal systems represented three degrees of openness. First, until 2008, Lithuania did not authorise the publication of separate opinions at all. Second, in Latvia only constitutional court judges may express a dissenting opinion, and it is not published together with the opinion of the court, but once a year in the official collection of judgments.[292] Finally, Estonia, the most open of the three countries from this point of view, allows public expression of dissent in almost the entire judiciary. In this country, there is no separate constitutional court, but there is a special section (the Constitutional Review Chamber) of the Supreme Court that decides on the constitutionality of laws.[293]

Estonia is one of the few countries in East-Central Europe which also allows its lower ordinary courts to publish separate opinions (*eriarvamus* in Estonian) in lower ordinary courts as well; what is more, this even extends to lay judges.[294] The right to write separately is provided by the civil and criminal procedural codes,[295] while there is no explicit rule for administrative and misdemeanour procedures.[296] Even so, lower courts do not use it as often as the Supreme Court. According to Julia Laffranque, this is related to the heavy caseload of judges in

291 The judgments, together with the separate opinions, are included on the main computer database in the Czech Republic (called ASPI), but the names of dissenting Justices are redacted out, and only their initials appear. I thank Mark Gillis for this information.

292 Art 225 of the Rules of Procedure of the Constitutional Court provides that dissenting opinions shall be kept attached to the case file for three months and after that are published; and art 33(2) of the Constitutional Court Act provides that once a year the Constitutional Court shall publish a collection of judgments of the Constitutional Court, including all judgments in full and individual opinions of justices attached to cases.

293 There are 19 justices in the Supreme Court, appointed to office by the Parliament (*Riigikogu*) on the proposal of the Chief Justice of the Supreme Court. Every justice is a member of one of the Administrative Law, Civil or Criminal Chambers. The Constitutional Review Chamber is comprised of nine justices. The Chief Justice of the Supreme Court is the chairman of the Constitutional Review Chamber. Other eight members of the Chamber are appointed by the Supreme Court *en banc*. See the Booklet about the Supreme Court of Estonia (2004), <www.nc.ee/vfs/22/RK_2004.pdf> accessed 19 January 2017.

294 Laffranque (n 280) 166.

295 Art 16(6) of the Code of civil procedure of 1998 which establishes the right to write separately. Art 230(1) provides that the judgment has to specify which judge(s) delivered a separate opinion and a summary of these, signed by their author, has to be included. In criminal cases, on the other hand, separate opinions are not published together the judgment, just included in the case dossier (art 266 of the Code of criminal procedure).

296 Laffranque (n 280) 166–67.

the lower courts and to the fact that the issues of principle, where the likelihood of expressing a dissenting opinion is higher, are in the last instance decided by the Supreme Court.[297]

Lithuania, on the other hand, represents the other end of the spectrum: it did not allow the publication of separate opinions until a reform in 2008. It is a peculiar case because Lithuania followed the German model of constitutional justice in other respects. Indeed, the reasons for not allowing the disclosure of dissent might have been similar to those discussed by the German legislature in the 1950s:[298] the constitutional court must first achieve authority before it can resist public influence that can be triggered by dissenting opinions.[299] Unlike in Romania, where the law was silent on the matter, the publication of dissent was explicitly forbidden in Lithuania until 2008.[300] This rule could also be considered a guarantee of judicial independence,[301] but the authority argument seems to be stronger. This is confirmed by the fact that, in 2008, on the proposal of the Constitutional Court itself, the Lithuanian Parliament decided to modify the rule and allow the judges to write separately.[302] Thus, one and a half decades after the Constitutional Court had been set up, both the Court and the legislature seemingly determined that such authority had been achieved. This reform might have been urged by the fact that ordinary and administrative judges already had this possibility,[303] so the prohibition was limited to the Constitutional Court. The Constitutional Court Act today provides that:

> A justice of the Constitutional Court, who has a different opinion about an act adopted by the Constitutional Court, shall have the right to set forth in writing his reasoned dissenting opinion within five working days of the pronouncement of the corresponding act in the courtroom. If such an opinion has been received not later than prior to the pronouncement of the act of the Constitutional Court, the Chairperson of the hearing shall state this fact in the courtroom after the act adopted by the Constitutional Court has been pronounced.[304]

297 Laffranque (n 280) 167.

298 See Section 2.1.1 in this Chapter.

299 Laffranque (n 280) 165, fn 20.

300 Art 53 of Act no I-67 of 3 February 1993 provided for the rule of confidentiality of the deliberation, and prohibited the publication of separate opinions or of voting results.

301 Nida Gelazis, 'Defending Order and Freedom: The Lithuanian Constitutional Court in Its First Decade' in Sadurski (n 269) 395, 400.

302 Act no X-1806, 11.11.2008, Valstybės žinios (*Official Gazette*), 2008, No 134–5179 (22.11.2008). Consequently, the Constitutional Court modified its Rules of Procedure inserting a Section VII entitled 'Dissenting opinion of a Justice of the Constitutional Court' (Decision of 26 November 2008).

303 Viktorija Staugaitytė, 'Dissenting Opinion in the Constitutional Justice: Collegiality of the Court *vs.* Personal Independence of the Judge' (2008) 9(111) *Jurisprudencija* 125, 130.

304 Art 55(4). The five working days rule was also part of the constitutional judges' proposal, who believed that it was important to read the majority's reasoning before one can prepare a separate opinion. Thus, separate opinions are not published together with the judgment

The deliberation and the voting results remain confidential, but now article 53(3) specifies that separate opinions cannot be considered a violation of this rule.

4.2.2. The Slovak story: precedent becomes law

In Czechoslovakia, after the breakdown of the socialist regime, judges of the Federal Constitutional Court could express their disagreement. A summary of their reasons was included in the court record. The record was, however, not accessible to the public.[305] The rule allowing for confidential separate opinions was continued by the newly partitioned state of Slovakia in 1993. That rule was liberalised in August 2000, so that now dissenting opinions may be published.[306]

This opening to publishing dissents can be explained in part by a controversial case decided by the Constitutional Court the year before. The facts can be summarised as follows. In August 1995, the son of President Michal Kováč was abducted. In March 1998, then Prime Minister Vladimír Mečiar, who was rumoured to have arranged the kidnapping, granted an amnesty for any criminal offenses related to that abduction.[307] However, in 1998, the new government abolished the amnesty. This led to a decision to prosecute a former high-ranking member of the secret service. The individual petitioned the Constitutional Court to vacate the prosecution. The Court agreed, notwithstanding the self-serving nature of the amnesty.[308] It was also controversial since, after six years of constant refusal to annul any decision contested by means of petition, this was the first time the Court decided to do so. As Radoslav Procházka wrote, '[t]he ruling was so out of line with the Court's case-law and so lacking in persuasive legal argumentation that it prompted some of the best legal minds of the country to label it as a direct attack on the rule of law'.[309] Judge Ján Klučka[310] was disappointed with the decision, thus he decided to write a dissenting opinion; this was noted

---

in the *Official Gazette*, but they are available on the website of the court and both the parties and the media are informed about it (art 55(5)). Section 145 of the Rules of Court, moreover, limits the possibility to write separately to decisions on the merits and to three types of procedural decisions, namely: dismissal after a case has been considered at a hearing and the interpretation or review of an earlier ruling, conclusion or decision.

305 Art 9(5) of Act no 491/1991 concerning the plenary session, and art 10(5) concerning the chambers.

306 Art 31(1) of the Slovak Constitutional Court Act. Initially, this Act provided for the same type of confidential separate opinion as the previous federal law.

307 Vladimír Mečiar granted an amnesty as President of the Republic *ad interim*, after President Michal Kováč (1993–98) ended his term. Art 105(1) of the Slovak Constitution provides that certain powers of the President shall pass to the government if the office of the President is vacant.

308 Decision no I ÚS 48/99 of 20 December 1999.

309 Radoslav Procházka, *Mission Accomplished: On Founding Constitutional Adjudication in Central Europe* (Central European UP 2002) 196–97.

310 Ján Klučka, a professor of International Law and Politics, was a member of the constitutional court from 1993 to 2004. From 2004 to 2009 he was a judge at the Court of Justice of the EU.

in the record. Since the record was not public, and the plenum of the Court rejected to publish his opinion in the official collection, Judge Klučka published an article in a law review in which he criticised the judgment. It was following this episode that the Slovak legislature decided to lift the ban on the publication of dissenting opinions.

4.2.3. The Yugoslav story: a separate way

Another interesting case is that of the former Socialist Federal Republic of Yugoslavia. In 1963, uniquely in Eastern Europe, the Yugoslav Federal Assembly set up a Federal Constitutional Court; the assemblies of the federal republics established their own constitutional courts.[311] During the socialist era, publication of dissenting opinions had been allowed at all levels of constitutional review. However, the Federal Constitutional Court did not consider dissenting opinions to be an important part of its constitutional review activity. So, step by step, separate opinions turned into confidential documents. They were announced at the Court's session by the dissenting judge, but the text was kept under special separate cover as a confidential part of the case dossier. From 1974 to 1990 separate opinions were not published anymore simply because no judge requested the publication of his dissent.[312]

After the dissolution of the Socialist Federal Republic of Yugoslavia, all former republics kept their respective constitutional courts. The Slovenian Constitutional Court, in particular, became very inclined towards activism. In the first period following the adoption of a new constitution in 1991, it decided many politically sensitive cases with a 5:4 vote and a high number of separate opinions. According to Miro Cerar, activism was the result of the prominence of a triumvirate of judges, who in a period of eight years each in turn held the presidency of the Court.[313] In the aforementioned cases in which the Court was divided, the majority formed around this 'triumvirate'. These decisions were criticised for being overtly in line with the interests of the then governing right-wing political parties. Indeed, all three members of the triumvirate took up ministerial posts after their term of office expired.[314]

4.3. The law in action: the use of dissenting opinions

4.3.1. What do the numbers show?

As Jaakko Husa pointed out, for a comparatist 'the empirical reality and normativity of law are intertwined', and 'the significance of positive law only opens up

311 However, these constitutional courts did not have the power to annul a legislative provision. Miro Cerar, 'Slovenia's Constitutional Court Within the Separation of Powers' in Sadurski (n 269) 213, 214.

312 I am thankful to Arne Mavčič, former Head of the Analysis and International Cooperation Department of the Slovenian Constitutional Court, for this information.

313 Cerar (n 311) 217.

314 Cerar (n 311) 218.

in legal practice'.[315] As the cases of Germany and Romania demonstrate, it is not sufficient to look at the law in the books. It may well happen, as in these two countries at the dawn of constitutional adjudication, that there is no mention of separate opinions in the positive law, while dissent is disclosed in some form in practice. The contrary might also occur: the law allows judges to disclose their dissent, but they do not take advantage of this possibility. This was the case in Yugoslavia in the last two and a half decades of the socialist era.[316] In this book, statistical data has been gathered from the following eight East-Central European countries' constitutional courts: the Czech Republic, Estonia, Hungary, Latvia, Lithuania, Poland, the Slovak Republic and Slovenia. The data, however, does not always cover the same period and lacks many details that would be needed to carry out a comparative analysis. Nonetheless, we can still learn something from these numbers.

LATVIA

The Latvian Constitutional Court, with its dissent rate of 7%,[317] seems to represent an exception among the last generation of constitutional courts. It seems that Latvian constitutional judges feel less pressing the need to express their disagreement publicly or, less likely, they find a way to agree on the decision in most cases.[318] Furthermore, the low number of separate opinions might be, at least in part, due to the low number of judges. In fact, the Latvian Constitutional Court is composed of only seven members, which makes it the smallest constitutional court in Europe. All other constitutional courts operate with at least nine judges. It is obviously easier for a smaller panel to reach unanimity than for a larger one.

LITHUANIA

In Lithuania, where the judges have been allowed to write separately since 2008, there was a rather high dissent rate in the first years following the reform, peaking at 35% in 2010; it dropped to an average of 7% in 2013.[319] This initial high rate might be due to the enthusiasm of Lithuanian constitutional judges about the possibility of writing individual opinions; this is something they had proposed

315 Jaakko Husa, *A New Introduction to Comparative Law* (Hart 2015) 39–40.

316 See Section 4.2.4.

317 Data related to the period from 2003 to 2010. Benjamin Bricker, 'Breaking the Principle of Secrecy: An Examination of Judicial Dissent in European Constitutional Courts' (2017) 39 *Law & Policy* 170, 174.

318 According a former law clerk of the Latvian court, the reason may lie in two circumstances: the similar educational and professional background of the judges which brings to a similar attitude on constitutional issues, and in the lack of time that they can spend on writing separate opinions.

319 Statistical data on file with the author. I thank Andrius Valuta and Vaidas Lubauskas for providing me with these data.

to the legislature. This enthusiasm diminished after a few years, and the practice normalised. Now the dissent rate of Lithuanian judges is even lower than the region's average.

ESTONIA

The data from Estonia, where dissenting opinions can be delivered in the entire judiciary, seem to show that constitutional cases trigger more dissent than other cases. As we have seen, there is no separate constitutional court, but a special constitutional review chamber operates within the ordinary Supreme Court. The publication of separate opinions is not limited to this chamber, though used more frequently by this than by the other three chambers.[320] This statistical fact seems to confirm that the publication of dissent is required more by judges when they discuss constitutional issues than when they decide civil or criminal law matters, as in the latter cases the judgment has a smaller impact on the legal system. During the first one and a half decades after independence from the Soviet Union, there was at least one separate opinion in 13.75% of the cases decided by the Supreme Court's Constitutional Review Chamber, while this percentage was only 1.85 in the Civil Law Chamber, 0.6 in the Criminal Law Chamber, and 0.85 in the Administrative Law Chamber.[321] The dissent rate increased over time, though it is not clear whether this apparent trend only results from lower levels of dissent in the early years.[322]

POLAND

Until 2010, the dissent rate was similar in the Polish Constitutional Tribunal (13.4%).[323] Leszek Garlicki observed that, considering the political changes in the Polish Parliament, the Tribunal's composition is the result of appointments made at different times by different majorities, and this is reflected in the number of separate opinions. In the period of four years from December 1993 to November 1997 there were 47 such opinions expressed in 29 cases, while in the following period of three years (from December 1997 to December 2000) the Polish constitutional judges wrote separately in 22 cases, producing a total of 45 dissenting and concurring opinions.[324] This means that the number of

320 The Civil, Criminal and Administrative Law Chambers. Laffranque (n 193) 22.
321 Until 2003. Data from Laffranque (n 193) 22.
322 Chris Hanretty, 'Judicial Disagreement need not to be Political: Dissent on the Estonian Supreme Court' (2015) 67 *Europe-Asia Studies* 970, 976. Hanretty, a political scientist, found that dissent on the Estonian Supreme Court is characterised by disagreements over plaintiff-friendliness which cannot be reduced to disagreements about left-right political issues, and which are related to judges' background in particular areas of law. He concluded that the Estonian pattern of dissent is not political in nature. Ibid. 984.
323 Data related to the period from 2003 to 2010. Bricker (n 317) 174.
324 Leszek Lech Garlicki, 'The Experience of the Polish Constitutional Court' in Sadurski (n 269) 265, 269.

separate opinions remained roughly the same after 1997, a turning point in Polish history for two reasons: the victory of conservative liberals at the parliamentary elections, and the adoption of a new Constitution which introduced important reforms in the system of constitutional justice.[325] More recent statistics show that the dissent rate increased considerably after 2011, peaking at 33% in 2012.[326] There might be a link between the recent constitutional reforms, which brought to a crisis of Polish constitutional justice,[327] and the increased dissent rate. Keeping an eye on the practice of dissenting opinions may provide us with a better insight into that crisis.

SLOVENIA AND THE CZECH AND SLOVAK REPUBLICS

The data from the constitutional courts of these three countries are fragmented but to a certain extent comparable. The average dissent rates are similar in Slovenia (25.7%) and the Czech Republic (29.5%).[328] The Slovenian Constitutional Court publishes 20–30 separate opinions a year on average,[329] and the number of separate opinions published per year is similar in the Slovak Republic.[330] In both Slovenia and Slovakia, separate opinions may be attached to any type of decision, while in the Czech Republic the rejection of manifestly ill-founded petitions – understandably – requires unanimity.[331] Interestingly, in Slovakia most of the dissenting opinions are expressed on admissibility, while in the Czech Republic the dissent rate is considerably higher in cases decided on the merits in plenary session. The explanation for this difference is two-fold. First, a debate took place within the Slovak Constitutional Court concerning the admissibility petitions against procedural delays after the termination of the procedure. The only judge

325 The new Polish Constitution was approved by a referendum held on 25 May 1997. The two most important changes concerned the Tribunal's composition: the number of judges was increased from 12 to 15, and the term of office from eight to nine years.
326 Considering the dissent rate in cases decided with a judgment on the merits. The rate is lower for cases decided with a procedural decision. Statistical data on file with the author. I thank Marek Domagała for providing me with these data.
327 Andrzej Kowalczyk, 'Crisis Over the Constitutional Tribunal in Poland' (*KOD*, 17 October 2016) <www.kod.ngo/crisis-constitutional-tribunal-poland/> and Opinion no 860/2016 of the Venice Commission on the Act on the Constitutional Tribunal of 14 October 2016 (CDL-AD(2016)026) <www.venice.coe.int/webforms/documents/default.aspx?pdffile=CDL-AD(2016)026-e> accessed 19 January 2017.
328 Data related to the period from 2003 to 2010. Bricker (n 317) 174.
329 In 2005, for example, there were 24 separate opinions. I am thankful to Arne Mavčič for the data.
330 The Slovak Constitutional Court published four separate opinions in 2001, 16 in 2002, 22 in 2003, 17 in 2004, 32 in 2005 and 34 in 2006. This shows a growing tendency. As mentioned above, separate opinions are published since August 2000 only. I am thankful to Ján Štiavniczký for the data.
331 Art 14 of the Czech Constitutional Court Act refers to decisions by the plenum only, but in practice the Court does publish separate opinions in cases decided by a panel too. A legal basis for this practice may be art 19(2), which provides that panels decide by majority. See also Chapter 2, Section 2.

who was in favour of admitting these petitions within two months was Juraj Babjak, the Slovak Court's 'Great Dissenter'. Of the 125 separate opinions published between 2001 and 2006, 87 were authored by him.[332] Second, a peculiarity of the Czech practice is that only the most important matters are reserved for the plenary session, which decides not more than 15–20 cases a year. The fact that these matters are the most divisive at the same time is demonstrated by the very high dissent rate: in most cases decided by the plenum in the last years there has been at least one separate opinion.[333] In these cases, the Czech court dealt with issues of general public interest, such as compulsory vaccination of children,[334] step-child adoption by same-sex couples,[335] and the pensions system.[336]

HUNGARY

The Hungarian Constitutional Court's average dissent rate in the first 21 years of its operation (1990–2010) can be considered relatively low in the region (10.96%). The Hungarian Court decided a total of 3,571 cases in full court, and in only 380 of these was the Court openly divided.[337] The practice of this Court will be analysed in detail in the next section.

4.3.2. The role of dissenting opinions in the development of constitutional law

While it can be useful to observe trends in the statistical data to gain insight into a court's practice, the numbers do not show the relevance of the individual separate opinions for the legal system. There have been cases in which a separate opinion later became the official position of the court. At times, a dissent or a concurrence could convince the majority a few years later. An example is offered by a 2005 decision of the Polish Constitutional Tribunal concerning the constitutionality of a law restricting access to documents of communist security agencies.[338] This decision was heavily influenced by the dissenting opinions delivered by Judge Zdzisław Czeszejko-Sochacki in two lustration cases in 1998.[339] The Court, just as Judge Czeszejko-Sochacki seven years earlier, found that the

332 I am thankful to Ján Štiavniczký for the data. Juraj Babjak was a member of the Court from January 2000 to January 2007.
333 In 13 out of 18 cases in 2013, in 13 out of 14 cases in 2014, and in 10 out of 15 cases in 2015. Statistical data related to these three years on file with the author. I thank Ľubomír Majerčík from the Analytics Department of the Czech Constitutional Court for providing me with these data.
334 Decisions Pl ÚS 16/14 and Pl ÚS 19/14 of 27 January 2015.
335 Four separate opinions delivered in the recent case Pl ÚS 7/15 of 14 June 2016.
336 Decision Pl ÚS 5/12 of 31 January 2012.
337 See Table 6 in the next section.
338 Decision no K 31/04 of 26 October 2005 <http://trybunal.gov.pl/fileadmin/content/omowienia/K_31_04_GB.pdf> (in English) accessed 9 August 2016. No separate opinions.
339 In East-Central Europe, by 'lustration' we mean the screening of public officials to establish whether they in the past collaborated with the communist secret services. Decisions

determination of the veracity of persons submitting lustration declarations is not the principal aim of lustration. The aim, instead, is to ensure the transparency of public life. There is no explicit reference to Judge Czeszejko-Sochacki's dissenting opinions, but his influence can be clearly traced in the reasoning.[340]

Sometimes separate opinions have blazed a new trail in the law. An example of a trailblazing concurring opinion is offered by Slovenian constitutional justice, where certain principles and legal institutions were first described in a separate opinion and only later included into an opinion of the court. The principle of proportionality appeared for the first time in a concurring opinion of Judge Matevž Krivic, delivered in a case concerning the constitutionality of the law on employment relations.[341] He used the same argument in a dissenting opinion, written in the same month, in a case related to the legality of a municipal regulation.[342] The Court began to use the principle of proportionality two years later.[343]

Just as judgments do, separate opinions may also exercise influence beyond national borders. They are available to anybody, within and outside the court that published it. A good example is offered by Latvian constitutional justice. As mentioned, the Latvian Constitutional Court publishes very few separate opinions. But in one of the most important cases of the Court's history, the Latvian constitutional judges ruled 4:3.[344] The decision concerned a provision of the electoral law excluding anyone who had been active in a communist organisation after the independence of Latvia or who had belonged to the regular staff of the USSR intelligence services from being eligible for the national parliament or local government. The majority considered the restriction to be in conformity with the principle of proportionality, because it concerned activities aimed to destroy the democratic state system rather than the expression of a political opinion.[345] In their joint separate opinion, the three dissenting judges referred to a lustration case decided by the Polish Constitutional Tribunal[346] in their argument sustaining that 10 years

no K 24/98 of 21 October 1998 and no K 39/97 of 10 November 1998. (No English translation is available.) On the Polish lustration cases Wojciech Sadurski, *Rights Before Courts: A Study of Constitutional Courts in Postcommunist States of Central and Eastern Europe* (2nd edn, Springer 2014) 352–66.

340 In particular, in para 7 of the reasoning, where the Court discusses the aim of lustration.

341 Decision no U-I-51/90 of 14 May 1992.

342 Decision no U-I-4/92 of 28 May 1992.

343 For the first time in case no U-I-135/92 of 30 June 1994, on the constitutionality of a law granting to deputies of the National Assembly more favourable possibilities for acquiring and asserting the rights arising from old-age insurance, and soon thereafter in case no U-I-77/93 of 6 July 1995, on the constitutionality of the Privatisation Act.

344 Decision no 2000–03–01 of 30 August 2000, available in English at <www.satv.tiesa.gov.lv/wp-content/uploads/2000/03/2000-03-01_Spriedums_ENG.pdf> accessed 19 January 2017.

345 For a comment on the case (in Italian) see Mauro Mazza, 'La giurisprudenza costituzionale nei Paesi baltici: profili processuali' (2006) *Diritto pubblico comparato ed europeo* 994, 1008–10.

346 Decision no K 39/97 of 10 November 1998. This is the second lustration case in which Judge Czeszejko-Sochacki dissented (see n 339).

after Latvia gained its independence there was no need for such restrictions in the electoral law. The dissenters considered these restrictions on the passive right to vote disproportionate, since it would be possible to adopt softer measures.[347] The question later reached the European Court of Human Rights, which, in the case *Ždanoka v. Latvia*, supported the dissenting judges' argument. Both the First Section which first heard the case, and the Grand Chamber referred explicitly to that dissenting opinion.[348] The Latvian government invoked the Constitutional Court's decision in its defence, while the applicant relied on the dissenting opinion.[349] In its final decision, the Court of Strasbourg ruled for the Latvian government, and found that the restriction on passive suffrage did not violate the Convention.[350] The Latvian Constitutional Court heard a similar case again in 2006. The opinion of the Court refers explicitly to the Strasbourg judgment and invites the legislature to rethink the necessity of such restrictions, as recommended by the ECtHR.[351] Judge Jelāgins, one of the three dissenters of the first case, wrote separately again, offering a detailed analysis of the Strasbourg judgment.[352]

Thus, it seems that dissenting opinions not only contribute to the development of constitutional law at home, but may also serve as a channel of communication between different jurisdictions, both at the national and the international level.[353] This is especially true in relation to the interpretation of fundamental rights and freedoms. Such rights and freedoms have assumed, at least in part, transnational character in Europe, also thanks to the influential role of the two European courts discussed in the previous section.

5. A country study: separate opinions in the Hungarian Constitutional Court (1990–2010)

In this part, the Hungarian Constitutional Court will be the object of a thorough analysis, based on quantitative and qualitative data collected by the author.[354]

347 The dissenting opinion delivered jointly by Judges Endziņš, Jelāgins and Ušacka is available in English at <www.satv.tiesa.gov.lv/wp-content/uploads/2000/03/2000-03-01_Atsevis kas_domas_ENG.pdf> accessed 19 January 2017.

348 *Ždanoka v. Latvia*, App no 58278/00, [First Section] 17 June 2004, para 49, [GC] 16 March 2006, para 63. It is, in fact, not rare that the ECtHR refers to a dissenting opinion of a domestic judge. The Court usually does that when it presents the domestic background of the case.

349 Para 62 of the First Section judgment and para 81 of the Grand Chamber judgment.

350 A comment on the case is offered by HG Hoogers, '*Ždanoka v. Latvia* – European Court of Human Rights: The Boundaries of the Right to Be Elected under Article 3 of the First Protocol to the European Convention on Human Rights' (2007) 3 *European Constitutional Law Review* 307, and Alessio Pecorario, 'Il rovescio del giudizio della *Grand Chamber*, in tema di violazione dell'art 3 primo protocollo e degli articoli 10 e 11 della convenzione, svela la complessità della transizione lettone' (2006) <http://archivio.rivistaaic.it/cronache/giurisprudenza_comunitaria/lettonia/index.html> accessed 19 January 2017.

351 Decision no 2005–13–0106 of 15 June 2006, para 16.1 <www.satv.tiesa.gov.lv/wp-con tent/uploads/2005/06/2005-13-0106_Spriedums_ENG.pdf> accessed 19 January 2017.

352 No English translation of the dissenting opinion is available.

353 In this sense, also Di Martino (n 14) 446.

354 I hand-collected quantitative data from the official annual collection of the Hungarian Constitutional Court's decisions (*Alkotmánybírósági Határozatok*, publisher: Magyar

A careful examination of the data concerning the practice of separate opinions provides food for thought about the role and meaning of judicial dissent. The present analysis concerns the first two decades of the Court's life and does not include an examination of the practice after 2010. The reason for this is that a clear demarcation line can be drawn between the first two decades and the period after the 2010 constitutional amendment.

A number of changes occurred after that, which would significantly alter the composition of the Court, and thus call for a separate analysis. In particular, the 2010 constitutional amendment made it possible for the government to unilaterally nominate new members.[355] While until June 2010 the parliamentary committee nominating the candidates was composed of one deputy from each political party represented in the parliament,[356] after that the composition of the committee was to reflect the weight of the political parties in the parliament.[357] In addition, in June 2011, the constitution was amended once again in order to increase the number of judges from 11 to 15 and to enable the government to appoint four new judges according to the new rules.[358] These and other important changes introduced by the new Fundamental Law,[359] in force since 1 January 2012, call for separate treatment of the practice of the post-reform Constitutional Court, the majority of which have been appointed unilaterally by the governing coalition.[360]

During the first two decades, on the other hand, the legal framework determining the Court's composition and powers did not change. In that period, constitutional judges were appointed for a nine-year term, thus two decades cover a bit more than two terms. While the first nine-year period shows a more stable

---

Hivatalos Közlönykiadó, Budapest). For a summarising table of these data see Tables 5 and 6 in this Chapter. The oral history is based on interviews conducted by the author between 2006 and 2008 with seven (current or former) judges of the Court and one law clerk.

355 Amendment of 5 July 2010, modifying art 32/A of the Constitution then in force.

356 This system of appointment was not perfect either. In practice, it was not able to achieve the objective that judges should be appointed on the basis of a political compromise, as the committee decided by a majority vote, and the opposition parties outnumbered the government parties. This gave rise to long vacancies on the Court. See Katalin Kelemen, 'Appointment of Constitutional Judges in a Comparative Perspective – With a Proposal for a New Model for Hungary' (2012) 54 *Acta Juridica Hungarica* 5, 22, where I proposed the introduction of the split model of appointment that would involve and ensure a balance between all three branches of government in the appointment procedure.

357 The new Fundamental Law, which entered into force on 1 January 2012, does not include any provision concerning the nominating committee, but now it is regulated by art 7(1) of the new Constitutional Court Act.

358 Art 3 of Act no LXI of 2011. There was also a vacancy to be filled, so the parliament elected five new judges in June 2011. They took up office in September 2011.

359 Other relevant changes are: the president is not chosen by the members of the Court from among themselves anymore, but appointed directly by the Parliament; the possibility of re-election has been abolished, but the term of office has been increased from nine to 12 years and the compulsory retirement age has been abolished.

360 An analysis of the post-reform practice has been carried out by a group of Hungarian NGOs (the Hungarian Helsinki Committee, the Hungarian Civil Liberties Union and the Eötvös Károly Institute), published only in Hungarian: *Egypárti alkotmánybírák a kétharmad szolgálatában* [Partisan constitutional judges at the service of the two-thirds majority] (2015)

composition,[361] the second one is characterised by frequent changes. Although the Court was composed of 11 members at the time, during the second period a total of 17 different judges sat on the bench at some point. Second, the Court's practice in the first nine years was strongly influenced by the personality of its first president. As explained in the first chapter,[362] László Sólyom had set the goal of delivering mostly unanimous decisions and his efforts can be seen in the statistics. Thus, there is a perceptible difference between the results of the first and the second decade.

This difference is also determined by the fact that in the first decade the Hungarian Constitutional Court had to face and, in fact, took the lead in transitioning from a socialist system to a democratic one. That period presented at least two serious challenges to the Court: it had to find its role and position within the public sphere, delimiting and widening its own powers, and it had to solve difficult transitional issues. Unlike in Germany, in Hungary dissenting opinions were born and have grown up together with the Constitutional Court itself. In this first formative period, the practice of separate opinions went through some changes and consolidated only after a few years. In the first years, the majority of the judges, including the Court's president, were hostile to the idea of publishing individual separate opinions that criticised the majority harshly. Consequently, the Court laid down in its internal rules that separate opinions were to be discussed by the full court alongside the draft of the majority opinion.[363] Moreover, in the first two years, the tendency when writing separately was to co-author the separate opinions with like-minded judges. So, the first separate opinions had typically multiple authors, and the practice of simply joining another judge's separate opinion developed later.[364]

5.1. *The challenges of a quantitative analysis*

In Hungarian practice the public can have knowledge about the dissent only if the dissenter decides to write separately. The voting results are not disclosed, and it is not compulsory for the dissenter to state her/his reasons in written form.[365]

<http://tasz.hu/files/tasz/imce/2015/ab_kiadvany_70_oldalas_vegleges.pdf> accessed 19 January 2017.

361 The first judges were appointed in 1989–90. Three of them left the Court prematurely: Pál Solt left after eight months in office to become President of the ordinary Supreme Court, Péter Schmidt reached the mandatory retirement age of 70 in 1996, after six years in office, and Géza Herczegh was appointed to the International Court of Justice in 1993, after three years in office. The vacancy left by Judge Solt was not filled until 1996, while the other two vacancies were filled only in 1997.

362 See Chapter 2, Section 1.2.

363 Interview with Judge D (Budapest, Hungary, 14 November 2006).

364 The first case of simple joining dates back to November 1991: the decision in the landmark *Jánosi* case (Decision no 57/1991 (XI.8.) AB of 5 November 1991), in which Judge Schmidt joined a dissenting opinion of Judge Kilényi concerning the concept of 'living law'. See also Chapter 1, Section 2.3, n 100, and n 458 in this chapter.

365 According to a former law clerk at the Constitutional Court from its first year of functioning, after some time it had become very rare that a dissenter would not write separately. Interview with a law clerk (Budapest, Hungary, 26 September 2007).

The decisions are signed by all judges who participated in the case, even by those who remained in minority. This rule can be considered a trace of the civil law attitude that requires loyalty by the judges towards the court as an institution. Thus, the lack of separate decisions does not necessarily mean that the court was unanimous. The only case in which we can be completely sure about the voting results is when the majority is the slightest possible, and all dissenters decide to write separately.[366]

There are other complicating factors as well. It is quite common that a dissenter disagrees with the majority only in part, as many cases involve more than one constitutional issue. It is very common that the Court hears more than one petition in the same procedure and decides them jointly. Also, the same petition may raise a number of constitutional issues. Thus, when looking for divided decisions, one cannot only consider the number of dissenting opinions. It may well happen that they disagree with the majority in relation to different issues. This happened, for example, in case no 44/2004 in which the Court examined the constitutionality of the Police Act.[367] There were three dissenting opinions, signed by five judges, so the opinion of the Court was apparently shared by a slight majority of six judges. But if we look into the substance of these opinions, we can see that they are at variance with the majority on different points.[368]

Still, in certain cases, it is clear that the Court has been split on a given issue. For example, a real 6:5 vote decided on the validity of the initiative to abolish conscription.[369] In 1994, when the Court temporarily operated with nine members, it ruled by a 5:4 vote on the constitutionality of a provision that allowed courts to oblige an employer to withdraw from the salary of a judgment debtor the sum corresponding to the allowance for the maintenance of children.[370] Similarly, the Court ruled by a 5:4 vote on the constitutionality of the incompatibility of the office of mayor with the parliamentary mandate.[371]

There are also examples of plurality opinion in Hungarian constitutional caselaw. This kind of decision, as already explained in relation to American practice,[372] is approved by a relative majority, that is a majority limited to the outcome of the case. The reasoning is not supported by a majority of the judges. A striking example is decision no 25/2004 on the legality of a referendum aimed to reduce the number of MPs.[373] Three separate opinions were attached to this decision:

366 For the Hungarian Constitutional Court it meant a 6:5 decision until 2012, and it means an 8:7 decision today, after the number of judges was increased to 15.
367 Decision no 44/2004 (XI.23.) AB of 22 November 2004.
368 The case was, indeed, a very complex one, involving seven constitutional issues. The Court ruled by a 6:5 vote on one of these only. Another example is case no 22/1999 (VI.30.) AB of 29 June 1999, examining the constitutionality of numerous provisions of the media law then in force (Act no I of 1996).
369 Decision no 50/2001 (XI.29.) AB of 26 November 2001.
370 Decision no 20/1994 (IV.16.) AB of 12 April 1994. See also n 429.
371 Decision no 55/1994 (XI.10.) AB of 8 November 1994. See also n 466.
372 See Chapter 3, Section 3.3.
373 Decision no 25/2004 (VII.7.) AB of 6 July 2004.

two concurrences and one dissent. Nine members of the Court participated in this decision, and five of them did not share the reasoning,[374] which was supported by only four judges. However, one must be cautious here as well, as only considering the numbers may be misleading. Concurring opinions, as already explained,[375] are very often not in disagreement with the majority's reasoning, and might not offer an alternative reasoning but rather explanatory comments and additional remarks.

The calculation of dissent rates also poses challenges to researchers, as the absolute number of cases decided a year is influenced by several legal and non-legal factors, such as changes in the court's jurisdiction or social and political phenomena of constitutional relevance. The number of separate opinions that a judge delivers can also depend on the type of cases decided by the court that year. For example, if there is a series of similar cases heard by the court in the same year, a judge might repeat the same separate opinion in many cases.[376] Similarly, the remarkably low dissent rate in 2010 can be explained with a number of factors.[377] First, that year the Court decided a high number of simple cases related to referendum issues in which the judges had no difficulties to reach consensus. Second, the policy of the newly appointed president, Péter Paczolay, that the Court should aim at unanimity in the more important and far-reaching cases,[378] coupled with a few persistent vacancies on the Court that year,[379] also contributed to the lower number of separate opinions.[380]

Concluding, quantitative data might be very useful to detect trends and striking similarities or differences that otherwise would be difficult to notice, but a correct interpretation of the data requires qualitative research as well.[381] Oral history gathered from judges and law clerks and a careful examination of the substance of the judgments and separate opinions may shed light on aspects that are otherwise hidden. In particular, judges and law clerks may offer explanations on which we could otherwise only speculate.

374 The two concurring opinions were authored by Judges Erdei and Harmathy, while the dissenting opinion was authored by Judge Kukorelli and joined by Judges Bihari, Holló and Kiss. Judge Erdei disagreed with the Court's reasoning only in part, but he considered the rest of the decision to be sufficient to justify the decision.

375 See Chapter 1, Section 1, text to n 1.

376 For example, the concurring opinions of Judge Holló in four consecutive cases, all related to referendum issues: decision nos 148, 149, 150 and 151/2008 (XII.3.) AB of 1 December 2008.

377 3.72% compared with the average of 10.96%. See Table 6 below.

378 Paczolay was elected president by his peers in July 2008. Interview with President Paczolay: Károly Lencsés, 'Paczolay: Az Alkotmánybíróság döntései mindenkire kötelezőek' [Paczolay: The Decisions of the Constitutional Court Bind Everyone] *Népszabadság* (Budapest, 29 July 2012) <http://nol.hu/belfold/paczolay__az_alkotmanybirosag_dontesei_mindenkire_kotelezok-1321579> accessed 16 January 2017.

379 The Court operated with nine judges in the first half of 2010 and with 10 judges in the second half of that year, instead of 11 as provided by the law.

380 I am thankful to Botond Bitskey, Secretary General of the Hungarian Constitutional Court, for this explanation.

381 As also Jaakko Husa pointed out in his introductory book on comparative law, 'quantitative methods do not offer freedom from independent and creative thinking', and a critical evaluation of the statistics is required. Husa (n 315) 200.

Table 4.2 Hungarian constitutional judges and separate opinions (1990–2010)[382]

	Own opinion[383] */ joining*	*Dissenting / concurring opinion*	*Separate opinions in total*[384]	*Rapporteur judge*[385]
FIRST DECADE				
Ádám Antal (11/1989 – 11/1998)[386]	12/3	9/6	15	392/10
Herczegh Géza (7/1990 – 5/1993)	3/0	0/3	3	43/0
Kilényi Géza (11/1989 – 11/1998)	15/5	16/4	20	394/12
Lábady Tamás (6/1990 – 7/1999)	12/10	16/6	22	166/21
Schmidt Péter (7/1990 – 12/1996)	9/1	7/3	10	216/1
Solt Pál (11/1989 – 6/1990)	–	–	0	10/0
Sólyom László (11/1989 – 11/1998)	19/1	10/10	20	137/20
Szabó András (7/1990 – 2/1998)	8/5	9/4	13	98/7
Tertyánszky Ödön (6/1990 – 7/1999)	22/4	19/7	26	239/14
Vörös Imre (6/1990 – 7/1999)	16/2	15/3	18	157/2
Zlinszky János (11/1989 – 3/1998)	**43/6**	33/16	49	182/6
SECOND DECADE				
Bagi István (6/1997 – 6/2006)	14/21	27/8	35	112/3
Balogh Elemér (11/2005 – 11/2014)	12/16	19/9	28	203/7
Bihari Mihály (6/1999 – 7/2008, 7/2010 – 2/2013)[387]	36/18	37/16	53	413/34
Bragyova András (9/2005 – 9/2014)	54/26	60/19	79	231/9
Czúcz Ottó (12/1998 – 5/2004)	8/15	20/3	23	110/2
Erdei Árpád (3/1998 – 3/2007)	17/12	23/6	29	208/27
Harmathy Attila (12/1998 – 4/2007)	49/9	39/18	57	148/15
Holló András (11/1996 – 4/2013)[388]	58/30	57/29	86	557/43

(*Continued*)

Table 4.2 (Continued)

	Own opinion[383] */ joining*	*Dissenting / concurring opinion*	*Separate opinions in total*[384]	*Rapporteur judge*[385]
Kiss László (3/1998 – 3/2016)[389]	68/21	67/22	89	567/23
Kovács Péter (9/2005 – 9/2014)	28/9	20/17	37	259/16
Kukorelli István (6/1999 – 7/2008)	35/24	39/20	59	227/25
Lenkovics Barnabás (4/2007 – 4/2016)	11/8	14/5	19	284/17
Lévay Miklós (4/2007 – 4/2016)	11/16	18/9	27	167/10
Németh János (6/1997 – 8/2003)	12/4	10/6	16	49/5
Paczolay Péter (2/2006 – 2/2015)	19/13	22/10	32	207/23
Strausz János (12/1998 – 12/2004)	9/7	15/0	15	216/10
Stumpf István (7/2010 – current)	1/1	1/1	2	5/0
Tersztyánszkyné Vasadi Éva (6/1999 – 2/2006)	19/10	24/5	29	215/15
Trócsányi László (2/2007 – 10/2010)[390]	26/8	24/10	34	134/11
TOTAL		515/207	722	

382 Prepared by the author on the basis of the official annual collections of the Hungarian Constitutional Court's decisions (*Alkotmánybíróság határozatai*), available at <http://alkotmanybirosag.hu/ugyek_stat/kiadvanyok/abh-eves-kotetek> accessed 20 December 2016. The number of separate opinions delivered by each judge have been included in the official statistics published by the Court since 2011 only. These statistics are available at <http://alkotmanybirosag.hu/dokumentumok/statisztika/2016> accessed 19 January 2017.

383 When two or more judges co-author a separate opinion, it is counted as an own opinion for each co-author.

384 Including simple joinings. The total number of separate opinions published in the annual collection of decisions is 608 (see Table 6).

385 The first number refers to the cases in which the given judge was rapporteur, while the second number refers to the cases in which the given judge was rapporteur and there was at least one separate opinion. The discrepancy from the total number is due the fact that in several cases the judge designated as rapporteur asked a fellow judge to share this task with her/him, thus in these cases there were two rapporteur judges.

386 Between brackets the period in which the judge sat on the Constitutional Court.

387 Bihari was re-elected for a second term in 2010, but left the Court in 2013 when he reached the mandatory retirement age.

388 Re-elected for a second term in November 2005.

389 Re-elected for a second term in March 2007.

390 Judge Trócsányi left the Court when he was appointed ambassador to France.

5.2. The data on separate opinions from 1990–2010

The following table shows the number of separate opinions for each judge, including the proportion between own opinions and joinings, that between dissents and concurrences, and the number of times they were rapporteur in a non-unanimous case.

It is noteworthy how often a judge joins another judge's opinion instead of writing individually. The level of 'individualism' of a judge is shown not only by the number of separate opinions written, but also by the proportion between the cases in which s/he joins another opinion and those in which s/he writes one on her/his own. In the first two decades there were only four judges out of 30 who preferred joining rather than writing.[391] One of them, Judge Bagi, in the first three years of his term actually never wrote separately, while he joined another judge's opinion in six cases. Remarkably, Judge Bagi was the only member of the Court who had been neither a scholar nor a judge before, but a practising business lawyer.

As Table 4.2 demonstrates, the 'great dissenter' of the first period was Judge János Zlinszky who expressed his disagreement on 49 occasions: 43 times writing for himself and only six times joining the opinion of another judge. This number is especially high, considering that the second 'great dissenter' of the Court in that period was Judge Ödön Tersztyánszky who expressed a separate opinion only in 26 cases. The second period, instead, has more than one 'great dissenter'. Judges András Bragyova, András Holló and László Kiss contend for this title. Considering the number of own opinions, Judges Holló and Kiss rank first with 58 and 68 own separate opinions, respectively.[392] However, one has to consider that they sat on the Court for two terms, as they both were re-appointed after their first term expired. In proportion to the number of years spent at the Court, Judge Bragyova wrote separately more often, almost ten times a year on average, compared with Judge Holló and Kiss, who did so in approximately four and five cases a year respectively.[393]

5.3. The two forms of separate opinion: dissents and concurrences

The following table shows the total number of separate opinions for each year in the examined period, indicating the dissent rates and the number of dissenting and concurring opinions separately.

Expressions of dissent constitute 70.9% of all expressions of disagreement, if we consider both written opinions and simple joinings. Considering the number

391 Judges István Bagi, Elemér Balogh, Ottó Czúcz, and Miklós Lévay.

392 Judge Holló, who expressed his disagreement in more cases than Judge Harmathy, wrote less separate opinions himself. As mentioned in Chapter 2, text to n 112, Judge Harmathy was known for writing most of the opinions alone, requiring less help from his clerks. It seems that he was a lone writer in every sense, as he joined the opinion of a fellow judge in a small number of cases.

393 They are closely followed by Judge Attila Harmathy who wrote separately in four cases a year on average.

Table 4.3 Separate opinions on the Hungarian Constitutional Court 1990–2010

Presidency	*L. Sólyom (7/1990–11/1998)*									*J. Németh (11/1998–8/2003)*				*A. Holló (8/2003–11/2005)*			*M. Bihari (11/2005–7/2008)*			*P. Paczolay (7/2008–)*		*average*	*TOTAL*
Year	*1990*	*1991*	*1992*	*1993*	*1994*	*1995*	*1996*	*1997*	*1998*	*1999*	*2000*	*2001*	*2002*	*2003*	*2004*	*2005*	*2006*	*2007*	*2008*	*2009*	*2010*		
Full court decisions total:	54	100	99	84	98	101	89	92	103	139	111	137	167	193	204	175	237	275	377	333	403	170	3571
Chamber decisions total:	59	169	90	157	122	144	143	95	171	90	119	125	119	90	105	89	121	121	160	109	115	123	2513
President decisions:	–	7	6	11	6	6	7	4	8	–	–	–	–	2	7	1	54	19	12	11	16	11	
TOTAL (cases):	113	276	195	252	226	251	239	191	282	229	230	262	286	285	316	265	412	415	549	453	534	298	6261
Concurrences (opinion+ joining)	7	15	0	7	6	4	7	8	13	1	11	10	21	15	16	12	10	44	39	13	16	13	275
Dissents (opinion+ joining)	3	26	8	21	21	8	12	13	18	29	12	45	40	57	56	26	70	50	72	59	24	32	670
Dissents and concurrences in total:	**10**	**41**	**8**	**28**	**27**	**12**	**19**	**21**	**31**	**30**	**23**	**55**	**61**	**72**	**72**	**38**	**80**	**94**	**111**	**72**	**40**	**45**	**945**
Full court cases with separate opinion(s)	4	14	5	15	13	9	11	9	10	11	8	21	19	23	27	18	34	39	41	34	15	18	380
Rate:	7.4%	15%	5%	17.9%	13.3%	8.9%	12.6%	9.8%	9.7%	7.9%	7.2%	15.3%	11.4%	11.9%	13.2%	10.29%	14.30%	14.18%	10.86%	10.21%	3.72%	10.96%	
Chamber cases with separate opinion(s)	–	1	–	–	–	–	–	–	–	–	–	–	–	–	–	–	–	–	–	–	–		
Rate:		0.59%																					
Concurring opinions	6	14	–	5	5	4	7	4	7	1	9	9	11	11	14	8	7	27	23	10	13	10	195
Dissenting opinions	3	11	7	16	10	10	6	9	11	15	9	29	20	37	33	19	45	31	38	37	17	20	413
Separate opinions in total:	**9**	**25**	**7**	**21**	**15**	**14**	**13**	**13**	**18**	**16**	**18**	**38**	**31**	**48**	**47**	**27**	**52**	**58**	**61**	**47**	**30**	**29**	**608**

of written opinions, regardless the number of judges joining them, dissenting opinions constitute 67.9% of all separate opinions. Thus it seems that judges feel more compelled to write separately when they are in complete disagreement with the majority than when their disagreement is limited to the reasoning. It is even more interesting if we consider that Hungarian constitutional judges, similarly to their foreign colleagues, make very free and varied use of concurring opinions. In most cases, a concurrence is not a 'parallel reasoning', as it is formally called in Hungarian, rather a simple addition to the reasoning of the majority. In these concurring opinions, the judge either offers additional (rather than alternative) grounds for the decision, or further explains the court's position. Thus, most of the concurring opinions fall within the categories of supplementary reasoning and explanatory opinion.[394]

These two 'mutant' forms of concurrence are especially common in hard cases that deal with traditional constitutional issues of fundamental importance, such as right to life or the principle of equality. In fact, the four concurring opinions attached to the famous death penalty decision were at least in part explanatory opinions.[395] According to one judge then sitting on the Court, President Sólyom encouraged his colleagues to write separately in order to enrich the Court's reasoning.[396] Indeed, the arguments used therein served as a source of inspiration in many later cases. Also, in the first abortion case, there were four explanatory opinions and one supplementary reasoning.[397] In the second abortion case, there was one explanatory opinion and one partly explanatory/partly alternative reasoning.[398] In a landmark sexual orientation case, there was one explanatory opinion and one supplementary reasoning (besides two dissents).[399]

The distinction between dissenting opinion and concurring opinion, however, is not always so clear-cut. Even if Hungarian constitutional judges must give a

394 See Chapter 1, Section 1.

395 Decision no 23/1990 (X.31.) AB of 24 October 1990. Besides a dissenting opinion by Judge Schmidt, there were four concurring opinions: one co-authored by Judges Lábady and Tersztyánszky, and three individual opinions by President Sólyom, Judge Szabó and Judge Zlinszky. See also n 462.

396 Interview with Judge D (Budapest, Hungary, 14 November 2006). Considering the importance of the case, the majority opinion is very short, which shows that the judges reached a compromise on the core of the reasoning, but the individual judges felt the need to explain their reasons more in detail in a concurring opinion.

397 Decision no 64/1991 (XII.17.) AB of 9 December 1991, delivered by ten judges. Concurring opinions of Judges Ádám, Herczegh, Kilényi, Zlinszky (explanatory) and Lábady (supplementary).

398 Decision no 48/1998 (XI.27.) AB of 18 November 1998. Dissenting opinions by Judges Lábady and Tersztyánszky, and concurring opinions by Judges Ádám (explanatory) and Holló (partly explanatory/partly supplementary). See also Chapter 2, Section 2.2, nn 84 and 100, and n 404 in this chapter.

399 Decision no 37/2002 (IX.4.) AB of 3 September 2002, annulling a provision of the Penal Code that criminalised consensual sodomy between an adult and a minor. Dissenting opinions of Judges Strausz and Tersztyánszkyné, and concurring opinions of Judge Kiss (supplementary) and President Németh (explanatory).

title to their separate opinion, choosing between defining it as a dissent or a concurrence, this choice may at times be hard and debatable. A dissenting opinion of Judge Balogh may well illustrate this point. Judge Balogh wrote a separate opinion, entitling it 'dissenting opinion', in a case in which the Court examined the constitutionality of a legislative provision determining an exception to the rule that weapons may be used against a prisoner who tries to escape.[400] According to the provision, weapons may not be used against minors or female prisoners. The petitioner argued that this exception is discriminatory against men and violates their right to human dignity. The Court found that it could not annul such a legislative provision because that would extend the possibility of using weapons against child or female prisoners, and it would go against the role of the Court as a guardian of constitutional rights. According to Judge Balogh, the majority did not examine the main constitutional issue: if the challenged provision is discriminatory or not. He explains which questions should have been examined and answered, but he does not answer these questions himself, so it is not clear whether he finds the challenged provision unconstitutional or not. The choice of labelling his separate opinion 'dissent' suggests a positive answer, but nothing in the text confirms this.

5.4. Why does a judge decide to write separately?

A judge may have several reasons for writing separately. Each judge has her/his own philosophy and working method regarding dissenting opinions. It is not compulsory for any Hungarian constitutional judge to write separately in case of disagreement. Judges may well decide to remain silent, in the eyes of the public, even if they vote against the decision. In that event no one, except her peers, will know that she dissented. One is naturally led to wonder: What are the factors influencing the judges' choice to write separately? The oral history gathered from former judges and clerks of the Hungarian Constitutional Court may provide some food for thought.

One might intuitively consider that the perceived importance of the issue at hand is a relevant factor for a judge to write separately. It emerges From the Hungarian judges' accounts that it is true that the importance of the issue matters, but it may matter in opposite ways. There are judges who draft a dissenting opinion only if the disagreement regards questions of fundamental importance, while there are others who refrain from writing separately precisely in these very cases, for solidarity and to increase legal certainty. Judge Y, for example, refrained from writing separately on ideologically loaded issues, since he considered his personal convictions inappropriate to be expressed publicly.[401] Other judges are skeptical about the possibility to divide cases according to their relevance (as Judge X).[402]

400 Decision no 103/B/1999 AB of 16 October 2006.

401 Interview with Judge Y (Budapest, Hungary, 3 November 2006). He called these 'questions of world view' (*világnézeti kérdések*).

402 Interview with Judge X (Budapest, Hungary, 6 November 2006).

Judge D aptly summed up this dilemma. According to him, in deciding whether to express a dissent two opposing principles are at stake: loyalty towards colleagues and personal integrity,[403] and everyone has to find the balance between these two values according to one's own convictions. Loyalty towards the institution certainly does play a role for many judges. A judge might be reluctant to write a separate opinion to a decision that is the fruit of long discussions and a compromise. S/he might not agree with the majority opinion in its entirety, but her/his view has been taken into consideration and is reflected in the reasoning.[404]

Besides the perceived importance of the case at hand, other factors come into play, such as the judge's field of expertise. Judge Attila Harmathy, for example, considered himself to be a member of the Court both as an expert in private law and as a constitutional judge. He remained a private lawyer on the Constitutional Court too, which brought a divergence of approach between him and his fellow judges and eventually made him one of the 'great dissenters' of the Court.[405] Many of his separate opinions are ascribable to this divergence of approach. He often disagreed with the majority on questions of private law which brought him to a different conclusion also from a constitutional perspective.[406] Judge Péter Kovács, a scholar of international law and a current judge of the International Criminal Court, often wrote separately to call attention to the international law aspects of a case. Sometimes he reached a different conclusion because he gave more weight to the sources of international law than most of his colleagues.[407]

Therefore, expertise certainly plays a role. According to Judge Y, judges with an expertise in public law tend to agree among themselves, and the same can be said about judges with a background in private law.[408] Indeed, the Court often

403 Interview with Judge D (Budapest, Hungary, 14 November 2006).

404 In an interview, Judge Vörös explained that he did not write separately in the second abortion case (no 48/1998 (XI.27.) AB of 18 November 1998) for this reason. Gábor Halmai and Csaba Tordai, 'Kevesebb lesz az elegáns röpködés a jogrendszer fölött. Vörös Imre távozó alkotmánybíróval Halmai Gábor és Tordai Csaba beszélget' [There Will Be Less Elegant Fluttering Above the Legal System. A Conversation of Gábor Halmai and Csaba Tordai With the Outgoing Constitutional Judge Imre Vörös] (1999) 2 *Fundamentum* 60, 63.

405 In nine years, he expressed his disagreement publicly in 57 cases, writing or joining 39 dissenting and 18 concurring opinions. See Table 5.

406 An example is case no 23/2000 (VI.28.) AB of 26 June 2000 dealing with the constitutionality of a municipal ordinance ordering that the inhabitants of a block of flats could keep dogs only with the consent of the neighbours. The rapporteur of the case was Judge Kukorelli, a constitutional law scholar. Judge Harmathy would have found the ordinance unconstitutional for lack of competence of the municipality, and in his dissenting opinion he also examined the ordinance's conformity with the Civil Code.

407 For example, in case no 88/B/1999 AB of 27 June 2006 the Court upheld the constitutionality of a legislative provision denying the right to strike to workers of the courts, the police and the military. Judge Kovács found that such a general, undifferentiated exclusion is contrary to the Hungarian state's duties under international law.

408 Interview with Judge Y (Budapest, Hungary, 3 November 2006). In fact, for example Judge István Bagi, a former business lawyer, joined Judge Harmathy's separate opinion or voted in the same way in many cases. See, for example, decision no 58/2001 (XII.7.) AB of 3 December 2001 concerning the right to one's name.

seemed divided along these lines, as for example in the already presented case decided by the casting vote of President Holló, who supported the group of judges specialised in public law.[409] At the end of the 1990s and the beginning of 2000s, however, Judge Harmathy and Judge Bagi were the only experts in private law among the judges, while there has never been a lack of experts in public law. In the first period, there was also a panel of three judges specialised in cases concerning local self-governments, a so-called 'public law panel', composed of judges with expertise in this area of law.[410] In fact, the members of this panel often shared the same opinion even in cases decided by the plenum.[411]

Concurring opinions form a special category. The motivation behind writing a concurrence is usually different from the reasons for a dissent. At times, a judge writes a concurrence to communicate something to the public. A good example is a concurring opinion of Judge Zlinszky attached to a decision of inadmissibility. In it, he instructed the petitioner how to proceed to find a remedy, while complaining that this should have been included by the majority in its opinion.[412] Similarly, Judge Kiss wrote separately in order to call the legislature's attention to a drafting error in a case in which he wrote for the majority.[413] He wrote a concurrence in two more cases where he was the rapporteur judge, and thus he authored the opinion of the court as well.[414] It seems that in these cases Judge Kiss was unable to convince his colleagues of his position in its entirety, so the parts not shared by the majority ended up in a separate opinion. Another example is a concurrence of Judge Kovács in a case concerning the compatibility of the Gambling Act with EU law. Interestingly, this concurring opinion was joined by one other judge. That shows that Judge Kovács, as the rapporteur of the case, circulated those additional arguments as well which finally ended up in a separate opinion.[415]

409 Decision no 62/2003 (XII.15.) AB of 15 December 2003. See Chapter II, Section 2.1, n 63.

410 This 'public law panel' was more like a custom, as neither the Constitutional Court Act nor the Rules of Procedure provided for the composition of the panels or for a specialisation of these.

411 More specifically, there was a certain convergence of opinion between Judges Holló, Kiss and Kukorelli, the three members of the 'public law panel' that existed at the time. See, for example, case no 54/2001 (XI.29.) AB of 26 November 2001, in which Judges Holló and Kiss co-authored a dissenting opinion joined also by Judges Czúcz and Kukorelli, and Decision no 55/2001 (XI.29.) AB, delivered the same day, to which Judge Kukorelli attached a dissenting opinion joined by Judges Czúcz and Kiss and partly shared by Judge Holló.

412 Decision no 1079/H/1995 AB of 22 April 1996. Similarly, in case no 261/D/2005. AB of 21 February 2006 Judge Balogh, while he agreed that the constitutional complaint was inadmissible, wrote that the legality of the challenged decision could have been examined by the head of the local public administration office.

413 Decision no 827/B/2000 AB of 16 February 2004.

414 The concurring opinions of Judge Kiss in case no 24/2000 (VII.6.) AB of 4 July 2000 and case no 2/2001 (I.17.) AB of 16 January 2001.

415 Decision no 1053/E/2005 AB of 16 June 2006.

Thus, concurring opinions are an especially powerful tool for a judge to express his own thoughts and even to set a personal 'agenda'. As already mentioned, Judge Kovács, a respected scholar of international law, wrote many times separately to draw attention to the international law aspects of a constitutional issue and to present and discuss the case-law of international courts. He did so from the very beginning of his mandate and in a total of 16 cases in less than two-and-a-half years.[416] Thus it seems that the majority usually did not deem such arguments important enough to be included in the opinion of the court. In one case, however, his concurring opinion, in which he presented the relevant decisions of the European Court of Human Right and of other countries' constitutional courts, was joined by the rapporteur judge.[417]

5.5. The style of separate opinions

As explained previously, all cases that reach the constitutional court are assigned to a judge who will act as rapporteur, but they are discussed by a panel of judges or by the plenum. The judgment, even when written by one single judge (usually the rapporteur of the case), is the result of this discussion and the opinion-writer does not enjoy complete freedom. Intuitively, the judgment should reflect the opinion of the court, not her/his personal position, and ultimately must meet with the panel's approval. In fact, judgments usually have an impersonal style and use more technical language than individual separate opinions, which are more the expression of their author's convictions and personality. It is also worth mentioning that the first draft of the judgment is usually prepared by one of the rapporteur judge's law clerks and then revised and supplemented by the judge herself/himself. This is certainly the common practice at the Hungarian Constitutional Court. Thus, the opinion of the Court is not the product of the rapporteur judge, but it is the result of close cooperation between multiple actors: first, within the team of the rapporteur, between clerk and judge; then during the discussion of the case, between the members of the panel. Therefore, we should look at separate opinions rather than at judgments to understand the personality and style of their authors.

Indeed, in their separate opinions judges tend to use a more direct and animated tone which sometimes may event turn into a provocative or ironic style. Both the first and the second terms of the Hungarian Constitutional Court had its leading figures. Judge Géza Kilényi, member of the Court during the first nine years, wrote many opinions revealing a strong and determined personality. To cite an example illustrating his style, in a dissenting opinion delivered in 1994 he stated: 'I apply self-restraint and do not continue the list of examples that

416 He delivered the first concurring opinion in October 2005, a month after being appointed to the Court. Only one of the 17 separate opinions authored by him in this period did not touch upon international law or foreign solutions.

417 Decision no 72/2006 (XII.15.) of 12 December 2006 concerning the status of public employees.

sustain my argument; the classification of legal persons provided by art 6 is arbitrary, desultory, discriminatory, and therefore unconstitutional.'[418] Judge Kilényi, one of the first five judges appointed to the Constitutional Court in 1989, was a potential candidate to become the Court's first president. The position at the end was assigned to László Sólyom whose personality determined the course of Hungarian constitutional justice in the period of democratic transition.

Separate opinions are often written in the informative and educational tone of student textbooks. The reason is clear: most of the judges have an academic background and are therefore accustomed to discussing legal issues systematically and with methodological rigour. In fact, the didactic tone has characterised especially the opinions of professors of law, such as Judges Kiss, Kukorelli and Bihari, who used to divide their opinions in chapters with a title.[419] Thus it is clear that judges are freer when they write individually than when they write in the name of the majority. Judge Kiss, in particular, often wrote with a passionate tone, sometimes being even ironic. The same is not true for Judge Harmathy who expressed himself in a more restrained and moderate style. Judge Kiss's dissenting opinion in case no 620/B/1998 of 2005[420] is a typical example. Contrary to the majority of the Court, he held unconstitutional a legal rule providing for a disproportionate increase of the electricity bill at the expense of users who stole electricity or made an irregular use of it. The reasoning illustrates well the pragmatism and literary style of his opinions. He severely criticised the opinion of the Court (incidentally, written by Judge Harmathy) stating that he had 'serious theoretical objections' to the arguments supporting the decision, and concluded indicating that: 'I do not support irregular users. They have to face the legal consequences of their action. However, in a modern state based on the rule of law, they cannot suffer from the shadow of Hammurabi.'[421] Judge

418 In the original Hungarian: 'Önmérsékletből nem folytatom ama példák felsorolását, amelyek mind azt támasztják alá: a jogi személyeknek a 6.§ szerinti kategorizálása önkényes, ötletszerű, diszkriminatív, s ezért alkotmányellenes.' (My own translation.) Dissenting opinion of Judge Kilényi attached to decision no 35/1994 (VI.24.) AB of 21 June 1994. It was a preventive review initiated by the President of the Republic. The Constitutional Court had to review the constitutionality of the Land Ownership Act restricting the size of land private persons can acquire.

419 For example, the dissenting opinion of Judge Kukorelli, joined by Judges Czúcz, Kiss and in part by Judge Holló, attached to decision no 55/2001 (XI.29.) AB of 26 November 2001 on the freedom of assembly (see also n 411), and the joint dissenting opinion of Judges Kiss and Kukorelli published in case no 35/2002 (VII.19.) AB of 12 July 2002 reviewing the constitutionality of legal provisions aiming to prevent disorder in sports grounds. Also Judge Bihari's dissent on the parliamentary speech case (decision no 12/2006 (IV.24.) AB of 24 April 2006) is a notable example. Besides being a professor of political science, Judge Bihari was also at the time the only member of the Court who had previously been a member of the parliament.

420 Decision no 620/B/1998 AB of 10 January 2005.

421 In the Hungarian original: 'Nem pártolom a jogosulatlan áramvételezőket, azoknak számolniuk kell tettük hátrányos jogkövetkezményeivel. Ez utóbbiakra azonban egy modernkori jogállamban nem vetülhet rá Hammurabi árnyéka.'

Kiss meant that such a disproportionate sanction runs the risk of getting close to the *lex talionis*, the law of retaliation.

The expressive freedom of judges can be seen not only in the style and tone, but also in other, more formal aspects, such as the opinion's structure and length. At times a separate opinion is longer than the judgment.[422] Moreover, judges decide for themselves if they title their separate opinion a dissenting or a concurring one, and the choice between joining another judge's opinion and writing individually is also rather flexible. It may happen that the latter choice is hard to make, and a judge decides to do both: he joins another judge's opinion *and* writes separately individually. This may be done in different forms. Joining is usually done by writing one sentence at the bottom of the separate opinion, saying 'I join the dissenting/concurring opinion', followed by the signature. Judge Kukorelli once decided to add a few more sentences to this statement, thus supplementing Judge Harmathy's dissenting opinion with an additional point of criticism towards the majority.[423] The simpler way, however, to combine joining and writing is to start the separate opinion with a statement of joining. Thus, the dissenter first states that s/he agrees with another dissenter, and then adds her/his own thoughts.[424] It also happens that there is only one judge indicated as the opinion's author, but s/he explicitly writes in the name of the joiner as well.[425] This inconsistent practice represents a challenge for an accurate statistical analysis of the rate between own opinions and simple joinings.[426]

422 For example, Decision no 18/1999 (VI.11.) AB of 7 June 1998, which is long five and a half pages, while the dissenting opinion of Judge Kiss is six-and-a-half pages long, and the nine-page long dissent of Judge Kovács attached to a five-page long judgment (in case no 2/2006 (I.30.) AB of 30 January 2006, see also n 448). (The number of pages refers to the official annual collection of the Constitutional Court's decisions.) This actually goes against the Rules of Court adopted by the Court itself, which provides that the length of a separate opinion cannot exceed the length of the decision. Today this provision is contained in art 59(4) of the Rules of Court adopted by Decision no 1001/2013 (II.27.) AB.

423 Decision no 1/2005 (II.4.) AB of 1 February 2005.

424 For example, Judge Bragyova's dissenting opinions in case no 8/2007 (II.28.) AB of 27 February 2007 and in case no 55/2008 (IV.24.) AB of 22 April 2008, in which he also joins Judge Holló's dissenting opinion, and Judge Holló's dissent in case no 47/2007 (VII.3.) AB of 3 July 2007, joining Judge Kukorelli's dissenting opinion.

425 For example, dissenting opinion of Judge Zlinszky delivered in case no 874/B/1994 AB of 29 April 1996. Judge Kilényi is not indicated as a co-author, but it seems that he simply joined Zlinszky's dissent. However, Judge Zlinszky writes in first person plural ('according to our position') throughout the whole opinion.

426 In Decision no 7/2004 (III.24.) AB of 23 March 2004, for example, three judges decided to write two concurring opinions. One was authored by Judge Bihari and joined by Judges Harmathy and Tersztyánszkyné, while the other one was authored by Judge Harmathy and joined by Judges Bihari and Tersztyánszkyné. This case brought to differing numbers in the different statistical calculations. The two concurring opinions are counted as two separate opinions, while they are calculated as one concurring opinion for each of the three judges. Moreover, Judges Bihari and Harmathy had both an own opinion and an expression of joining, while the two concurrences are counted as one single joining for Judge Tersztánszkyné.

5.6. The internal dynamics of decision-making

Separate opinions reveal not only the personal views of their authors but also the interaction and relationship between judges. The number of cases in which two judges agree and co-author a dissenting opinion or simply join the opinion of one another, can show possible affinities.[427] It is exactly due to their separate opinions that the contrast between Judge Imre Vörös and President László Sólyom became well-known. In half of the cases in which Vörös wrote a dissent (in nine out of 18), Sólyom was the author of the judgment. Considering that the Court was composed of 11 members at that time, this number clearly points in the direction of an intense disagreement.[428] One may also notice that they never joined one another's separate opinion, however once they both joined the dissent of a third judge.[429] They left their mark in Hungarian constitutional history as the judges representing the two ends of the spectrum of judicial policy-making: President Sólyom is remembered as an activist judge, while Judge Vörös opposed him calling for self-restraint.[430]

It is also remarkable that President Sólyom was inclined to assign to himself the cases that he deemed most important. In the first two decades of life of the Hungarian Court Sólyom was the only president who made use of his power of assignment to keep the most important cases for himself.[431] In fact, he was the

427 For example, Judge Holló and Judge Bragyova joined each other's opinions in a striking number of cases.

428 According to Gábor Halmai, both President Sólyom and Judge Vörös shared liberal views and an interest in theoretical questions, and this situation of 'two pipers in one tavern' might have increased the conflicts. Moreover, Halmai argues, it resulted in a lower number of separate opinions authored by Judge Vörös in the second half of his term, because he got tired of playing second fiddle to the president. Consequently, many decisions from that period remained without a liberal critique. Gábor Halmai, 'Az aktivizmus vége? A Sólyom-bíróság kilenc éve' [The End of Activism? The First Nine Years of the Sólyom Court] (1999) 2 *Fundamentum* 5, 25, fn 7. Indeed, the data show that 12 of Judge Vörös's 18 separate opinions are from the first three years of his nine years on the Court.

429 In case no 20/1994 (IV.16.) AB of 12 April 1994 they both joined Judge Lábady's dissenting opinion, together with Judge Szabó. See also n 370.

430 Judge Vörös stated himself in an interview that around 70% of his dissenting opinions were about competence issues. Halmai and Tordai (n 404) 62. An illustrative example is case no 4/1997 (I.22.) AB of 21 January 1997, in which Sólyom wrote for the majority that ruled that the Constitutional Court had the power to review the constitutionality of an international treaty after its ratification. Judge Vörös disagreed, arguing that the Constitutional Court Act allows only a preventive review of international treaties. In his conclusion, he cites several former dissents in which he called for self-restraint, and points out that the Constitutional Court cannot exercise any power not explicitly conferred to it by law, as this goes against the principle of legal certainty.

431 For a similar practice of certain Chief Justices of the US Supreme Court see Chapter 3, Section 2.2. Judge Holló, on the other hand, as president of the Court in one particular case deliberately did not assign the case to himself, as the main issue (the constitutional review of the Supreme Court's uniformity decisions) was one of his favourite topics. The case was assigned to Judge Árpád Erdei who, however, asked him to act as co-rapporteur (case no 42/2005 (XI.14.) AB of 12 November 2005). Interview with Judge M (Budapest, Hungary, 9 November 2006).

rapporteur judge of the second highest number of cases in which at least one separate opinion was expressed in the first period.[432] Considering the total number of cases in which he wrote the majority opinion, Sólyom can actually be defined as the most 'disputed' member of the entire examined period of 21 years.[433] The judges who followed him in the presidency had a lower rate of disputed opinions of the Court.[434] The very low number of non-unanimous judgments (two) authored by Judge Vörös is also worthy of notice.[435] It might be due to the fact that President Sólyom kept the authorship of the most important, and therefore most divisive, cases for himself, but it also suggests that an activist judge triggers more dissent than one who calls for self-restraint.

As regards certain specific issues, it is possible to notice an out-and-out split within the Court which persists in time and re-emerges every time the same issue is under debate. In these cases the publicity of judicial dissent translates into transparency. An out-and-out split within the Court shows that the question at hand is a difficult and debated one. It also makes a future overruling rather likely, as the composition of the Court is constantly changing, so a limited and weak majority may be overturned by the appointment of a new judge who has a different opinion. An emblematic example is the interpretation of the right to social security[436] and, in particular, the question of pension escalation that the Court had to discuss in several cases during the first decade of its operation. The first case reached the Court in 1991, when it decided to suspend the proceedings because the pension system was under recodification.[437] On that occasion four judges, including the rapporteur (Judge Zlinszky), expressed a joint dissenting opinion.[438] In this dissent the four judges expressed their regret for the fact that the Court did not

432 In a total of 20 cases. He is preceded by Judge Lábady who was rapporteur in 21 such cases. See Table 5.

433 As one can deduct from the data in Table 5. The rate between unanimous and divided decisions authored by President Sólyom is 14.59%, while for Judge Lábady it is 12.65%. The most 'disputed' members of the second period were Judge Erdei, with a rate of 12.98%, Judge Paczolay, with a rate of 11.11%, and Judge Kukorelli, with a rate of 11.01%.

434 During his nearly five years of presidency, President Németh was the rapporteur judge in only five cases in which at least one separate opinion was delivered. At the same time, he also authored a considerably low number of judgments than Sólyom. In any event, a separate opinion was delivered in 10.2% of the cases in which he was a rapporteur. During his nearly three years of presidency, President Holló was the rapporteur judge in only three cases in which disagreement between the judges was disclosed.

435 He wrote a total of 157 majority opinions while on the Court. Thus Judge Vörös is one of the less disputed members of the first Court, as only two of the judgments he authored are followed by a separate opinion. His rate of 'disputedness' is only 1.27% compared with the average of 6.62% of all judges in the examined period.

436 The right to social security was provided by art 70/E of the old Constitution. Today, it is enshrined in art XIX of the Fundamental Law as a programmatic norm rather than as a fundamental right.

437 Decision no 24/1991 (V.18.) AB of 7 May 1991. Joint dissenting opinion by Judges Kilényi, Szabó, Vörös and Zlinszky. It was a 6:4 decision.

438 Since it was a procedural decision, it is likely that the draft judgment prepared by Judge Zlinszky became a dissenting opinion after the voting that brought to a different result than

decide the case on the merits. According to them it would have been necessary to set constitutional limits for the legislature. In a second case, two years later, the Court decided the issue on the merits, and the dissenters had once again the opportunity to explain their position, even if this time they did so separately, not in one single joint opinion.[439] Judge Kilényi pointed out that the constitutional issue at hand is the same that had already been addressed in the 1991 case and that had shed light on a 'considerable divergence of opinion' within the Court. According to Judge Kilényi, this divergence of opinions made the need to express the minority opinion on the right to social security even more pressing.

The 'Bokros package' case, involving the constitutional review of a series of austerity measures proposed by then Minister of Finance Lajos Bokros, however, brought the Court's approach to social security rights to a turning point. In a unanimous decision, signed by eight judges, the Court revisited its self-restraint and, with reference to the principle of legal certainty, set certain limits to the reform of the social security system.[440] Three of the previous dissenters joined the majority this time (and one of them, Judge Kilényi, co-authored the majority opinion with President Sólyom), while the fourth dissenter, Judge Vörös, did not participate in this decision.[441] This line of cases shows the mutual influence that the judges exercise on each other. In this particular case, the minority was able to change the Court's orientation. The otherwise activist President Sólyom showed a surprising self-restraint in relation to social security rights in the first years, but his approach changed with this third case.[442] The division between judges, however, did not disappear completely. The following year, the Court rejected a petition claiming an omission of the legislature concerning the pension system.[443] In this case only Judge Zlinszky wrote separately. His concurring opinion, aiming to supplement the Court's reasoning, consists in large part of literal quotations from the dissenting opinions delivered in the second case. At last, in 1997 three of the dissenters expressed once again their disagreement in two dissenting opinions.[444] Judge Kilényi underlined that his position had not changed, therefore he could not accept the decision of the Court. He expressly referred to his own dissenting opinion delivered four years earlier. In their joint dissenting opinion, Judges Szabó and Zlinszky also maintained their position expressed in the previous case.

---

the one proposed by him. In any event, this dissent represents an exception. The general practice has been that a rapporteur who remains in minority with her/his view does not write for the majority.

439 Decision no 26/1993 (IV.28.) AB of 19 April 1993. Dissenting opinions by Judge Kilényi, by Judges Szabó and Zlinszky (jointly) and by Judge Vörös. It was a 6:4 decision. The majority opinion was written by Judge Lábady.

440 Decision no 43/1995 (VI.30.) AB of 30 June 1995.

441 Judge Zlinszky, however, wrote a concurring opinion in which he argued that the Court should have carried out a more comprehensive theoretical analysis of the law under review.

442 In this sense, also Halmai (n 428) 11.

443 Decision no 1067/B/1993 AB of 17 June 1996.

444 Decision no 277/B/1997 AB of 27 May 1997. Dissenting opinions by Judge Kilényi and by Judges Szabó and Zlinszky (jointly).

It is worth noting that in the last two of this line of cases Judge Vörös, who expressed his dissent on the first two occasions, abstained from writing separately. This shows that judges may well decide to avoid writing a dissenting opinion even when they disagree with the majority, especially if they have already expressed their disagreement in the past. A scheme elaborated by Maurice Kelman, an American scholar, in the 1980s offers a systematic analysis of this phenomenon. Kelman identified three possible different paths of judicial dissent. First, the '*stare decisis* option', when the judge abandons past dissent under the pressure of the rule of binding precedent. And this is the option that Judge Vörös chose in the social security rights cases. Second, the 'never-say-die option', when a judge renews the first dissent holding true to her/his own doctrinal position, without compromising or relinquishing her/his views. And this was the option Judge Zlinszky chose. Finally, there is the option of temporary acquiescence, when the judge decides to abstain from writing separately until the court considers overruling, awaiting a time when she may win over the majority.[445] Kelman himself supports this last option in which the judge avoids the rataplan of her/his dissent and quietly awaits the moment of victory. At the same time, Kelman suggests to the judge to clarify in a concurring opinion the interim nature of her/his shifted position, so that it will not be misunderstood for a '*stare decisis* option'.[446]

In the practice of the Hungarian Constitutional Court there are several examples of dissenting opinions expressly referring to a previous dissent. We can find one already in the third year of the Court's functioning: a joint dissenting opinion of Judges Kilényi and Schmidt cites a previous separate opinion delivered by them four months earlier.[447] Similarly, Judge Kovács repeats his position in a second dissenting opinion concerning the role of the National Electoral Commission (*Országos Választási Bizottság*) in evaluating initiatives related to the recognition of national and ethnic minority groups. Kovács insisted that the Commission must examine if the group launching the initiative complies with the legal requirements, but avoided repeating all arguments. He simply referred to his previous nine-page long dissent in half a page in the second case.[448] In a 2006 case, Judge Harmathy also expressly upheld his previous dissent on the power of the Constitutional Court to review the Supreme Court's uniformity decisions.[449] Thus Hungarian constitutional judges seem to choose the 'never-say-die option' rather often.[450]

445 Maurice Kelman, 'The Forked Path of Dissent' (1985) 6 *Supreme Court Review* 227.

446 Kelman (n 445) 298.

447 Dissenting opinion attached to Decision no 8/1992 (I.30.) AB of 28 January 1992. The previous dissent had been delivered in case no 48/1991 (IX.26.) AB of 23 September 1991, co-authored by Judge Vörös.

448 Both cases were decided in 2006: decision no 2/2006 (I.30.) of 30 January 2006, see also n 422, and decision no 27/2006 (VI.21.) of 19 June 2006.

449 Case no 70/2006 (XII.13.) AB of 11 December 2006. The first dissent was expressed in case no 42/2005 (XI.14.) AB of 12 November 2005 (see also n 431).

450 One more example is the repeated dissent of Judge Holló in cases no 28/2006 (VI.21.) AB of 16 June 2006, 29/2006 (VI.21.) AB of 16 June 2006, and 63/2006 (XI.23.) AB of 20 November 2006, all related to the regulation of family doctor practice.

5.7. When a separate opinion becomes precedent

As in the experience of other European constitutional courts,[451] we can find examples of trailblazing separate opinions also in Hungary. Sometimes a dissent becoming majority opinion is clearly due to a change in the court's composition. A good example is an early dissenting opinion of Judge Imre Vörös,[452] which became the official position of the Court six years later.[453] The question concerned the relationship between qualified majority laws and simple majority laws. At the time of the second case, the rapporteur of the first case, President Sólyom, had already ended his term of office, while Judge Vörös was still sitting on the Court. It seems that in this case the dissenter succeeded in convincing the rapporteur judge of the new case (Judge Erdei) and a majority of his fellow judges. There were, however, three judges who continued to sustain the previous majority position and wrote a dissenting opinion. Two of them had already sat on the Court in the first case.[454] The composition of the Court between the two cases changed considerably. Only three of the judges participating in the decision of the first case, including Judge Vörös, were still on the Court when the second case was decided. And the fact that Judge Vörös's position prevailed after President Sólyom left the Court is a further sign of the long-lasting contrast between the two. In the second judgment, there is no explicit mention of the dissenting opinion, but two arguments are copied from it almost literally.[455] according to one judge then sitting on the Court, there was no explicit reference because of a general negative attitude towards dissenting opinions which most of the judges considered a 'deal with the devil' that weakens the Court's authority.[456] Thus, the majority did not want to acknowledge the influence of a dissenting opinion on a later decision.

This might seem a hypocritical attitude, as it is clear to a careful reader that the second decision is, at least in part, based on the arguments used by Vörös in his earlier dissent. At the same time, it shows how highly institutional loyalty is valued by the Court. It demonstrates that Hungarian constitutional judges, probably in part due to their legal education, are reluctant to build up a system of binding precedents as it ought to be, including the use of the techniques of overruling in a clear and coherent manner. A common law court usually states clearly which precedent it overrules and for which reasons. This is considered to be

451 See Section 4.3.2.

452 The dissenting opinion in question was attached to decision no 4/1993 (II.12.) AB of 8 February 1993.

453 Decision no 1/1999 (II.24.) AB of 23 February 1999.

454 Dissenting opinion written by Judge Lábady, joined by Judges Bagi and Tersztyánszky.

455 The first states that the list of legislative matters that require a qualified majority was created by the constitution-maker under political considerations, but this does not make the given constitutional provision less binding. The second argument concerns the formal aspects of legislative procedure and the legal consequence of non-compliance (both in para II/3 of the reasoning).

456 Interview with Judge D (Budapest, Hungary, 14 November 2006).

driven by the need for legal certainty which in this case prevails over institutional loyalty. Remarkably, there are no examples of explicit reference to a separate opinion in the Hungarian Constitutional Court's decisions. Thus, it is necessary to examine the content to discover possible influences.[457]

We can detect such an influence also in relation to the doctrine of 'living law'. In 1991, the Court established that when considering the constitutionality of a legislative provision, it will examine the law as interpreted and applied in practice, rather than its pure wording. Two judges expressed their dissent in the leading *Jánosi* case that first adopted this doctrine.[458] According to the dissenters, the Constitutional Court does not have the power to declare unconstitutional a provision that has a potentially constitutional reading. If the ordinary courts interpret the law in a way that contradicts the constitution, the Constitutional Court can only state this in the reasoning of its decision, explaining which interpretation would be in conformity with the constitution instead. The Court later softened its approach and elaborated a two-step process. In a 1993 case and in a position adopted by the plenary session the same year, the Court stated that it would first limit itself to declaring that a certain interpretation is contrary to the constitution, but without annulling it if a constitutional interpretation is also possible. It would annul the provision only if the ordinary courts continued to apply the interpretation declared as contrary to the constitution.[459]

As in Slovenia,[460] it happened in Hungarian constitutional justice as well that a principle was first defined in a separate opinion, and then applied by the majority in later cases. In particular, the first president of the Court, László Sólyom, wrote some especially influential separate opinions of this kind. The necessity test, for example, which later became one of the fundamental pillars of Hungarian

457 In the examined period (1990–2010), there are, however, three separate opinions citing another judge's separate opinion written in a previous case. Two were authored by Judge Kiss, while the third endorses a previous opinion delivered by him. First, in 1999, Judge Kiss endorsed an earlier concurring opinion of Judge Vörös in his dissenting opinion (joined by Judge Bihari), where he wrote: 'As a starting point, I share the view expressed by former Judge Imre Vörös in his concurring opinion delivered in case no 56/1995 (XI.15.) of 12 September 1995, according to which a heavy reduction of national insurance services is, in itself, not a constitutional issue as long as it does not concern the system in its entirety or the categories of beneficiaries.' (Decision no 39/1999 (XII.21.) of 21 December 1999, at para 2/d) Second, in a 2006 dissent he quotes literally an entire page from the dissenting opinion of Judge Lábady (joined by three other judges, including the president of the Court) delivered in a 1994 case concerning the right to privacy in child maintenance enforcement procedures (Decision no 576/D/2000 AB of 7 November 2006, para 1 of Judge Kiss's dissenting opinion). Finally, in case no 99/2007 (XII.6.) of 4 December 2007, Judge Trócsányi states that he agrees with a certain argument used by Judge Kiss in his concurring opinion delivered in case no 26/2007 (IV.25.) of 24 April 2007. Not unexpectedly, Judge Kiss joined this concurring opinion.

458 Decision 57/1991 (XI.8.) AB of 5 November 1991. Dissenting opinion of Judge Kilényi, joined by Judge Schmidt. See also Chapter 1, Section 2.3, n 100, and n 364 in this chapter.

459 Decision no 38/1993 (VI.11.) AB of 8 June 1993 and Position of the plenary session no 1/1993 (IX.13.) Tü Áf.

460 See Section 4.3.2 in this chapter.

constitutional justice, was first applied by him in a dissenting opinion delivered in 1990.[461] This dissenting opinion was, at the same time, the first one in the Court's history. His concurrence in the death penalty case, delivered the same year, has also become famous.[462] It was in this opinion that he first exposed the concept of 'invisible constitution', which has been subject to harsh criticism by many scholars.[463] Even if the concept itself as such has never been explicitly used in a majority opinion, its legacy is tangible. The Court has, in fact, found certain principles by reading between the lines of the constitutional provisions. The principle of separation of powers is one of these. It is an 'invisible' concept in the sense that there was no explicit mention of it in the constitutional text. The Constitutional Court, even though it did not use the concept of 'invisible constitution', made this principle 'visible' for the first time in December 1990,[464] and applied it as part of the principle of rule of law (enshrined in art. 2(1) of the Constitution) in several other cases later on.[465] Consequently, complainants also soon began to rely on this principle.[466] Sólyom's concurrence in the death penalty case

461 Case no 2/1990 (II.18.) AB of 12 February 1990. It was also the first separate opinion of Judge Sólyom. In this first dissent, however, he examines only three aspects of the restriction of constitutional rights (relevance, necessity and inevitability), and does not discuss reasonableness and proportionality. Albert Takács, 'Egy alkotmányos forradalmár. Sólyom László – a tudós, az alkotmánybíró, az elnök' [A Constitutional Revolutionist. László Sólyom – The Scientist, the Constitutional Judge, the President], in Gábor Halmai (ed), *A megtalált alkotmány? A magyar alapjogi bíráskodás els kilenc éve* [The Constitution Found? The First Nine Years of Hungarian Constitutional Review on Fundamental Rights] (INDOK 2000) 99, 107–8.

462 Decision no 23/1990 (X.31.) AB of 24 October 1990. The length of Sólyom's concurring opinion (12 pages) is the double of that of the decision. There were four more separate opinions attached to the decision (one dissenting and three concurring), authored by five judges. The Court was composed of ten members at the time. As mentioned above, President Sólyom encouraged his colleagues to write separately in this case (see n 395).

463 The concept of 'invisible constitution' has divided Hungarian legal scholarship. Those who deem it unacceptable argue that it is a tool for the Constitutional Court to disregard the written constitution. For example, András Sajó, 'Reading the Invisible Constitution: Judicial Review in Hungary' (1995) 15 *Oxford Journal of Legal Studies* 253. Others, like András Holló, argued that the concept of 'invisible constitution' has been misunderstood by its critics, as it does not mean that the Constitutional Court could disregard the written constitution. Instead, the 'invisible constitution' is an 'interpreted constitution' based on constitutional principles. It would mean that the constitution is self-interpretive, and the Constitutional Court's job is to make this visible. András Holló, *Az Alkotmánybíróság. Alkotmánybíráskodás Magyarországon* [The Constitutional Court: Constitutional Justice in Hungary] (Útmutató 1998), 63–4. He defended the concept also in a recent book: András Holló, *Az alkotmányjognak asztalánál. Az Alkotmánybíróság belülnézetben* [At the Table of Constitutional Law: The Constitutional Court Seen From the Inside] (HVG-ORAC 2015) 143.

464 Decision no 31/1990 (XII.18.) AB of 11 December 1990. The rapporteur of the case was Judge Kilényi.

465 For example, decision no 16/1991 (IV.20.) AB of 18 April 1991 and decision no 64/1992 (XII.11.) of 8 December 1992, in which President Sólyom wrote for the majority and made explicit reference to the 31/1990 decision. The principle of separation of powers was later incorporated into the new Fundamental Law (art C(1)).

466 For example, decision no 55/1994 (XI.10.) AB of 8 November 1994 concerning the compatibility between the office of mayor and the parliamentary mandate. See also n 371.

offered at least one more remarkable concept: that of the law's tolerance towards situations of necessary choice between human lives. Judge Holló, in a dissenting opinion of 2004,[467] explains how this concept has made its way into the Court's case-law, including the first abortion decision.

5.8. *Conclusion*

A careful examination of the Hungarian practice shows that Hungarian constitutional judges, who had no previous experience of writing separately, became comfortable with it rather quickly. The Court published dissenting opinions from the very first year of its operation. The number of separate opinions rose quickly, peaking at 17.9% in 1993, which is a relatively high rate compared to other European constitutional courts, even if still far from the US Supreme Court's 62%. This increase in the number of dissents shows a gradual individualisation of the Court which was accompanied by a certain degree of personalisation of its decisions. It is in part due to the strong personality of some of its members, especially of the first president, László Sólyom, and his antagonist, Judge Imre Vörös. The second Court also had its distinguished personalities, like Judges Harmathy and Kiss, whose opinions have become well-known. The tendency of writing separately together also diminished after the first two years, and co-authored separate opinions have become less common.

Notwithstanding this gradual individualisation and some significant separate opinions in the most important cases, the Hungarian Constitutional Court was able to gain a certain prestige in and outside Hungary, and was soon seen as a model by the other constitutional courts of the region and in international literature.[468] This prestige lasted until the recent reforms adopted by the conservative government in 2010–11 and a successful operation of 'court-packing' by the same.[469] This fact and the experience of other courts show that dissenting and concurring opinions in themselves are not harmful to a constitutional court's legitimacy, but rather enrich constitutional debate and make a more honest and complex dialogue possible between the court and the outside world. Rather than the presence or absence of separate opinions, it is the quality of these, the majority judgment and the arguments used therein that determine the court's prestige and authority.

467 Delivered in case no 9/2004 (III.30.) AB of 29 March 2004.

468 László Sólyom, 'The Role of Constitutional Courts in the Transition to Democracy: With Special Reference to Hungary' (2003) 18 *International Sociology* 133, 134.

469 See my series of posts on the blog *Diritti Comparati* <www.diritticomparati.it> accessed 19 January 2017. This loss of prestige is demonstrated by the severe criticism and concerns expressed by many Hungarian and international scholars not only about the constitutional and legislative reforms but also in relation to concrete decisions delivered by the 'packed' Court. For example, Sadurski (n 339) 10–11, and the writings of a number of Hungarian constitutional scholars, like Gábor Halmai, 'In memoriam magyar alkotmánybíráskodás. A pártos Alkotmánybíróság első éve' [In Memoriam Hungarian Constitutional Justice: The First Year of the Partial Constitutional Court] (2014) 1–2 *Fundamentum* 36.

5 Comparative reflections

1. The publication of dissenting opinions: pros and cons

Many authors who examine the phenomenon of judicial dissent present and weigh the different arguments that one can use for and against the publication of separate opinions.[1] It can be useful to go through these arguments, as they touch upon fundamental values and principles, but one should keep in mind that the pros and cons of disclosing judicial dissent have to be evaluated in the context of one concrete jurisdiction. The merits of separate opinions are usually discussed in relation to principles and concepts, such as transparency, judicial independence, legitimacy and authority. A pro-con discussion on judicial dissent reveals the interconnectedness of these principles and concepts.[2] Dissenting opinions have at least four functions: I will call them the stimulatory, the communicative, the dialectical, and the transformative functions.

Dissent occurs in collective bodies such as a court panel. It is natural that judges disagree on legal issues of a certain importance and difficulty. The question is if it is reasonable to conceal dissent. Judges undoubtedly discuss the cases among each other and influence one another's opinion. These discussions are needed to reach a decision and to find a solution to a legal problem at hand. Judges can benefit from the arguments brought up by the previous members of the court only if there is the possibility to write separately. Thus, dissenting opinions also constitute a kind of 'marketplace of ideas',[3] a precious source for possible arguments and alternative interpretations. It is argued, as we have seen for example

1 The list is very long. A few examples are John Alder, 'Dissents in Courts of Last Resort: Tragic Choices?' (2000) 20 *Oxford Journal of Legal Studies* 221; Josef Azizi, 'Unveiling the EU Court's Internal Decision-Making Process: A Case for Dissenting Opinions?' (2011) 12 *ERA Forum* 49; William J Brennan Jr, 'In Defense of Dissents' (1985) 37 *Hastings Law Journal* 427; Kurt H Nadelmann, 'The Judicial Dissent: Publication vs. Secrecy' (1959) 8 *American Journal of Comparative Law* 415; Sergio Verdugo R, 'Aportes del Modelo de Disidencias Judiciales al Sistema Político' (2011) 18 *Revista de Derecho Universidad Católica del Norte* 217.

2 As also pointed out by Hjalte Rasmussen and Louise Nan Rasmussen, 'Comment on Katalin Kelemen – Activist EU Court "Feeds" on the Existing Ban on Dissenting Opinions: Lifting the Ban is Likely to Improve the Quality of EU Judgments' (2013) 14 *German Law Journal* 1373.

3 Brennan (n 1) 430.

in relation to the Court of Justice of the European Union which bans separate opinions,[4] that the possibility of publishing dissent may improve the quality of the judgment by forcing the majority to deal with the hardest questions urged by the dissenters.[5] In this way dissenting opinions reinforce collegiality rather than undermine it, as they ensure that all members of the panel are treated equally and their arguments are taken into account.[6] This may be called the stimulatory function of judicial dissent,[7] directed to insiders, the other members of the court. One can wonder whether internally circulated but unpublished separate opinions may fulfil the same function. While unpublished dissenting opinions may contribute to a more lively discussion within the court, they probably do not have the compelling force of a published opinion. It follows that published separate opinions help keeping judges accountable by guaranteeing the public that they are on the job and participate in the deliberative process.[8]

Dissenting opinions also have an important informational or communicative function towards outsiders. They may help those who must abide by the court's judgment, the parties to the case and other legal actors who are affected by the precedential value of the decision, most importantly lower courts,[9] to better understand the reasons that brought to the decision and to predict a possible future change in the court's orientation. In fact, a separate opinion – especially a concurring opinion – may offer further explanations and supplement the majority's reasoning with details that help to obtain a more complete picture of the court's reasons. Moreover, it is not uncommon, as we could see, that a dissenting or concurring opinion is addressed to the lawmakers, making recommendations on how to correct or improve the law, or to the losing party, instructing her on where to seek relief.[10]

Legal doctrine is also among the beneficiaries of separate opinions. In fact, legal scholars often dedicate much of their attention to these opinions which, as

4 See Chapter 4, Section 3.2.

5 In this sense, also Brennan (n 1) 430.

6 Alder (n 1) 240. More generally it is argued that majoritarianism is more conducive to equality and fairness of participation than consensus, because it does not require anyone's view to be played down or put at rest. Jeremy Waldron, *Law and Disagreement* (Oxford UP 1999) 111.

7 As Lauterpacht put it, the possibility of dissent is 'a powerful stimulus to the maximum effort of which a tribunal is capable'. Hersch Lauterpacht, *The Development of International Law by the International Court* (Cambridge UP 1982) 66–67. Karl Llewellyn argued that it stimulates legal inventiveness. Karl N Llewellyn and Paul Gewirtz, 'The Case Law System in America' (1988) 88 *Columbia Law Review* 989, 1001.

8 Llewellyn and Gewirtz (n 7) 1002.

9 The dissenter may furnish litigants and lower courts with practical guidance, such as ways of distinguishing subsequent cases. Brennan (n 1) 430.

10 For examples from the Hungarian Constitutional Court's case-law see Chapter 4, Section 5.4. Another concrete example is an explanatory memorandum of the Estonian Ministry of Justice attached to a legislative proposal referring to a dissenting opinion (delivered in a case decided by the plenary session of the Supreme Court on 7 July 2001, RT III 2002, 2, 8). Julia Laffranque, 'Dissenting Opinion in the European Court of Justice' (2004) 9 *Juridica International* 14, 15.

we have seen, often have a similar style as academic writings. There is an even more special relationship between constitutional courts and legal doctrine. Many judges come from academia, and legal scholars may well aspire to become a constitutional judge. Thus, there is a strong interaction between constitutional justice and the academia both on the personal and on the substantive level. Dissenting opinions become part of a larger dialogue between judges and scholars on the various legal topics, therefore they also assume a kind of dialectical function.

Finally, dissenting opinions may exercise an important transformative function. Legal scholars who praise the publication of judicial dissent often consider it a useful vehicle of legal development.[11] A dissenting opinion or, more importantly, the presence of more dissenting opinions may be a precursor to future overruling, as it reveals a discordance of opinions inside the court. The composition of the court changes, and dissenters may become the majority. It is not a remote possibility. As we have seen, it does happen sometimes. Some scholars describe dissenting opinions as an important tool for the recognition of pluralism and an expression of the democratic principle.[12] Being able to manifest dissent publicly undoubtedly guarantees greater transparency of judicial decision-making.

These four functions of dissenting opinions are commonly used as an argument in favour of their publication. But besides benefits, the disclosure of judicial dissent has its costs too. The most powerful argument against the publication of dissent is that it damages the judgment's authoritativeness and, indirectly, the court's authority. On the other hand, however, one can say that if disclosure of dissent is allowed and no judge writes separately, the force of the decision is considerably stronger than in a system where dissenting opinions are banned and unanimity is uncertain. Real, and not only apparent, unanimity enhances the judgment's authoritativeness. As we have seen, exactly for this reason Chief Justice Warren worked hard to reach unanimity in the delicate case of *Brown v. Board of Education*.[13] He knew that in such an important issue regarding such a sensitive social problem the decision of the federal Supreme Court should show unity to be authoritative and enforceable. In that case the public acceptance of the decision could have been compromised by hiding divergent opinions, since it would have prevented the Court from strengthening the authoritativeness of a judgment by demonstrating real unanimity.[14] In England, Lord Mansfield, Lord Chief Justice in the 18th century, was an early advocate of judicial unanimity for the same reason. In *Millar v. Taylor*, a landmark copyright case decided by the

11 For example, Llewellyn and Gewirtz (n 7) 1000 ff, and Laffranque (n 10) 15.

12 For example, Brennan (n 1) and Alder (n 1) 223.

13 347 U.S. 483 (1954). See Chapter 2, Section 2.2.

14 As explained by Justice Scalia in a speech held at a conference on judicial dissent in Italy: 'United States Supreme Court lore contains the story of Chief Justice Warren's heroic and ultimately successful efforts to obtain a unanimous court for the epochal decision in *Brown v. Board of Education* (. . .). [T]hat unanimity was important to achieving greater public acceptance. But would it have had that effect if *all* the decisions of the Supreme Court, even those decided by 5:4 vote, were announced as unanimous? Surely not.' Antonin Scalia, 'Remarks on Dissenting Opinions' in Adele Anzon (ed), *L'opinione dissenziente* (Giuffrè 1995) 411, 413.

King's Bench in 1769, he wrote that unanimity (not achieved in that case) 'gives weight and dispatch to the decisions, certainty to the law and infinite satisfaction to the suitors'.[15] Thus, a dissenting opinion might be harmful to a given judgment's authoritativeness, but banning separate opinions does not benefit the authoritativeness of the single judgments. Also from the point of view of the court as an institution, dissenting opinions, one can argue, enhance rather than diminish its authority and prestige, because they increase public confidence.[16] The presence of dissenting opinions, the argument goes, provides reassurance that the courts are staffed by judges who make their decisions according to their understanding of the law.[17]

Another possible argument against separate opinions is that their preparation requires time, so they distract judges from their other duties. Considering the huge workload that European constitutional courts must deal with, this argument is not to be underestimated. It is to be weighed against the benefits of publishing dissent. One might argue that it is reasonable to permit the disclosure of a contrary vote publicly to protect the judge's right not to be forced to join a disliked majority opinion and, thus, her/his freedom of conscience. However, it would also be reasonable to require the judge to state her/his reasons elsewhere, for example in an article or an interview. Permitting more than this, the argument goes, would cost substantial resources in terms of judge time, court money, and public disrespect.[18] It gives a judge an opportunity for self-publicity at the public expense.[19]

As John Alder points out, the arguments against publishing dissent take a different view of the nature of authority and concentrate upon empirical disadvantages of dissents, while the proponents of dissenting opinions tend to focus on the democratic concerns related to the judiciary.[20] It seems, however, that, the civil law tradition has had more difficulties in handling judicial disagreement.[21] The aim of this chapter is to discuss the merits of dissenting opinions from the perspective of the civil law tradition and, in particular, of constitutional courts within that legal tradition. I will do this by examining judicial dissent from the point of view of some fundamental principles and values, namely judicial independence, transparency, legal certainty and free speech.

15 *Millar v. Taylor* (1769), 4 Burrows 2302, 98 ER 201.
16 For example, Charles Evans Hughes, *The Supreme Court of the United States* (Princeton UP 1928) 67.
17 Andrew Lynch, 'Is Judicial Dissent Constitutionally Protected?' (2004) 4 *Macquarie Law Journal* 81.
18 Rory K Little, 'Reading Justice Brennan: Is There a "Right" to Dissent?' (1999) 50 *Hastings Law Journal* 683, 699.
19 Alder (n 1) 243.
20 Alder (n x) 242.
21 The practice of dissenting opinions is not uncontroversial in the common law tradition either. See, for example, the changes in the practice of the Privy Council, discussed in Chapter 3, Section 2.1.

2. Independence vs transparency: a difficult balance

Dissenting opinions are usually discussed in the light of their impact on the legitimacy of the judiciary, whether constitutional or ordinary. The question of democratic legitimacy is crucial for an accurate analysis of the phenomenon of judicial dissent.[22] However, much depends on our understanding of the concept of legitimacy. In relation to the legitimacy of constitutional courts, Wojciech Sadurski discusses its 'meta-constitutional' character. He explains that since constitutional courts are explicitly endowed with the power of judicial review by their respective national constitutions, the issue of legitimacy of these courts cannot have a 'formal' character, and in this sense, their legitimacy is much stronger than that of the US Supreme Court. Therefore, as regards constitutional courts, 'the question is not whether these courts exercise their powers in accordance with the constitution and other laws but whether the constitution *should* endow them with such powers'.[23] In this context the notion of legitimacy at work is 'meta-constitutional' because the objection is addressed to the constitution-makers, not to constitutional judges. However, the objection of illegitimacy is addressed to constitutional judges as well on the ground that they exceed the limits determined by the constitution. Here the notion of 'judicial activism' comes into play, which again can be interpreted in different ways.[24]

Another distinction made by Sadurski is between input and output legitimacy.[25] Input legitimacy is related to the way constitutional courts are set up (the appointment procedure and the composition), while output legitimacy concerns their decision-making and its impact on the legal system and the society. Judicial dissent is clearly an aspect of the problem of output legitimacy. Sadurski, however, does not include dissenting opinions in his analysis of output legitimacy, but instead focuses on the distinction between separation-of-powers issues and rights adjudication, explaining that constitutional courts' legitimacy is higher in relation to the first.[26] Other authors discussing the problem of legitimacy do not deal with dissenting opinions either. They focus on input legitimacy and

22 I discussed these questions in my article Katalin Kelemen, 'Dissenting Opinions in Constitutional Courts' (2013) 14 *German Law Journal* 1345.

23 Wojciech Sadurski, 'Constitutional Courts in Transition Processes: Legitimacy and Democratization' (2011) Sydney Law School Legal Studies Research Paper No 11/53, 4.

24 The notion of judicial activism in relation to legitimacy has been discussed mostly by political scientists. See, for example, Christian Boulanger, 'Europeanization Through Judicial Activism? CEE Constitutional Courts' Legitimacy and the Return to Europe' in Wojciech Sadurski et al (eds), *Spreading Democracy and the Rule of Law? Part II* (Springer 2006) 263, and Shannon Ishiyama Smithey and John Ishiyama, 'Judicial Activism in Post-Communist Politics' (2002) 36 *Law and Society Review* 719, 720.

25 Sadurski (n 23) 4.

26 It was also explicitly declared by László Sólyom, the first President of the Hungarian Constitutional Court. See András Mink, 'Interview With László Sólyom' (1997) 6 *East European Constitutional Review* 71, 72.

judicial activism.[27] Empirical research on dissenting opinions might help us to understand the dynamics of legitimacy, since the publication of dissent affects the authoritativeness of the decisions and the public image of the courts.

There are two principles which come into play when discussing the problem of legitimacy. Both are strictly related to the issue of dissenting opinions: judicial independence and transparency of decision-making. These two principles are considered to be the cornerstones of a democracy, and at the same time, they are difficult to balance. How do these values influence the assessment of dissenting opinions?

2.1. Dissenting opinions and judicial independence

In modern democratic societies, judicial independence is a fundamental constitutional principle, but there is no consensus about its meaning and requirements.[28] Judicial independence has an intertwining external and internal aspect. One can analyse the independence of the judiciary from the other powers (the external aspect) or the judges' independence from their colleagues and superiors (the internal aspect). Furthermore, a distinction can also be made between the institutional and the individual aspects of judicial independence. We can talk about the independence of courts as institutions (institutional independence) or about the independence of judges as individual persons (individual independence).[29] The multi-faceted nature of the notion of judicial independence makes it more complex to relate it to judicial decision-making and, in particular, to the practice of dissenting opinions. In fact, the independence argument has been used both in favour and against the disclosure of dissent.[30] It is important to be aware of which facet of judicial independence we take into consideration when discussing the issue of dissenting opinions.

On the one hand, the publication of dissent can be objected to on the ground that it compromises the impartiality of the judge. This argument is based on the external aspect of judicial independence, and for constitutional courts it is mainly expressed in terms of fear of political pressure on the judges, but it can also be related to the risk of economic or social pressure exercised by publicly influential interest groups and the media. As to the danger of political pressure, the issue of dissenting opinions is often discussed in connection with the possibility of re-election

27 For example, Sergio Bartole, 'Conclusions: Legitimacy of Constitutional Court: Between Policy Making and Legal Science' in Wojciech Sadurski (ed),*Constitutional Justice, East and West* (Kluwer Law International 2003) 409.

28 Diana Woodhouse, 'The Constitutional Reform Act 2005 – Defending Judicial Independence the English Way' (2007) 5 *International Journal of Constitutional Law* 153, 156.

29 Shimon Shetreet, 'Judicial Independence and Accountability: Core Values in Liberal Democracies' in HP Lee (ed), *Judiciaries in Comparative Perspective* (Cambridge UP 2011) 3.

30 Julia Laffranque, 'Dissenting Opinion and Judicial Independence' (2003) 8 *Juridica International* 162, 168.

of constitutional judges. As a result, the Venice Commission and several scholars have recommended a prohibition against re-election, since it may undermine the independence of a judge.[31] If judges are allowed to run for a second term, they will want to be popular among their nominators in order to be re-elected.[32] Dissenting opinions come into play because they reveal the opinion of the single judges. In a system where the publication of dissent is not permitted, it will be difficult for the nominators to understand the position of the members of the court, since all decisions appear as unanimous and, consequently, anonymous. On the other hand, a separate opinion expresses a judge's personal opinion, even if it is sometimes written together with another judge or expressed in the form of simply joining the opinion of another judge. So, if judges can publish their dissent, the possibility of re-election becomes even more dangerous to their independence. This has been sometimes used as an argument against dissenting opinions. However, it should rather be used as an argument in favour of a ban on re-election. Indeed, there is a clear tendency in Europe to abolish the possibility of re-election.[33] And, as we have seen, those advocating the abolition of the ban on dissenting opinions in the CJEU, at the same time, call for the abolition of re-eligibility.[34]

On the other hand, the principle of judicial independence may also be used as an argument in favour of dissenting opinions. In this case, the internal expect of judicial independence comes into play. Dissenting opinions are an expression of the judge's independence from her/his fellow judges. As a former Chief Justice of the US Supreme Court, Charles Evans Hughes put it, merely formal unanimity, which is recorded at the expense of strong, conflicting views, is not desirable, because what must ultimately sustain the court in public confidence is the character and independence of the judges.[35]

2.2. Dissenting opinions and transparency of decision-making

When the democratic legitimacy of constitutional courts is questioned, an important question emerges: can the democratic legitimacy argument be also employed

31 European Commission for Democracy through Law (Venice Commission), 'The Composition of Constitutional Courts' (1997) in Science and Technique of Democracy No 20, 11 <www.venice.coe.int/webforms/documents/CDL-STD(1997)020.aspx> accessed 19 January 2017.

32 Eli M Salzberger and Stefan Voigt, 'On the Delegation of Powers: With Special Emphasis on Central and Eastern Europe' (2002) 13 *Constitutional Political Economy* 25, 38.

33 The most recent examples are the European Court of Human Rights and the Hungarian Constitutional Court, which functioned with re-eligible judges until 2010 and 2011, respectively. Art 2, Protocol no 14 ECHR, which modified art 23 of the Convention and entered into force on 1 June 2010, and art 6, para 3 of the new Hungarian Constitutional Court Act. In both cases the abolition of the possibility of re-election was accompanied by an extension of the term of office.

34 See Chapter 4, Section 3.2.

35 He added that 'while it may be regrettable that [the judges] cannot always agree, it is better that their independence should be maintained and recognized than that unanimity should be secured through its sacrifice'. Hughes (n 16) 67–68.

to the decision-making process of courts, and, in particular, of constitutional courts? The requirement of giving reasons for the decision serves a function within the judicial process similar to that served by the electoral process with regard to the political branches of government. It keeps judges accountable to the law.[36] Moreover, the need for a certain extent of democratic legitimacy of constitutional courts is clearly reflected in the appointment procedure of constitutional judges, which is an openly political and interest-laden process.[37] But how far can democratic requirements go in relation to constitutional courts? The notion of majority rule is central to traditional conceptions of democracy, and indeed, also applies to judicial decisions. When a decision is made by a panel of judges, the opinion of the majority prevails. No system requires unanimity in every case, even where the publication of dissent is prohibited. While the members of the Austrian Constitutional Court, for example, are not allowed to write dissenting opinions, the Constitutional Court Act nonetheless expressly provides for majority voting.[38] Unanimity is only required from the chambers when they reject hearing a constitutional complaint or dismiss a complaint on the ground that no constitutional right has evidently been infringed.[39] In Italy, where dissenting opinions are also banned and the Constitutional Court does not hear constitutional complaints of individuals, unanimity is never required. The Italian Constitutional Court Act provides for simple majority voting as a general rule,[40] and the only exception is for the removal of its members from office, where two-thirds majority is required.[41] The fact that in some systems, politically sensitive cases and cases of primary constitutional importance require a qualified majority indicates an effort to introduce a democratic element into the court's decision-making process. Germany, for example, requires a two-thirds majority for impeachment proceedings against the federal President or against ordinary

36 Brennan (n 1) 435.

37 According to Zdeněk Kühn and Jan Kysela, this acknowledges that European constitutional courts are major actors of domestic politics. The political scrutiny of nominees is made possible also by the fact that constitutional judges are generally seasoned lawyers, scholars or politicians with a clear background and a record of mature opinions. See Zdeněk Kühn and Jan Kysela, 'Nomination of Constitutional Justices in Post-Communist Countries: Trial, Error, Conflict in the Czech Republic' (2006) 2 *European Constitutional Law Review* 183, 185.

38 'All orders shall be passed with a definite majority' (art 31 of the Austrian Constitutional Court Act [VfGG)]. The Act acknowledges the possibility of the emergence of diverging opinions and contains detailed rules on how to proceed if none of the opinions reached the majority required for a decision (arts 31–32). For the removal from office of a constitutional judge two-thirds majority is required (art 10(4)).

39 Art 31. In a similar way, unanimity is also required from the chambers of the German Federal Constitutional Court if they refuse to decide an application by an ordinary judge and when they decide on the admissibility of constitutional complaints. Arts 81a, 93d of the German Federal Constitutional Court Act (BVerfGG).

40 Art 16, Act no 87 of 11 March 1953.

41 Art 7 of the Italian Constitutional Court Act (Supplementary Norms). The same rule can be found in Austria (art 10(4) VfGG).

judges, proceedings to determine the constitutionality of political parties, and decisions regarding the forfeiture of basic rights.[42]

The *sui generis* nature of constitutional courts, however, suggests that the democratic legitimacy argument cannot be employed in exactly the same way as towards representative bodies. Nobody expects the same degree of transparency from constitutional courts. The medieval English practice of *seriatim* opinions delivered by the individual judges without having discussed the case with each other before is not upheld anymore.[43] Today it would clearly violate the democratic principles and how we expect our judges to make their decisions. Every judgment has to be the product of a reasoned discussion between the judges. However, a complete publicity would put the effective functioning of the courts at risk. Not even the US Supreme Court deliberates in public, even if its decisions are far more transparent than those of the European constitutional courts. According to Henry J Abraham, 'the secrecy of the [US Supreme] Court's proceedings behind that "Purple Curtain" is a necessary by-product of its work'.[44] Or, as Justice Frankfurter explained, 'the Supreme Court should not be amenable to the forces of publicity to which the Executive and the Congress are subjected is essential to the effective functioning of the Court.'[45] They both mean that publicity, and undue popular pressures on judges that it may entail, could endanger the court's independence. However, there are commentators of the US Supreme Court's caselaw who consider the Court's secrecy excessive.[46] But even if decisions are made behind closed doors, the final result is completely public and transparent. In fact, from a comparative perspective, the US Supreme Court follows a rather unique practice. On the famous Opinion Day, the Court announces the decisions it has reached. In this occasion, every judge, commencing with the junior Justices, and proceeding in order of seniority, reads, paraphrases or summarises her/his opinion.[47] Consequently, it is no secret which judges approved the ruling and which ones remained in the minority. The identity of the opinion-writer judge is also public. The judgment is written as the 'opinion of the Court', but it is authored by one judge who delivers the decision in the name of the majority.[48]

42 Art 15(4) BVerfGG.

43 See Chapter 3, Section 2.1.

44 Henry J Abraham, *The Judicial Process* (7th edn, Oxford UP 1998) 239.

45 Felix Frankfurter, 'Mr. Justice Roberts' (1955) 104 *University of Pennsylvania Law Review* 311, 313.

46 David Lazarus, 'The Supreme Court's Excessive Secrecy: Why It Isn't Merited' (*FindLaw*, 30 September 2004) <http://writ.news.findlaw.com/lazarus/20040930.html>, and Pema Levy, 'This Is How the Supreme Court Decides Which Cases to Announce When' (*Mother Jones*, 24 June 2015) <www.motherjones.com/politics/2015/06/supreme-court-explained-obamacare-gay-marriage> both accessed 19 January 2017.

47 Abraham (n 44) 240.

48 Tie votes are an exception to this rule. In these cases no opinion is written at all, and the Court does not announce on which side of the tie the Justices stood. Abraham (n 44) 219. The so called *per curiam* opinions are another exception to the rule. A *per curiam* is an unsigned, usually brief opinion for the Court, applying *res judicata*, and amount to 15–25% of all judgments. Ibid. 201–2.

No European constitutional court follows this practice. The secret nature of deliberation within constitutional courts includes the secrecy of voting. Every judge must sign the decision.[49] As a rule, the result of the voting is not made public. An exception to this rule is the German practice, in which the court may decide to reveal the number of votes for and against. There are, however, two important differences from the American practice: the court may state the number of votes in the decision, but it is not obliged to do so, and in any case, the identity of the judges who voted for and against the decision is not revealed. In the European constitutional courts' practice, the identity of judges remaining in the minority is revealed only if they write a dissenting opinion. Otherwise, if they decide not to write separately, the public will never know who voted against the decision, since it is signed by every judge who participated in the decision-making.

So, there may be different degrees of transparency within the final stage of the decision-making process. The first degree is to allow judges to publish their dissent. The rule is that they cannot simply state their disagreement but must also give reasons for it, even if just in the form of joining another judge's separate opinion. The second degree of transparency is the possibility of additionally revealing the number of the votes in favour and against the decision. This is implemented in Germany, even if in a limited way, since there it is not a duty but a possibility. Finally, the third degree of transparency is represented by the American (and English) practice in which the vote of every judge is public, whether they choose to write their own dissent or not. A special case is represented by Greece, where all courts have to disclose dissent, so it is an obligation and not a possibility.[50] The rationale behind this exceptional Greek rule is to ensure transparency, without however putting the individual judges in the spotlight, because separate opinions are published anonymously.[51]

However, even in countries where dissenting opinions can be published by the judges of the constitutional court, there are some instances in which they are prohibited. A ban on the publication of dissent is usually provided for in cases in which the decision concerns the criminal or disciplinary responsibility of a judge or other high official of the state.[52] It seems that in these cases the publication of dissent is considered to be inappropriate. The same approach applies in the English criminal appeals, where it has been long regarded as imperative that 'the discomfiture of the unsuccessful appellant should not be aggravated by an overt division of opinion among the judges.'[53] As regards the criminal or disciplinary

49 For example, art 30(1) BVerfGG.

50 Art 93(3) of the Constitution provides that 'publication of the dissenting opinion shall be compulsory'.

51 Art 35(1) of Act no 184/1975. European Parliament, Directorate-General for Internal Policies, *Dissenting Opinions in the Supreme Courts of the Member States* (PE 462.470, November 2012) 24 <www.europarl.europa.eu/committees/en/supporting-analyses-search.html> accessed 19 January 2017.

52 See Chapter 4, Section 4.2.4.

53 Louis Blom-Cooper and Gavin Drewry, *Final Appeal: A Study of the House of Lords in Its Judicial Capacity* (Clarendon Press 1972) 81. See Chapter 3, Section 2.1, text to n 31.

responsibility of high public officials and judges, the question is even more delicate and has also political implications. In these cases, the overt expression of disagreement in the court could lead to friction between the judiciary and the other two branches of power.

3. Judicial dissent and legal certainty

In the civil law tradition, the standard attitude is that the law is certain and should appear so, and that this certainty would be impaired by noting dissents and by publishing separate opinions. The principle of legal certainty is a kind of dogma and a fundamental goal. At the same time, using the expression of John Merryman, it is like a queen in chess, it can move in any direction.[54] This metaphor may be well illustrated by the paradoxical and counter-intuitive relationship between legal certainty and the possibility of publishing separate opinions. There is a paradox, because even if an apparently unanimous decision seems to enhance legal certainty, as the court speaks with one voice and gives only one answer to each legal question at hand, at the same time, it endangers the predictability of the law, as future changes in case-law are more difficult to foresee. Thus, from the perspective of non-unanimous judgments, there is a contrast between the two most basic elements of legal certainty: consistency and predictability.

The difficulty of discussing the principle of legal certainty lies in the fact that it covers conceptually heterogeneous legal issues. From the perspective of judicial dissent the relevant issues are: the possibility of knowing the exact content of legal provisions, the predictability of legal rulings, the possibility of being aware in advance of how legal decisions are made, and the stability of law over time (legal continuity). There is no widely shared definition or common understanding of the principle of legal certainty.[55] Besides being a manifold principle, legal certainty bears a different weight in different legal traditions. The importance of legal certainty in relation to other principles is itself a matter of debate.[56]

The most obvious contrast is between how the civil law and common law traditions understand this principle. While for the former legal certainty is an abstract value, which is commonly emphasised in order to make the law judge-proof, the latter discusses legal certainty in more functional terms. There it is not a dogma, but a value which has its limits and stands in competition with other values. In the common law, certainty is achieved by giving force of law to judicial decisions, something theoretically forbidden in civil law.[57] For common lawyers, case-law provides more certainty about the law. Thus, the desire for certainty is

54 John H Merryman and Rodrigo Pérez-Perdomo, *The Civil Law Tradition* (3rd edn, Stanford UP 2007) 48.

55 Stefano Bertea, 'Towards a New Paradigm of Legal Certainty' (2008) 2 *Legisprudence* 25, 26.

56 John Alder argues that for this reason it cannot be a reason for excluding the publication of dissent. Alder (n 1) 243.

57 Merryman and Pérez-Perdomo (n 54) 49.

an argument in favour of the rule of binding precedent, while it is an argument against it in civil law. In the common law, it is more generally recognised that certainty frequently implies rigidity, and as such it competes with the desire for flexibility. The desire for molding the law in response to changed circumstances or bending it to the requirements of a particular case is considered to be equal to the desire for certainty. For the same reason, the common law tradition confers equitable powers on judges, while the civil law tradition considers that incompatible with the judicial function. In essence, it seems that how legal certainty is conceived also depends on the legal tradition.

If dissenting opinions are viewed as an attack to legal certainty, which is still considered to be a fundamental value, it seems difficult to understand why its use is spreading in the civil law tradition. Does it mean that legal certainty has lost its dogmatic character? It is an especially relevant question for the civil law tradition, which has traditionally venerated this principle. Nonetheless, there has been no substantial debate on this issue among legal scholars of civil law background. It may be because the publication of dissenting opinions, apart from a few sporadic historical exceptions, is a relatively recent phenomenon in continental Europe and in many civil law systems is limited to constitutional courts.

3.1. Legitimacy, the majority principle and the 'consistency' element of legal certainty

There is a clear tension between the normative content of legal certainty and the practice of the law. The 'consistency' element of certainty meets considerable difficulties in practice. Some pragmatic theorists, such as Jürgen Habermas,[58] argue that discussing legal certainty is pointless and should be of no concern to legal theorists. Stefano Bertea argues that legal certainty should be regarded as an intrinsically theory-laden notion, which needs to be discussed in relation to particular theories, and not treated as a largely pre-theoretical idea.[59] In the context of judicial dissent, in particular, the concepts of legitimacy and democracy come into play.

US Supreme Court Justice Antonin Scalia defended dissenting opinions by stating that the authority of a bench of judges, like the authority of a legislature, depends simply upon a grant of power from the people. And if the terms of the grant are that the majority vote shall prevail, then *that* is all authority that is required.[60] He argues that the authority of a court does not depend upon unanimity, even though it may well be that the people will be more inclined to accept it without complaint. Scalia's analogy with the legislature is at least problematic, as the judicial power is essentially different from the legislative power. The legislature creates the law, while the judges' principal role is to interpret the law, their

58 Jürgen Habermas, *Between Facts and Norms* (Polity 1992) 201.
59 Bertea (n 55) 27.
60 Scalia (n 14) 413.

law-creation is much more limited.[61] Others argue that the authority of a court is based on the content of its decisions, rather than on democratic legitimacy.[62] It is especially true for the common law tradition, where it is argued that the legitimacy of judicial decision-making derives from its great transparency.[63] The same argument, obviously, could not be used in the civil law tradition where the judicial decision-making is far from being transparent. However, also the civil law tradition emphasises the importance of the content of judicial decisions which must prove that the decision is based on the positive legal sources.

At the same time, even if judicial dissent cannot be made public, the procedural rules do not require unanimity. Judicial benches make their decisions by majority in the civil law as in the common law tradition. Even if a court might use voting in *extrema ratio* and aim at reaching consensus in every case,[64] this is not always possible. Thus, unanimity is sometimes – or often, we cannot know, – only apparent. Therefore, civil law judgments give the illusion of legal certainty, as they pretend to be based on a consensus among the judges, but it does not necessarily reflect reality. Even if unanimity were imposed by procedural rules, it is sometimes hard to achieve that in practice. And there is more: it would clearly violate judicial independence. Judges are expected to make their decisions based on the law *and* according to their conscience. Their interpretation of the law cannot be determined by other judges, even if these other judges constitute the majority of the bench in a given court at a given moment in time. As long as the interpretation is based on the positive legal sources and applies reasonable canons of interpretation, it is a lawful interpretation.

The majority rule is necessary for an effective functioning of the court, but it – in itself – does not make the court a political institution. In fact, in constitutional courts with a strong sense of collegiality that thrive for consensus in every case, like the Italian and German constitutional courts, voting is not a routine practice.[65] It is considered to be an *extrema ratio*. According to this idea, rooted in the civil law tradition, in a court there are no pre-established majorities and minorities, but the deliberative process aims to accommodate the different views of all or most judges. The single judges' positions are unimportant. They work together to reach the largest consensus possible.[66]

3.2. The 'predictability' element of legal certainty

While the 'consistency' element of legal certainty is weakened by judicial dissent, the 'predictability' element seems to be enhanced by it. The desire for

61 On this argument see also Verdugo (n 1) 233.

62 Verdugo (n 1) 233.

63 Mitchell de S-O l'E Lasser, *Judicial Deliberations* (Oxford UP 2004) 1.

64 As we could see, this is the case in German and Italian Constitutional Courts. See Chapter 4, Sections 2.1.2 and 2.3.

65 See Chapter 2, Section 2.2.

66 Gustavo Zagrebelsky, 'La Corte costituzionale italiana' in Pasquale Pasquino and Barbara Randazzo (eds), *Come decidono le corti costituzionali (e altre Corti). How Constitutional Courts Make Decisions* (Giuffrè 2009) 59, 78–79.

predictability of the law means that people should be able to anticipate the content of judicial decisions. Or, more in general, it calls for the possibility of knowing in advance what legal consequences will follow from one's conduct. Certainty in law is thus associated with uniform treatment, regularity, and predictability.[67]

However, even in the common law tradition which recognises the binding nature of precedents, case-law is in continuous development. Precedents may be overruled; previous cases may be distinguished. So, when such a change occurs, the predictability of the law is harmed. The harm may be diminished by a dissenting opinion attached to the overruled precedent.[68] If dissents are kept secret, the legal community is deprived of the possibility to predict change. In this context dissenting opinions act as a preventive indicator of the likelihood of change in case-law. Judges are not immortal. The composition of courts changes in time, so do the majority and their interpretation of the law. In fact, in the common law tradition judgments relying on a slight majority of the court have a weaker precedential value than unanimous judgments.[69]

The role of dissenting opinions in enhancing predictability of the law is even clearer in relation to activist courts. As Hjalte Rasmussen argued, echoing Tom Bingham, one of England's greatest judges, when judges recast the law in a radically innovative fashion, they not only create legal uncertainty, but they divert from courts' purposes.[70] In the context of an activist court, the moderating influences of minorities are there to hold radicalisation in check. But this check is only effective if dissents are published. If the identity of the judges forming the majority is not disclosed, they are less motivated to 'invest all their intellectual capacity into delivering well-founded legal reasonings'.[71]

As mentioned above, the 'predictability' element of legal certainty is, however, not restricted to the predictability of judicial decisions. It concerns the interpretation of the law in general. The possibility to know the content of legal normative statements is a necessary condition for law to be certain. This aspect of predictability calls our attention to language, since the law owes some of its characters to the language that frames it.[72] The language-dependence of legal certainty was explained by Herbert Hart. For Hart, language is open-textured and this trait of

67 Bertea (n 55) 29–30.

68 A classic example is that of Justice Harlan's dissent in *Plessy v. Ferguson*, a judgment overruled sixty years later by *Brown v. Board of Education*. Even if the legal ground for the overruling of Plessy is not the same on which Justice Harlan would have based the decision, his dissenting opinion indicated that not all Justices supported the 'separate but equal' doctrine. See Chapter 3, Section 2.3.

69 The precedential value of plurality opinions, in which the reasoning is not supported in its entirety by a majority of judges, has been object of extensive doctrinal debate in American legal scholarship. For example, The Harvard Law Review Association, 'Plurality Decisions and Judicial Decision-making' (1981) 94 *Harvard Law Review* 1127; and Linda Novak, 'The Precedential Value of Supreme Court Plurality Decisions' (1980) 80 *Columbia Law Review* 756.

70 Rasmussen and Rasmussen (n 2) 1383.

71 Ibid. 1385.

72 Bertea (n 55) 30.

language is transmitted to law. Whichever device is chosen for the communication of standards of behaviour, these will, at some point, prove indeterminate.[73] This does not mean that Hart considers law completely indeterminate. He adopts a moderately skeptical attitude towards the possibility of achieving legal certainty, arguing that both officials and private individuals are guided by determinate rules which do not require from them a fresh judgment from case to case.[74]

3.3. Legal certainty and legal positivism

It seems that the phenomenon of judicial dissent, which is an undeniable reality, makes clear the tension between the two basic elements of legal certainty: consistency and predictability. The difficulty of the civil law legal systems to come to terms with judicial dissent is largely a legacy of legal positivism.[75] For the traditional positivist theory, interpretation of the law consists merely in an intellectual act of clarifying or understanding; as if the law-applying organ had to use only her reason but not her will. It has us believe that the law can supply only one correct decision and that the 'correctness' of this decision is based on the given source of law itself. Hans Kelsen, in his pure theory of law, criticised this traditional theory. He argued that the law to be applied constituted only a frame within which several applications are possible, whereby every act is legal that stays within the frame. Kelsen clearly asserted:

> The interpretation of a statute (. . .) need not necessarily lead to a single decision as the only correct one, but possibly to several, which are all of equal value, though only one of them in the action of the law-applying organ (especially the court) becomes positive law. The fact that a judicial decision is based on a statute actually means only that it keeps inside the frame represented by the statute.[76]

For Hans Kelsen, unlike for the traditional positivist theory, the judicial decision has a constitutive character.[77] A judicial decision is not pure law application, but it is law creation in the literal sense of the word,[78] even though to a lesser extent than law creation by the legislature.[79] It is the continuation, not the beginning, of the law-creating process.[80] Kelsen also observed that courts in a legal system where judicial decisions have the character of binding precedent

73 Herbert LA Hart, *The Concept of Law* (3rd edn, Oxford UP 2012) 127–28.
74 Bertea (n 55) 31.
75 Ibid. 27.
76 Hans Kelsen, *Pure Theory of Law* (trs Max Knight, University of California Press 1967) 351.
77 Kelsen (n 76) 236–42.
78 Hans Kelsen, *Introduction to the Problems of Legal Theory* (B Litschewski Paulson and SL Paulson trs, Clarendon Press 1992) 68.
79 Kelsen (n 78) 70.
80 Kelsen (n 76) 255.

are actually authorised to create general norms, but even courts whose decisions have no precedential value create individual norms.[81] Individual norms establish a material fact, determined *in abstracto* by the general norm (statute), as actually existing *in concreto*, and order a coercive act.[82] Both individual and general norms created by courts compete with the legislative organ and result in a decentralization of the legislative function. This radical decentralization of law creation is justified by the assumption that no case is exactly like any other case.[83] This system is distinguished by great flexibility, but lacks all legal certainty. For Kelsen, the principle of legal certainty (*Rechtssicherheit*) is in inverse relation to the principle of flexibility of law. A system in which the courts are authorised to create general norms in the form of precedential decisions represent a higher degree of decentralisation of the law-creating function and thereby a lower degree of the realisation of the principle of legal certainty.[84]

Kelsen stated explicitly that his pure theory of law rejects the view that interpretation is cognition of positive law, a way of deriving new norms from prevailing norms. He criticised the so-called jurisprudence of concepts (*Begriffsjurisprudenz*), represented by Puchta and von Jhering, that views the judicial function as the discovery of norms that already exist, and thus are simply to be uncovered in a particular way. Kelsen accuses the traditional positivist theory of striving to maintain the illusion of legal certainty.[85]

Kelsen did not engage in a discussion of judicial dissent, as his is a theory on how the law *should* be applied, not how it *is* applied. Based on his theory, we may presume that he considered the phenomenon to be obvious. However, it would be interesting to see what Kelsen would say about the ***publication*** of dissent. Even the most convinced positivists admit that judicial dissent exists, as some judges may be misled in their process of interpretation and not reach the (one and only) correct conclusion. But how can we ensure that it is the majority that reached the correct conclusion and not the dissenter? Not even the most convinced positivist would argue that the majority principle ensures the *legal* 'correctness' of law-application. As John Alder put is, 'a majority has predictive,

81 Ibid. 251.
82 Kelsen (n 78) 67.
83 This assumption is closely related to the concept of justice. Flexibility of the law is often demanded in the name of justice. 'Just' in this sense is said to be the decision of a concrete case if it takes into consideration all peculiarities of the case. Kelsen points out that if we accept this way of thinking, since no case is exactly like any other, the application of a general norm can never lead to a just decision. But if the law-applying organ is to make a 'just' decision, he can do this only by applying a general norm he considers as just. And in doing so he must proceed in the same way as a legislator who is guided by a certain ideal of justice. This ideal of justice is necessarily relative. A justification or foundation of the validity is only possible by showing that the individual norm conforms with a higher general norm presupposed to be just. This theory, according to Kelsen, ends up as a variant of the doctrine of natural law. Kelsen (n 76) 252–54.
84 Ibid. 251–54.
85 Kelsen (n 78) 84.

but not necessarily normative significance'.[86] The position on the publication of judicial dissent reveals a pitfall of legal positivism.

3.4. A brief remark on the indeterminacy of constitutional law

Legal certainty has special relevance in constitutional law, which has often been described as more abstract than other fields of law. Constitutions typically do not give direct answers to concrete legal problems, but they serve as a guideline for and a limit to the lawmaking power. Consequently, a constitution must be interpreted. However, the same is true for statutory law, especially in the civil law tradition, where codes contain general clauses that are at least as abstract as constitutional provisions. On the other hand, constitutions also contain procedural rules, which are of more concrete nature. Thus, the peculiarity of constitutional law is not in its abstract character, but in the greater number of abstract and general rules than in statutory law. As András Jakab convincingly argues, a sharp difference between constitutional and statutory law in terms of nature is rather a myth and a harmful one, as it leads to 'escaping from the control of usual methods [of interpretation], thus being able to smuggle one's own moral preferences masked as the result of some special kind of interpretation'.[87] Indeed, the question of indeterminacy of law has been a common theme in legal theory, especially among critical legal scholars.[88] Whether different or not from statutory interpretation, constitutional interpretation – or constitutional reasoning[89] – has become object of comparative research in Europe in the last few decades,[90] and this line of research undoubtedly benefits from the publication of dissenting opinions.[91]

86 Alder (n 1) 222.

87 András Jakab, *European Constitutional Language* (Cambridge UP 2016) 21–22.

88 For a critical account of the development of the indeterminacy thesis in critical legal scholarship see Lawrence B Solum, 'On the Indeterminacy Crisis: Critiquing Critical Dogma' (1987) 54 *University of Chicago Law Review* 462.

89 The distinction between constitutional interpretation and constitutional reasoning is subtle. The former aims to determine the content of a constitutional provision, while the latter serves this aim by arguing for or against a certain determination of content. Jakab (n 87) 17.

90 See, for example, Josè Juan Moreso, *Legal Indeterminacy and Constitutional Interpretation* (Springer 1998), and the CONREASON Project conducted by the German Max Planck Institute and the Hungarian Academy of Legal Sciences <www.conreasonproject.com/> accessed 19 January 2017. The principle output of this research project will be the forthcoming book András Jakab and Arthur Dyevre (eds), *Comparative Constitutional Reasoning* (Cambridge UP 2017).

91 Indeed, one of the questions included in the questionnaire used for the country reports in the CONREASON Project regards separate opinions. In particular, the frequency of dissent and the factors influencing it are under scrutiny. András Jakab, Arthur Dyevre and Giulio Itzcovich, 'CONREASON – The Comparative Constitutional Reasoning Project. Methodological Dilemmas and Project Design' (2015) MTA Law Working Papers 2015/9, 14 <http://jog.tk.mta.hu/uploads/files/mtalwp/2015_09_jakab.pdf> accessed 19 January 2017.

4. The judges' point of view

4.1. *The personal dimension of separate opinions*

Analysing the practice of dissenting opinions from the point of view of judicial independence and transparency involves studying its external impact. This kind of analysis considers the court's relationship with the other public powers and with the public in general. It attempts to understand the way and the extent to which the publication of dissenting opinions affects the court's external relationships, such as those with the parliament, the executive, the other courts, and public opinion. However, there is another dimension that deserves the attention of researchers: the internal one. The internal or personal dimension basically consists of the judges' point of view. When do judges decide to publish their dissent? How do they make use of this possibility? How does it affect their relationship with their colleagues? These questions have been of special interest to legal realists and political scientists.

The personal dimension is no less complex than the external one, for several reasons. First, judges are not obliged to publish their dissent even if they vote against the decision. Consequently, in constitutional courts, where the result of the voting is not public, it is not possible to compile complete statistics on the voting behaviour of judges. A researcher can only analyse the number and content of published separate opinions, but only the judges themselves know how many times they remained in the minority with their opinions. As already mentioned above, this is not the case for the US and UK Supreme Courts where the result of the voting is public, therefore making it possible to undertake a thorough analysis of voting behaviour. A common law judge can, however, decide to withhold her/his dissent, even if s/he does not truly share the opinion of the majority.[92] Thus, the real difference between a common law and civil law judge is that the former cannot vote against the judgment without stating her/his reasons for it, while the latter may well vote against a judgment and keep her/his reasons hidden. A judge sitting on a constitutional court allowing for the publication of dissent who finds herself/himself in the minority with her/his view has four options: (1) voting with the majority as a sign of respect and loyalty towards the majority and the court's authority, or the 'withheld dissent' option; (2) voting against the majority, without writing separately and remaining silent about her/his dissent in the eyes of the public, or the 'silent dissenter' option, not available to the Justices of the US and UK Supreme Courts; (3) voting against the judgment, without writing separately but joining the separate opinion of another judge, or the 'concurring dissent' option; and, finally, (4) voting against the majority and writing separately, or the 'full dissent' option. The fact that for judges it is a right and

92 Thus, the percentage of dissenting opinions is not necessarily a true reflection of all the occasions in which one judges disagrees with the majority in the common law courts either. Jon O Newman, 'Between Legal Realism and Neutral Principles: The Legitimacy of Institutional Values' (1984) 72 *California Law Review* 200, 204, fn 8.

not a duty to write a dissenting or concurring opinion leaves space for strategic behaviour. Judges are supposed to vote according to their conscience, but the lower dissent rates in European courts seem to suggest that sometimes their loyalty towards the institution supersedes their conscience. Alternatively, or in addition, it might also suggest that they work harder to reach an agreement than their American colleagues. In any event, it is a demonstration of loyalty and respect.

Another factor making the researcher's job more difficult is the secrecy of deliberation. Only the product (the judgment) is public, not the production (the decision-making process). This ties the external observer's hands to a considerable extent. Some insight into the court's deliberation process can be gained if a judge or a clerk breaches her/his duty of confidentiality and speaks out about events inside the court,[93] but the records are not within the reach of researchers. So, a systematic and comprehensive analysis of the decision-making process seems impossible. Dissenting opinions, on the other hand, still provide a remarkable insight into how courts work. The study on the Hungarian Constitutional Court included in the previous chapter has been an attempt of this kind.

Most scholars and judges agree that a system permitting the publication of dissent improves the quality of the majority opinion.[94] It is a constraint on the majority, because it ensures that minority views are taken into due regard. It is not a secret that both the majority opinion and separate opinions are circulated among judges before the final vote on the decision. They do not form their opinions in a complete isolation, but discuss it on several occasions. Consequently, majority and dissenting judges inevitably influence one another.[95] The question is: in which circumstances does a judge decide to break her/his loyalty towards her/his fellow judges and write a separate opinion? What is the degree or the nature of disagreement that induces a judge to publish her/his dissent? Or rather, does it depend on the importance or the nature of the issue under discussion? The question is even more intriguing in relation to European constitutional courts, where judges are more unwilling to write separately. The dissent rate in constitutional courts is remarkably lower than in the US Supreme Court.[96]

93 In the United States law clerks of the Justice have come to the spotlight in the last two decades. They started to gain the attention of commentators and scholars in the last two decades, since some of them revealed confidential information in relation to certain cases. See Chapter 3, Section 3.2.

94 For example, Scalia (n 14) 422. According to Justice Scalia, 'the mere *prospect* of a separate writing renders the writer of the majority opinion more receptive to reasonable suggestions on major points'.

95 In the words of Justice Brennan, '[f]or simply by infusing different ideas and methods of analysis into judicial decision-making, dissents prevent that process from being rigid or stale. And, each time the Court revisits an issue, the justices are forced by a dissent to reconsider the fundamental questions and to rethink the result'. Brennan (n 1) 436.

96 In the period 1990–2007, there were one or more separate opinions in 62% of the cases in the US Supreme Court. See Chapter 3, Section 3.4. On the German Federal Constitutional Court the dissent rate hardly reaches 7%. See Chapter 4, Section 2.1.2. In the Spanish Constitutional Court the dissent rate is somewhat higher, 16% recently, but it still does not come close the American level. See Chapter 4, Section 2.2.2.

As Donald Kommers explained in relation to the practice of the German Federal Constitutional Court:

> The institutional bias against personalized judicial opinions has tended to minimize published dissents. Dissenting judges – even if they have circulated written dissents inside the court – more often than not choose not to publish their dissents or even to be identified as dissenters partly out of a sense of institutional loyalty. The prevailing norm seems to be that personalized dissenting opinions are proper only when prompted by deep personal convictions.[97]

This means that German constitutional judges write separately only in exceptional circumstances, when the disagreement with the majority is so unbearable and the issue at stake is so important that the judge's conscience prevails over loyalty towards her/his colleagues. They show prudence in the use of dissenting opinions. Their mind-set differs from the mind-set of American judges, even though constitutional courts have many features in common with the US Supreme Court. The fact that constitutional courts exert more effort to reach unanimity calls for attention. Does this mean that constitutional judges make use of dissenting opinions to disclose unbearable disagreements inside the court? Does it help them to resolve internal conflicts that emerge between judges? As the title of the volume published by Judge Vörös, *Dixi et salvavi*, shows,[98] when a judge expresses her/his disagreement publicly, she sets her/his mind at rest, which can clearly help to improve her/his relationship with colleagues and to solve internal tensions within the court.[99]

4.2. *Judicial dissent and the freedom of expression*

The ability to publish dissent may also be perceived in terms of freedom of expression. It guarantees the judge's dignity, allowing her/his to express her/his opinion even if s/he remains in the minority. The importance of the judge's freedom of expression is felt especially strongly in the American legal tradition, where the right to dissent has been generally recognised as a fundamental right enshrined in the First Amendment of the federal Constitution.[100] For judges, in common law and

97 Donald P Kommers, *The Constitutional Jurisprudence of the Federal Republic of Germany* (Duke UP 1997) 26.

98 Imre Vörös, *Dixi et salvavi. Különvélemények, párhuzamos indokolások* [Dixi et salvavi: Dissenting and Concurring Opinions] (Logod Bt 2000).

99 Interesting research carried out by Canadian scholars analysed judicial opinions (both majority and separate opinions) in order to understand how emotion and anger are reflected in them. The authors state 'it is in dissent that emotion is most apparent because dissent expresses a difference in opinion'. Marie-Claire Belleau and Rebecca Johnson, 'Faces of Judicial Anger: Answering the Call' (2007) 1 *European Journal of Legal Studies* 20, 22.

100 The right to dissent is obviously not limited to judges. For a general discussion about the role of dissent in a democratic society see Cass R Sunstein, *Why Societies Need Dissent* (Harvard UP 2005).

civil law alike, the decision to publish their dissent is often a question of conscience. This is exemplified by the title of the aforementioned collection of dissenting opinions published by Judge Imre Vörös after the end of his term: *Dixi et salvavi.*[101] He decided to publish all of his separate opinions in a single volume in order to protect his personal integrity, which he describes as one of the main functions of the dissenting opinion.[102] 'Dixi et salvavi animam meam', which means 'I spoke and saved my soul', is a Latin saying based on a passage of the Bible,[103] and perfectly illustrates this argument. Even if the judge knows that her/his opinion will not bind anyone and will not become law, she still deems it important to express it publicly in order to safeguard her/his personal integrity and dignity.

As we have seen, judges are sometimes tenacious in their dissent and repeat the same opinion in several different cases.[104] Especially this kind of dissent, when a judge chooses the so-called 'never-say-die option',[105] seeks more than simply offer an alternative opinion. As Justice Brennan explained: 'It constitutes a statement by the judge as an individual: "Here I draw the line."'[106] This is sometimes explicitly offered as a justification for the decision to write separately, as Justice Daniel did in a concurrence in the *License Cases*,[107] where he wrote: 'I possess no sovereign prerogative by which I can put my conscience into commission. I must interpret exclusively as that conscience shall dictate.' But while in the civil law tradition the conscience of the judge has traditionally been considered to be sufficiently protected by the right to vote freely for or against a certain solution,[108] in the US and other common law systems there seems to be a constitutional right to make disagreement public, at least in the form of having it publicly noted in the judgment.

The right to write separately is not undebated in the common law tradition either.[109] While it is clear that judges do not lose their constitutional rights when they take on their robes, it is not straightforward how far these rights extend in relation to judicial decision-making.[110] In the US Constitution, the freedom of speech is covered by the First Amendment. As Rory Little argued, 'the First Amendment can support at most only a right for judges to express and publicly

101 Vörös (n x).

102 The other function, according to Judge Vörös, is the one related to the evolution of constitutional law. Vörös (n 98) 5–7. As we could see, it is due precisely to the publication of dissenting opinions that the contrast between Judge Vörös and the Court's influential President, László Sólyom, became well-known at that time. See Chapter 4, Section 5.6, text to n 425.

103 Ezekiel 3:19.

104 See Chapter 4, Section 5.6.

105 Maurice Kelman, 'The Forked Path of Dissent' (1985) 6 *Supreme Court Review* 227.

106 Brennan (n 1) 437.

107 46 U.S. (5 How.) 504, 612 (1847). See also Chapter 3, Section 2.3, n 66.

108 In the civil law tradition, the question of judicial dissent is rarely discussed in terms of free speech. Whether the judges' right to write separately falls within art 10 of the European Convention on Human Rights enshrining the freedom of expression seems to remain within the states' margin of appreciation. Alder (n 1) 234.

109 In the US, Little (n 18). In Australia, Lynch (n 17).

110 Little (n 18) 696.

note their dissents, not an additional right to publish their rationales for dissenting'.[111] On the other hand, from the perspective of the court's audience, simply noting dissent is of little value if the reasons are not explained. It can hardly fulfil any of the four functions identified above.[112] It is, in fact, the dissenter's opinion that may fulfil those functions, not a bare statement of disagreement. The latter might safeguard the dissenter's conscience, but it does not force the majority to deal with the hardest questions, it does not inform or communicate with anyone outside the court, it does not engage in a dialogue with legal doctrine, and it cannot be a useful vehicle of legal development. Expressing dissent without explaining the reasons, as Lauterpacht explained, 'presumes to substitute the authority of the individual judge for the strength of the argument underlying the dissent'.[113]

The judges' point of view, however, is not the only one when discussing the relationship between dissenting opinions and free speech. It may be examined from the citizens' point of view as well. The Hungarian Constitutional Court dealt with the question from this perspective when two persons wanted to initiate a referendum to ban the publication of dissenting opinions in the Constitutional Court. The National Electoral Commission (OVB) rejected the initiative on the ground that it would amount to a constitutional amendment as it violated freedom of expression enshrined in the Constitution.[114] In its reasoning the Commission argued that banning the publication of separate opinions would, in particular, violate the fundamental right of access to public data. Thus, it did not base its decision on the judges' but rather on the citizens' freedom of expression. It considered dissenting opinions to be information of public interest (*közérdekű információ*). The decision was challenged before the Constitutional Court,[115] which – with a remarkably concise reasoning – unanimously confirmed the Electoral Commission's conclusions.[116]

5. The role of dissenting opinions in the development of constitutional case-law

As we have seen, a possible function of dissenting opinions is to predict future change. Indeed, sometimes they offer the ground for overruling in a later case.

111 Little (n 18) 699. On the other hand, he finds the basis for a constitutional right to write separately in Article III, as the Framers expressly endorsed inferior federal courts and judges while they were familiar with the practice of seriatim opinions. Ibid. 701.

112 The stimulatory, the communicative, the dialectical, and the transformative functions. See Section 1.

113 Hersch Lauterpacht, *The Development of International Law by the International Court* (Cambridge UP 1982). See also, Chapter 4, Section 3.3, n 232.

114 Decision no 403/2009 (5 October 2009) <www.valasztas.hu/hu/parval2010/hatarozatok/2009/2009-2700.html> accessed 19 January 2016 (in Hungarian).

115 On the basis of art 130 of the Electoral Law and art 1(h) of the Constitutional Court Act then in force, which conferred this competence to the Constitutional Court. This competence is upheld by the new Constitutional Court Act (art 33).

116 Decision no 17/2010 (II.18.) AB of 16 February 2010.

Not all dissenting opinions have this fortune. Indeed, most of them do not. But even in those cases, simply by presenting different ideas and methods of analysis, dissents force the court to reconsider the fundamental questions and to rethink the result in every similar case that is brought before it at a later moment.[117] It is especially true in constitutional law that operates with abstract principles and values. As several political philosophers observed, it is impossible to create a rationally coherent scheme of values in a democratic legal system which is based on the interaction between competing wills and interests.[118] One of the principal tasks of a constitutional court is to arbitrate between competing values. Disagreement on these issues is not simply inevitable, but it is a driving force of both legal and political processes. Dissenting opinions, in this sense, draw attention to incommensurable values and keep alive choices for the future.[119]

Moreover, if dissenting opinions are more easily justified in a field of law which is built through case-law rather than through legislation, we can understand why they are more common in constitutional courts than in ordinary courts in the civil law tradition. That constitutional law develops through case-law is also demonstrated by the fact that overruling a precedent is more common when constitutional interpretation is involved.[120] Even if it is widely recognised by comparatists that the formal absence of the doctrine of binding precedent in the civil law tradition does not mean that precedents are not followed by civil law judges, and in practice the difference between the common law and the civil law in this respect is something like a 'folklore', as John Merryman puts it,[121] this 'folklore' still has some implications. And these implications are shown in the style of judgments. Merryman states that 'the distinction between the civil law and the common law judicial processes does not lie in what courts in fact do, but in what the dominant folklore tells them to do'.[122] This, in fact, explains why the civil law courts abandon a precedent (or 'overrule' it, according to the common law terminology) more often implicitly rather than explicitly: since precedents are not formally binding, there is no need to justify a change in the court's orientation. It is sufficient that the (second) decision is well-reasoned on the basis of the other, positive sources of law. If there is no need to justify an overruling, it is even less necessary to refer to a previous dissenting opinion as a basis for the judgment. As we have seen, civil law judges *are* persuaded by previous dissents sometimes,[123] but they rarely admit it.[124]

117 Brennan (n 1) 436.

118 Alder (n 1) 223.

119 Ibid. 224.

120 For a general discussion of this issue see Jon D Noland, 'Stare Decisis and the Overruling of Constitutional Decisions in the Warren Years' (1969) 4 *Valparaiso University Law Review* 101.

121 Merryman (n 54) 46–47.

122 Ibid. 47.

123 See Chapter 4, Sections 2.1.2 and 5.7.

124 This is true for the ECtHR as well. See, for example, cases *I v. The United Kingdom* App no 25680/94 (11 July 2002) and*Christine Goodwin v. the United Kingdom* App

6. Conclusive remarks: judicial dissent and the civil law tradition

The principle aim of this book has been to examine the phenomenon of judicial dissent in constitutional adjudication from the perspective of the civil law tradition. While the spread of dissenting opinions in this tradition makes the well-known convergence between the common law and the civil law more obvious, the way they are used by judges demonstrates that this convergence is still far from being complete. There are several features of the civil law tradition which make a difference in the practice of publishing separate opinions. On the other hand, it is also important to point out that neither the common law nor the civil law traditions are homogeneous, so we should be cautious with generalisations. As we could see in the previous chapters, any generalised finding presents exceptions. Moreover, this book focused on constitutional courts, which constitute a special type of court, and do not resemble ordinary courts in every aspect. A separate examination of ordinary courts and their decision-making process could bring to different conclusions and would certainly greatly contribute to a better understanding of the judicial function in the civil law tradition.

One common feature of the civil law tradition is the especially high prestige of academia and the intense dialogue between scholars and the judiciary. It is especially true for constitutional courts for at least two reasons. First, constitutional issues, even if emerging in the context of a concrete controversy, are of public importance, and their discussion necessarily involves the assessment of fundamental principles and values. Second, constitutional judges themselves often come from the academia. The dissenting opinions of judges with an academic background, as we have seen, usually have a different style,[125] and legal scholars might become more activist judges than their brethren,[126] but there seems to be no strong correlation between the dissent rate of the individual judges and their professional background.[127] Thus, apparently, career judges have no difficulties in adapting themselves to the different judicial environment of a constitutional court or, at least, they have no more difficulties than members of another legal profession.

Another relevant distinguishing feature of the civil law tradition, commonly discussed as such by comparatists, is the absence of the principle of binding

no 28957/95 (11 July 2002), concerning the right of transgender persons to have their gender changed on their birth certificate, in which the Court changed the margin appreciation applied in relation to arts 8 and 12 of the Convention, and the reasoning shows a clear affinity with the dissenting opinion of Judge Martens delivered in *Cossey v. the United Kingdom* App no 10843/84 (27 September 1990) and the one delivered by Judge Casadevall in *X, Y, and Z v. the United Kingdom* App no 21830/93 (22 April 1997). For a comment see Alessandra Di Martino, *Le opinioni dissenzienti dei giudici costituzionali. Uno studio comparativo* (Jovene 2016) 416.

125 See Chapter 4, Section 5.5.

126 See Chapter 4, Section 3.1.

127 See Benjamin Bricker, 'Breaking the Principle of Secrecy: An Examination of Judicial Dissent in European Constitutional Courts' (2017) 39 *Law & Policy* 170.

precedent. Even though comparatists do not hesitate to stress that this is only a formal difference, as civil law judges tend to follow precedents in practice, while common law judges can employ different techniques to avoid having to follow a precedent, it is still a difference. And formal differences do count in law. In this case, they have serious implications for the content and style of judgments. Civil law judges do follow precedents, but these are not presented as a starting point in their reasoning, rather as additional arguments sustaining a certain solution. While the argumentation of a common law judge is precedent-based, the same cannot be said about a civil law judgment. The latter applies deductive reasoning using positive law (the constitution and statutory law) as a starting point. Moreover, civil law judges do not feel themselves obliged to refer to precedents, thus their references are more selective. This has at least two consequences. First, in the very same case the majority and the dissenters may refer to different precedents, according to their own understanding of which precedents are the most relevant, while it happens rarely in common law courts. In the common law tradition, the case is usually that the dissenter interprets the precedents in a different way and reaches a different conclusion from these, rather than s/he bases her/his opinion on different precedents. Second, even if some dissenting opinions do become majority opinions, it is uncommon that the reasoning of the overruling is based on or even refers to a past dissenting opinion. This lack of transparency in the court's reasoning is a legacy of the rigid Montesquieuan idea of separation of powers which sees the judge as the mouth of the law, without any power to create law.

The extent to which a legal system's judges adhere to a more traditional view of the judicial role can be measured through the practice of writing separately. But even in jurisdictions that ban dissenting opinions completely, one can look at the deliberative culture within the court. For example, the fact that Italian constitutional judges usually do not refrain from writing the judgment in cases in which they remained in the minority shows a very high respect for the principle of collegiality and a high level of institutional loyalty. In other courts, judges feel less comfortable with authoring a decision they do not share.

As regards the judicial decision-making process in general, and the practice of dissenting opinions in particular, rather than a distinction between the civil law and the common law tradition, we can notice a difference between the United States and the rest of the Western legal tradition, including other common law countries. As we could see, a very high dissent rate, the phenomenon of 'canonisation' of dissents, and the frequent use of non-legal (social, political, moral) arguments are unique to the US practice.[128] In Europe, on the other hand, there is a clear trend to allow judges, especially constitutional judges, to write separately. If we examine the spread of dissenting opinions in the civil law tradition from a historical perspective, we see that among Western European

128 See Chapter 3, Section 3.4.

countries which designed their constitutional system following the end of the Second World War the trend was against the disclosure of dissent. This trend was inverted after the breakdown of Eastern European socialist regimes. The change of the German practice in the 1960s and the legislative reform permitting the publication of separate opinions in 1970 seem to play a decisive role in the inversion of trend. The German Federal Constitutional Court has served as a model for most European constitutional courts established since the 1970s, including the two Iberian and several Eastern European courts. The German experience has proved to be successful and the publication of dissent is seen by many as a requirement in well-established constitutional democracies of the 21st century.

While several Western European constitutional courts have not caught up with this trend yet, in East-Central Europe even those countries that were skeptical about the dissenting opinions, namely Lithuania and Romania, later decided to open towards it. But there has been a lively debate about the possibility of removing the ban on dissenting opinions also in France and Italy, as well as in relation to the CJEU. The European practice is, however, still far from being homogeneous. Each constitutional court must be examined in its specific legal and political context. We could see that the courts' internal organisation vary considerably, as does the distribution of workload between judges and the rest of the staff, including law clerks and the secretary general. These factors, together with the broader socio-political context in which the courts operate, are to be taken into consideration when examining the practice of dissenting opinions.

In essence, the European trend towards the disclosure of judicial dissent is to be examined and discussed as part of a larger picture in which transparency and accountability are at the centre.[129] This trend is accompanied by an intensified dialogue between courts, involving national supreme courts, constitutional courts and international courts.[130] Indeed, dissenting opinions and a more extensive use of comparative law by constitutional judges are two sides of the same coin. In a context of constitutional pluralism, dissenting opinions are the proof that courts are not immune to the debates taking place in society but, on the

129 The issue of separate opinions is only one of the many facets of transparency, which includes many other questions, such as the accessibility of information on the court's activity, the publicity of hearings, the accessibility of court documents, and the court's visibility in the press and the electronic media. Eszter Bodnár, 'Open Justice in the Digital Age – How Can ICT Enhance the Transparency of Constitutional Courts?' in Alexander Balthasar, Blaž Golob, Hendrik Hansen, Robert Müller-Török, András Nemeslaki, Johannes Pichler and Alexander Prosser (eds), *Central and Eastern European e|Dem and e|Gov Days 2016* (Austrian Computer Society 2016) 53.

130 The use of comparative law by courts has recently become a popular subject of research in Europe. See Elaine Mak, *Judicial Decision-Making in a Globalised World* (Hart 2013), Michal Bobek, *Comparative Reasoning in European Supreme Courts* (Oxford UP 2013), Mads Andenas and Duncan Fairgrieve (eds), *Courts and Comparative Law* (Oxford UP 2015).

contrary, they engage in them.[131] Constitutional pluralism is especially strong in Europe today.[132] Such pluralism compels judges to deal with a plurality of sources of constitutional authority. In this way, courts, and in particular constitutional courts, become part of a larger public discourse in which they participate actively not only through their judgments but also through the individual opinions of particular judges.

131 Lucrezia Palandri, 'Theoretical Reflections on Legal Pluralism and Global Constitutionalism: Their Possible Reconciliation in an Alternative Model of Plural Constitutionalism' (2013) 54 *Acta Juridica Hungarica* 58.

132 It has also been defined as 'multi-level constitutionalism'. The expression was coined by German scholars reflecting on the nature of European constitutionalism and the relationship between EU law and domestic constitutions. See, for example, Ingolf Pernice, 'Multilevel Constitutionalism in the European Union' (2002) 27 *European Law Review* 511.

Appendix

List of Western and East-Central European Constitutions, Constitutional Court Acts and Rules of Procedure of the respective constitutional courts[1]

Albania

Constitution of the Republic of Albania, 28 November 1998 (last amended in 2016)
<www.euralius.eu/en/library/albanian-legislation/send/9-constitution/171-new-constitution-of-the-republic-of-albania-21–7–2016-en> (provisional translation)
Law on the Organization and Functioning of the Constitutional Court, Nr. 8577 dated 10.02.2000
<www.gjk.gov.al/web/law_nr_8577_date_10_02_2000_84.pdf>

Austria

Federal Constitutional Law – Bundes-Verfassungsgesetz – B-VG, BGBI. Nr. 1/1930 (last amended in 2016)
<www.ris.bka.gv.at/Dokumente/Erv/ERV_1930_1/ERV_1930_1.pdf>
Constitutional Court Act 1953 – Verfassungsgerichtshofgesetz 1953 – VfGG, BGBI. Nr. 85/1953
<www.ris.bka.gv.at/Dokumente/Erv/ERV_1953_85/ERV_1953_85.pdf> (last amended in 2016)
Rules of Procedure of the Constitutional Court – Geschäftsordnung des Verfassungsgerichtshofes 1946
<www.ris.bka.gv.at/GeltendeFassung.wxe?Abfrage=Bundesnormen&Gesetzesnummer=10000208> (in German)

Belgium

Coordinated Constitution of 17 February 1994 (last amended in 2014)
<www.const-court.be/en/common/home.html>
Special Act of 6 January 1989 on the Constitutional Court (last amended in 2015)
<www.const-court.be/en/common/home.html>

1 All links have been last accessed on 17 January 2017. I am thankful to Camilla Cordelli for her assistance in the preparation of this list.

Bosnia and Herzegovina

Constitution of Bosnia and Herzegovina, 1995 (last amended in 2009)
<www.ccbh.ba/osnovni-akti/ustav/?title=preambula&lang=en>
Rules of the Constitutional Court of Bosnia and Herzegovina (last amended in 2014)
<www.ccbh.ba/osnovni-akti/pravila-suda/uvod/?title=uvod&second=true>

Bulgaria

Constitution of the Republic of Bulgaria, Promulgated, *State Gazette* No 56/13. 07.1991, effective 13.07.1991 (last amended in 2015)
Constitutional Court Act, Promulgated SG. 67/16 Aug. 1991 (last amended in 2014)
Both available at <http://constcourt.bg/en/LegalBasis>

Czech Republic

Constitution of the Czech Republic of 16 December 1992, No 1/1993 Sb. (last amended in 2013)
<www.usoud.cz/fileadmin/user_upload/ustavni_soud_www/Pravni_uprava/AJ/Ustava_EN_ve_zneni_zak_c._98-2013.pdf>
Charter of Fundamental Rights and Freedoms, Constitutional Act No 2/1993 Coll. as amended by Constitutional Act No 162/1998 Coll.
<www.usoud.cz/fileadmin/user_upload/ustavni_soud_www/Pravni_uprava/AJ/Listina_English_version.pdf>
Constitutional Court Act of 16 June 1993, No 182/1993 Sb. (last amended in 2012)
<www.usoud.cz/fileadmin/user_upload/ustavni_soud_www/Pravni_uprava/AJ/Constitutional_court_act_182_1993.pdf>

Croatia

Constitution of the Republic of Croatia, 1990 (consolidated text as of 2014)
<www.usud.hr/hr/ustav-RH> (only in Croatian, not yet available in English)
Consolidated text in English as of 2010: <www.usud.hr/sites/default/files/dokumenti/THE_CONSTITUTION_OF_THE_REPUBLIC_OF_CROA TIA_-_consolidated_text.pdf>
The Constitutional Act on the Constitutional Court of the Republic of Croatia, consolidated text, *Official Gazette* No 49/02 of 3 May 2002
<www.usud.hr/sites/default/files/dokumenti/The_Constitutional_Act_on_the_Constitutional_Court_of_the_Republic_of_Croatia_consolidated_text_Official_Gazette_No_49-02.pdf>
The Rules of Procedure of the Constitutional Court of the Republic of Croatia (editorially revised and consolidated text), 15 January 2015
<www.usud.hr/sites/default/files/dokumenti/Editorially_revised_and_consoli dated_text_of_the_Rules_of_Procedure_of_the_Constitutional_Court_of_the_Republic_of_Croatia.pdf>

France

Constitution of 4 October 1958
<www.conseil-constitutionnel.fr/conseil-constitutionnel/english/constitution/constitution-of-4-october-1958.25742.html>
Constitutional Court Act: Ordinance no 58–1067 constituting an Institutional Act on the Constitutional Council, Journal Officiel of 9 November 1958, p. 10129 (last amended in 2011)
<www.conseil-constitutionnel.fr/conseil-constitutionnel/root/bank_mm/anglais/en_ordinance_58_1067.pdf>
Decree no 59–1292 of 13 November 1959 on the obligations of the members of the Constitutional Council
<www.conseil-constitutionnel.fr/conseil-constitutionnel/root/bank_mm/anglais/decree59-1292_members.pdf>
Decree no 59–1293 of 13 November 1959 on the organisation of the Secretariat-General of the Constitutional Council
<www.conseil-constitutionnel.fr/conseil-constitutionnel/root/bank_mm/anglais/decree59-1293_organisation.pdf>

Germany

Basic Law for the Federal Republic of Germany, 1949 (last amended 2014)
<www.gesetze-im-internet.de/englisch_gg/basic_law_for_the_federal_republic_of_germany.pdf>
Law on the Federal Constitutional Court
<www.bundesverfassungsgericht.de/SharedDocs/Downloads/EN/Gesetze/BVerfGG.pdf?__blob=publicationFile&v=5>
Rules of Procedure of the Federal Constitutional Court of 19 November 2014 (Federal Law Gazette 2015 I, p. 286)
<www.bundesverfassungsgericht.de/SharedDocs/Downloads/EN/Gesetze/GO_BVerfG.pdf?__blob=publicationFile&v=3>

Hungary

The Fundamental Law of Hungary, 25 April 2011
<www.alkotmanybirosag.hu/rules/fundamental-law>
Act CLI of 2011 on the Constitutional Court
<www.alkotmanybirosag.hu/rules/act-on-the-cc>
Rules of Court: Decision by the Plenary Session no 1001/2013 (II.27) AB (last amended in June 2016)
<www.alkotmanybirosag.hu/jog/ugyrend> (in Hungarian)

Italy

The Constitution of the Italian Republic, 1948
<www.cortecostituzionale.it/documenti/download/pdf/The_Constitution_of_the_Italian_Republic.pdf>

Supplementary norms for the procedure before the Constitutional Court (Norme integrative per i giudizi davanti alla Corte Costituzionale), Gazzetta Ufficiale 7 November 2008, no 261

<www.cortecostituzionale.it/documenti/download/pdf/CC_Fonti_NORME_INTEGRATIVE%20_05032011.pdf> (in Italian)

Rules of Court: Regolamento generale della Corte Costituzionale, Gazzetta Ufficiale 19 February 1966, no 45, special edition)

<www.cortecostituzionale.it/documenti/download/pdf/CC_Fonti_REGGEN luglio_2009_05032011.pdf> (Italian)

Kosovo

Constitution of the Republic of Kosovo, 9 April 2008 (last amended in 2013)

<www.gjk-ks.org/repository/docs/Kushtetuta_RK_ang.pdf>

Law on Constitutional Court No 2008/03-L-121

<www.gjk-ks.org/repository/docs/Law_03-L-121_CCK.pdf>

Rules of Procedure of the Constitutional Court of the Republic of Kosovo (last amended in 2015)

<www.gjk-ks.org/repository/docs/gjkk_rregullore_e_punes_2015_ang.pdf>

Latvia

The Constitution of the Republic of Latvia, 1933 (last amended in 2014)

<www.satv.tiesa.gov.lv/en/2016/02/04/the-constitution-of-the-republic-of-latvia/>

Constitutional Court Law (last amended in 2014)

<www.satv.tiesa.gov.lv/en/2016/02/04/constitutional-court-law/>

Rules of Procedure of the Constitutional Court, Decision of the Plenary Sitting of the Constitutional Court of 5 February 2014

<www.satv.tiesa.gov.lv/en/2016/02/04/hello-world/>

Lithuania

The Constitution of the Republic of Lithuania, 25 October 1992

<www.lrkt.lt/en/about-the-court/legal-information/the-constitution/192>

The Law on the Constitutional Court, Law no I-67 of 3 February 1993 (last amended in May 2015)

<www.lrkt.lt/en/about-the-court/legal-information/the-law-on-the-constitutional-court/193>

Rules of the Constitutional Court of the Republic of Lithuania of 5 March 2004 (last amended in August 2015)

<www.lrkt.lt/en/about-the-court/legal-information/the-rules-of-the-constitutional-court/194>

Luxembourg

Constitution du Grand-Duché de Luxembourg, 17 octobre 1868 (last amended in 2016)

<www.legilux.public.lu/leg/textescoordonnes/recueils/Constitution/constitution_gdl.pdf> (in French)
Organisation de la Cour Constitutionnelle (Frieden), 27 juillet 1997
<www.legilux.public.lu/leg/a/archives/1997/0058/1997A17241.html> (in French)

Macedonia

Constitution of the Republic of Macedonia, 17 November 1991 (last amended in 2011)
Rules of Procedure of the Constitutional Court: Decision of the Constitutional Court no 394/92 of 7 October 1992
Both available at <www.ustavensud.mk/domino/WEBSUD.nsf>

Montenegro

Constitution of the Republic of Montenegro, *Official Gazette* of the Republic of Montenegro, br. 66/06
<http://www.ustavnisud.me/engleska/PDF/The%20Constitution%20of%20Montenegro.pdf>
Law of the Constitutional Court of Montenegro, *Official Gazette* of the Republic of Montenegro, br. 64/2008 of 27 October 2008
<http://www.ustavnisud.me/engleska/PDF/Law%20on%20the%20Constitutional%20Court%20of%20Montenegro%20.pdf
Rules of Procedure of the Constitutional Court, *Official Gazette* of the Republic of Montenegro no 33/2009 of 20 May 2009
<http://www.ustavnisud.me/engleska/PDF/Rules%20of%20Procedure%20of%20the%20Constitutional%20Court.pdf>

Poland

The Constitution of the Republic of Poland, adopted by the National Assembly on 2 April 1997
<http://trybunal.gov.pl/en/about-the-tribunal/legal-basis/the-constitution-of-the-republic-of-poland/>
The Constitutional Tribunal Act, 22 July 2016, Journal of Laws – Dz. U. item. 1157
<http://trybunal.gov.pl/en/about-the-tribunal/legal-basis/the-constitutional-tribunal-act/> and
<www.venice.coe.int/webforms/documents/default.aspx?pdffile=CDL-REF(2016)052-e>
NB: 11 August 2016 – the Constitutional Tribunal issued a judgment on the constitutionality of the Constitutional Tribunal Act of 22 July 2016 in the case ref. no K 39/16

Portugal

Constitution of the Portuguese Republic, adopted by the Constituent Assembly on 25 April 1974, Seventh Revision [2005]

<www.en.parlamento.pt/Legislation/CRP/Constitution7th.pdf>

Law of the Constitutional Court, Law no 28/82, of 15 November (modified by Law no 143/85, of 26 November, Law no 85/89, of 7 September, Law no 88/95, of 1 September, by Law no 13-A/98, of 26 February, and Organic Law no 1/ 2001)

<www.tribunalconstitucional.pt/tc/en/tclaw.html>

Romania

The Constitution of Romania of 8 December 1991, republished in 2003

<www.ccr.ro/constitutia-romaniei-2003>

Law No 47/1992 on the Organisation and Operation of the Constitutional Court

<www.ccr.ro/Legea-nr-471992>

Law No 124/2000 on the Structure of the Constitutional Court Personnel

<www.ccr.ro/Legea-nr-1242000>

Regulations on the Organisation and Functioning. Approved by Resolution no 6 of 7 March 2012 of the Plenum of the Constitutional Court and published in the *Official Gazette* of Romania, Part I, no 198 of 27 March 2012

<www.ccr.ro/Regulamentul-de-organizare-i-funcionare>

Serbia

Constitution of the Republic of Serbia, *Official Gazette* of the RS no 98/2006

<www.ustavni.sud.rs/page/view/en-GB/235-100028/constitution>

Law on the Constitutional Court, *Službeni glasnik RS*, Nos 109/07 of 28 November 2007 (last modified in December 2015)

<www.ustavni.sud.rs/page/view/en-GB/237-100030/law-on-the-constitutional-court>

Rules of Procedure: Decision of the Constitutional Court of 14 November 2013, *Official Gazette* of the RS, no 103/13

<www.ustavni.sud.rs/page/view/en-GB/238-101921/rules-of-procedure>

Slovakia

Constitution of the Slovak Republic, 1992 (latest amendment 2014)

<www.ustavnysud.sk/en/ustava-slovenskej-republiky>

Act no 38/1993 of 20 January 1993 on the Organisation of the Constitutional Court of the Slovak Republic, on the Proceedings before the Constitutional Court and on the Status of Its Judges

<www.ustavnysud.sk/en/o-ustavnom-sude-slovenskej-republiky>

Slovenia

Constitution, *Official Gazette* RS Nos 33/91-I, 42/97, 66/2000, 24/03, 69/04, 68/06, and 47/13

<www.us-rs.si/en/about-the-court/legal-basis/>

Constitutional Court Act (ZUstS), *Official Gazette* of the Republic of Slovenia, No 64/07

<www.us-rs.si/en/about-the-court/legal-basis/statutes/>

The Rules of Procedure, *Official Gazette* of the Republic of Slovenia, No 86/07, 54/10 and 56/11

<www.us-rs.si/en/about-the-court/legal-basis/the-rules-of-procedure-of-the-constitutional-court/>

Spain

Constitution, 1978 (latest amendment 2011)

<www.tribunalconstitucional.es/en/tribunal/normativa/Normativa/ConstitucionINGLES.pdf>

Organic Law no 2/1979 on the Constitutional Court of 3 October 1979 (last amended in 2015)

<www.tribunalconstitucional.es/en/tribunal/normativa/Normativa/LOTC-en.pdf>

Rules of Procedure: Reglamento de Organizatión y Personal del Tribunal Constitucional, Decision of the Plenum of the Constitutional Court of 5 July 1990, BOE no 185, 3 August 1990 (last amended in April 2016)

<www.tribunalconstitucional.es/en/tribunal/normativa/Normativa/ROPTC-consol.pdf> (in Spanish)

Bibliography

Abraham HJ, *The Judicial Process* (7th edn, Oxford UP 1998)

Alder J, 'Dissents in Courts of Last Resort: Tragic Choices?' (2000) 20 *Oxford Journal of Legal Studies* 221

Alemanno A and Stefan O, 'Openness at the Court of Justice of the European Union: Toppling a Taboo' (2014) 51 *Common Market Law Review* 97

Anand RP, 'The Role of Individual and Dissenting Opinions in International Adjudication' (1965) 14 *International and Comparative Law Quarterly* 788

Andenas M and Fairgrieve D (eds), *Courts and Comparative Law* (Oxford UP 2015)

Andrews N, 'The United Kingdom's Supreme Court: Reflections on the Role of the British Nation's Highest Tribunal' (2009) 14 *ZZP Int Zeitschrift für Zivilprozess International* 33

Andrioli V, 'Motivazione collegiale e dissensi dei giudici di minoranza' (1963) *Democrazia e diritto* 508

Anzon A (ed), *L'opinione dissenziente. Atti del seminario svoltosi in Roma nei giorni 5–6 novembre 1993, Palazzo della Consulta* (Giuffrè 1995)

——— 'Gli assistenti di studio dei giudici costituzionali' in P Costanzo (ed), *L'organizzazione e il funzionamento della Corte costituzionale*, vol 1 (Giappichelli 1996) 215

Appleby J and Ball T (eds), *Jefferson: Political Writings* (CUP 1999)

Atiyah PS, 'Judgments in England' in *La sentenza in Europa. Metodo, tecnica e stile* (Cedam 1988) 140

——— 'La sentenza in Inghilterra' in *La sentenza in Europa. Metodo, tecnica e stile* (Cedam 1988) 552

Azizi J, 'Unveiling the EU Court's Internal Decision-Making Process: A Case for Dissenting Opinions?' (2011) 12 *ERA Forum* 49

Baldassarre A, 'L'"opinione dissenziente" e l'intervista di Amadei' (1981) *Democrazia e diritto* 238

Balkin JM, '"Wrong the Day it Was Decided": Lochner and Constitutional Historicism' (2005) 85 *Boston University Law Review* 677

——— and Levinson S, 'The Canons of Constitutional Law' (1998) 111 *Harvard Law Review* 964

Bartole S, 'Conclusions: Legitimacy of Constitutional Court: Between Policy Making and Legal Science' in W Sadurski (ed),*Constitutional Justice, East and West* (Kluwer Law International 2003) 409

Belleau M-C and Johnson R, 'Faces of Judicial Anger: Answering the Call' (2007) 1 *European Journal of Legal Studies* 20

Benelli F, 'Una battaglia non decide la guerra (Nota in dissenso con la sentenza n. 116 del 2003 della Corte costituzionale)' (2003) Forum di Quaderni Costituzionali <www.forumcostituzionale.it> accessed 18 January 2017

Bertea S, 'Towards a New Paradigm of Legal Certainty' (2008) 2 *Legisprudence* 25

Bickel A, *The Least Dangerous Branch* (Bobbs-Merrill 1962)

Black HC, *Handbook on the Law of Judicial Precedents: Or, the Science of Case Law* (West Publishing Company 1912)

Blom-Cooper L, Dickson B and Drewry G (eds), *The Judicial House of Lords 1876–2009* (Oxford UP 2009)

Blom-Cooper L and Drewry G, *Final Appeal. A Study of the House of Lords in its Judicial Capacity* (Clarendon Press 1972)

Bloomfield M, 'Chambers' in KL Hall (ed), *The Oxford Companion to the Supreme Court of the United States* (2nd edn, Oxford UP 2005) 157

Bobek M, 'A Fourth in the Court: Why Are There Advocates-General in the Court of Justice?' (2011–12) 14 *Cambridge Yearbook of European Legal Studies* 529

——— *Comparative Reasoning in European Supreme Courts* (Oxford UP 2013)

Bodnár E, 'Open Justice in the Digital Age – How Can ICT Enhance the Transparency of Constitutional Courts?' in Alexander Balthasar et al, *Central and Eastern European e|Dem and e|Gov Days 2016* (Austrian Computer Society 2016) 53

Boulanger C, 'Europeanization Through Judicial Activism? CEE Constitutional Courts' Legitimacy and the Return to Europe' in W Sadurski et al (eds), *Spreading Democracy and the Rule of Law? Part II* (Springer 2006) 263

Brennan Jr WR, 'In Defense of Dissents' (1985) 37 *Hastings Law Journal* 427

Bricker B, 'Breaking the Principle of Secrecy. An Examination of Judicial Dissent in European Constitutional Courts' (2017) *Law & Policy* (Accepted Article)

Bruinsma FJ, 'Judicial Identities in the European Court of Human Rights' in A Van Hoek et al (eds), *Multilevel Governance in Enforcement and Adjudication* (Intersentia 2006) 203

——— 'The Room at the Top: Separate Opinions in the Grand Chambers of the ECHR (1998–2006)' (2008) *Ancilla Iuris* 32

——— and De Blois M, 'Rules of Law from Westport to Wladiwostok. Separate Opinions in the European Court of Human Rights' (1997) 15 *Netherlands Quarterly of Human Rights* 175

Calamandrei P, *Elogio dei giudici scritto da un avvocato* (first published 1935, Ponte alle Grazie 1935)

Cámara Villar G, *Votos particulares y Derechos fundamentales en la práctica del Tribunal Constitucional español (1981–1991)* (Secretaría General del Ministerio de Justicia 1993)

Cappelletti M, 'Ideologie nel diritto processuale' (1962) *Rivista trimestrale di diritto e procedura civile* 193

——— *Judicial Review in the Contemporary World* (Bobbs-Merrill 1971)

Carrubba CJ, Gabel M and Hankla C, 'Judicial Behavior under Political Constraints: Evidence from the European Court of Justice' (2008) 102 *American Political Science Review* 435

Cascajo Castro JL, 'La figura del voto particular en la jurisdiccion constitucional española' (1986) 17 *Revista española de derecho constitucional* 171

Castillo Vera P de, 'Notas para el estudio del comportamiento judicial. El caso del Tribunal Constitucional' (1987) 20 *Revista Española de Derecho Constitucional* 177

Cerar M, 'Slovenia's Constitutional Court Within the Separation of Powers' in W Sadurski (ed), *Constitutional Justice, East and West* (Kluwer Law International 2010) 213

Cheli E, 'Render noti i motivi del dissenso in giudizio' *Corriere della sera* (8 April 1973)

Clayton CW and Gillman H, *Supreme Court Decision-making. New Institutionalist Approaches* (University of Chicago Press 1999)

Cohen M, 'Reason-Giving in Court Practice: Decision-makers at the Crossroads' (2008) 14 *Columbia Journal of European Law* 257

——— 'Ex Ante Versus Ex Post Deliberations: Two Models of Judicial Deliberations in Courts of Last Resort' (2014) 62 *American Journal of Comparative Law* 401

Cohn EJ, 'Dissenting Opinions in German Law' (1957) 6 *International Comparative Law Quarterly* 540

Conley JM and O'Barr WM, 'Legal Anthropology Comes Home: A Brief History of the Ethnographic Study of Law' (1993–94) 27 *Loyola of Los Angeles Review* 41

Consultative Council of European Judges, 'Questionnaire for 2008 CCJE Opinion Concerning the Quality of Judicial Decisions: Reply Submitted by the Delegation of Poland' (March 2008) <https://wcd.coe.int> accessed 19 January 2017

Cordelli C, 'Judicial appointments to the Court of Justice of the European Union' (2013) 54 *Acta Juridica Hungarica* 24

Cosa significa fare il giudice costituzionale?, public conversation between Marta Cartabia, Sabino Cassese and Joseph Weiler (Rimini, 25 August 2015) <www.meetingrimini.org> accessed 18 January 2017

Council of Europe, Parliamentary Assembly, Committee on Legal Affairs and Human Rights, *Ad hoc Judges at the European Court of Human Rights: An Overview*, Information Report (Doc 12827, 23 January 2012)

Crawford J, *Brownlie's Principles of Public International Law* (8th edn, Oxford UP 2012)

Cruz Villalón P, 'El Tribunal Constitucional Espanol' in P Pasquino and B Randazzo (eds), *Come decidono le corti costituzionali (e altre Corti). How Constitutional Courts Make Decisions* (Giuffrè 2009) 85

Damle SV, 'Specialize the Judge, not the Court: A Lesson from the German Constitutional Court' (2005) 91 *Virginia Law Review* 1267

De Luca P, 'Che fine ha fatto l'introduzione dell'opinione dissenziente?' (2014) 11 *Forum di Quaderni Costituzionali* <www.forumcostituzionale.it> accessed 18 January 2017

Denti V, 'Per il ritorno al "voto di scissura" nelle decisioni giudiziarie' in C Mortati (ed), *Le opinioni dissenzienti dei giudici costituzionali ed internazionali* (Giuffrè 1964) 1–20

Der Kampf um den Wehrbeitrag (Institut für Staatslehre und Politik 1953) vol 2

Di Martino A, *Le opinioni dissenzienti dei giudici costituzionali. Uno studio comparativo* (Jovene 2016)

D'Orazio G, 'Corte costituzionale. Cronaca (1968–1974)' (1974) *Giurisprudenza costituzionale* 2838

Dumbrovský T, Petkova B and Van Der Sluis M, 'Judicial Appointments: The Article 255 TFEU Advisory Panel and Selection Procedures in the Member States' (2014) 51 *Common Market Law Review* 455

Epstein L, Landes WM and Posner RA, 'Why (and When) Judges Dissent: A Theoretical and Empirical Analysis' (2011) 3 *Journal of Legal Analysis* 101

European Commission, *Europeans and Their Languages Report* (Special Eurobarometer 386, 2012)

European Commission for Democracy through Law (Venice Commission), 'The Composition of Constitutional Courts' (1997) in Science and Technique of Democracy No 20, 11 <www.venice.coe.int> accessed 19 January 2017

European Parliament, Directorate-General for Internal Policies, *Dissenting Opinions in the Supreme Courts of the Member States* (PE 462.470, November 2012) <www.europarl.europa.eu> accessed 19 January 2017

Fabbrini F, 'Kelsen in Paris: France's Constitutional Reform and the Introduction of *a Posteriori* Constitutional Review of Legislation' (2008) 9 *German Law Journal* 1297

Ferreres Comella V, *Constitutional Courts and Democratic Values. A European Perspective* (Yale UP 2009)

Fish PG, 'Office of the Chief Justice' in KL Hall (ed), *The Oxford Companion to the Supreme Court of the United States* (2nd edn, Oxford UP 2005) 162

Flauss J-F, 'Les juges des pays d'Europe centrale et oriéntale à la Cour Européenne des droits de l'homme: vues de l'extérieur' in *Mélanges en hommage à Louis Edmond Pettiti* (Bruyland 1998) 344

Frankfurter F, 'Mr. Justice Roberts' (1955) 104 *University of Pennsylvania Law Review* 311

Funston RY, 'Benjamin Robbins Curtis' in KL Hall (ed), *The Oxford Companion to the Supreme Court of the United States* (2nd edn, Oxford UP 2005) 242

Gambaro A, 'Lo stile della sentenza francese' in L Vacca (ed), *Lo stile delle sentenze e l'utilizzazione dei precedenti* (Giappichelli 2000) 121

García de Enterria E, 'La posición jurídica del Tribunal Constitucional en el sistema español: Posibilidades y perspectivas' (2014) 100 *Revista Española de Derecho Constitucional* 39

Garlicki L, 'Constitutional Courts versus Supreme Courts' (2007) 5 *International Journal of Constitutional Law* 44

——— 'The Experience of the Polish Constitutional Court' in W Sadurski (ed), *Constitutional Justice, East and West* (Kluwer Law International 2010) 265

Garoupa N and Ginsburg T, 'Building Reputation in Constitutional Courts: Political and Judicial Audiences' (2011) 28 *Arizona Journal of International and Comparative Law* 539

——— *Judicial Reputation: A Comparative Theory* (University of Chicago Press 2015)

Garoupa N, Gomez-Pomar F and Grembi V, 'Judging under Political Pressure: An Empirical Analysis of Constitutional Review Voting in the Spanish Constitutional Court' (2011) 29 *Journal of Law, Economics, and Organization* 513

Gelazis N, 'Defending Order and Freedom: The Lithuanian Constitutional Court in its First Decade' in W Sadurski (ed), *Constitutional Justice, East and West* (Kluwer Law International 2010) 395

Gentili G, 'A Comparative Perspective on Direct Access to Constitutional and Supreme Courts in Africa, Asia, Europe and Latin America' (2010) 29 *Penn State International Law Review* 705

——— 'A Comparison of European Systems of Direct Access to Constitutional Judges: Exploring Advantages for the Italian Constitutional Court' (2012) 4 *Italian Journal of Public Law* 159

Giles OC, 'Book review of "Das Minderheitsvotum des überstimmten Richters" by Wolfgang Heyde' (1968) 31 *Modern Law Review* 232

Gill TD, *Litigation Strategy at the International Court* (Martinus Nijhoff 1989)

Gluckman M, 'Judicial Process. Comparative Aspects' (1968) 8 *International Encyclopedia of the Social Sciences* 291

Gorla G, 'La struttura della decisione giudiziale in diritto italiano e nella "Common Law": Riflessi di tale struttura sull'interpretazione della sentenza, sui "Reports" e sul "Dissenting"' (1965) *Giurisprudenza italiana* I/1, 1239

——— 'Le opinioni non "segrete" dei giudici dissenzienti nelle tradizioni dell'Italia preunitaria' (1982) 105(5) *Il Foro italiano* 97

Goutal JL, 'Characteristics of Judicial Style in France, Britain and the U.S.A.' (1976) 24 *American Journal of Comparative Law* 43

Granger M-P F, 'When Governments Go to Luxembourg . . .: The Influence of Governments on the Court of Justice' (2004) 29 *European Law Review* 3

Grementieri V and Golden CJ, 'The United Kingdom and the European Court of Justice: An Encounter between Common and Civil Law Traditions' (1973) 21 *American Journal of Comparative Law* 664

Grimm D, 'The German Constitutional Court' in P Pasquino and B Randazzo, *Come decidono le corti costituzionali (e altre Corti). How Constitutional Courts Make Decisions* (Giuffrè 2009) 41

Grzybowski K, 'Socialist Judges in the International Court of Justice' (1964) *Duke Law Journal*, No 3, 536

Habermas J, *Between Facts and Norms* (Polity 1992)

Halmai G, 'Az aktivizmus vége? A Sólyom-bíróság kilenc éve' (1999) 2 Fundamentum 5

——— 'In memoriam magyar alkotmánybíráskodás. A pártos Alkotmánybíróság első éve' (2014) 1–2 *Fundamentum* 36

——— and Tordai Cs, 'Kevesebb lesz az elegáns röpködés a jogrendszer fölött. Vörös Imre távozó alkotmánybíróval Halmai Gábor és Tordai Csaba beszélget' (1999) 2 *Fundamentum* 60

Hambro E, 'Dissenting and Individual opinions in the International Court of Justice' (1956/57) *Zeitschrift für ausländisches öffentliches Recht und Völkerrecht* 229

Hammond TH, Bonneau CW and Sheehan RS, *Strategic Behavior and Policy Choice on the U.S. Supreme Court* (Stanford UP 2005)

Hanretty C, 'Dissent in Iberia' (2012) 51 European Journal of Political Research 671

——— 'Judicial Disagreement need not be Political: Dissent on the Estonian Supreme Court' (2015) 67 *Europe-Asia Studies* 970

Harrison BF, *The Work of a Magistrate* (Shaw & Sons 1964)

Hart HLA, *The Concept of Law* (3rd edn, Oxford UP 2012)

Hendrick BJ, *Bulwark of the Republic: A Biography of the Constitution* (rev edn, Brown 1941)

Heyde W, *Das Minderheitsvotum des überstimmten Richters* (Verlag Ernst und Werner Gieseking 1966)

Holló A, *Az Alkotmánybíróság. Alkotmánybíráskodás Magyarországon* (Útmutató Kiadó 1998)

——— *Az alkotmányjognak asztalánál. Az Alkotmánybíróság belülnézetben* (HVG-ORAC 2015)

Holmes OW, *Opinioni dissenzienti. A cura di Carmelo Geraci* (Milano 1975)

Hoogers HG, '*Ždanoka v. Latvia* – European Court of Human Rights: The Boundaries of the Right to Be Elected under Article 3 of the First Protocol to the European Convention on Human Rights' (2007) 3 *European Constitutional Law Review* 307

Hönnige C, 'The Electoral Connection: How the Pivotal Judge Affects Oppositional Success at European Constitutional Courts' (2009) 32 *West European Politics* 963

Hughes CE, *The Supreme Court of the United States* (Princeton UP 1928)

Husa J, *A New Introduction to Comparative Law* (Hart 2015)

Hussain I, *Dissenting and Separate Opinions at the World Court* (Martinus Nijhoff 1984)

Ingman T, *The English Legal Process* (10th edn, OUP 2004)

Ishiyama Smithey S and Ishiyama J, 'Judicial Activism in Post-Communist Politics' (2002) 36 *Law and Society Review* 719

Jackson PE, *Dissent in the Supreme Court* (University of Oklahoma Press 1969)

Jackson VC and Tushnet M, *Comparative Constitutional Law* (Foundation Press 1999)

Jakab A, 'Judicial Reasoning in Constitutional Courts: A European Perspective' (2013) 14 *German Law Journal* 1215

——— *European Constitutional Language* (Cambridge UP 2016)

——— and Dyevre A (eds), *Comparative Constitutional Reasoning* (Cambridge UP 2017) (forthcoming)

——— Dyevre A and Itzcovich G, 'CONREASON – The Comparative Constitutional Reasoning Project. Methodological Dilemmas and Project Design' (2015) MTA Law Working Papers 2015/9 <http://jog.tk.mta.hu> accessed 19 January 2017

Janosik RJ, 'Seniority' in KL Hall (ed), *The Oxford Companion to the Supreme Court of the United States* (2nd edn, OUP 2005) 903

Kaidatzis A, 'Greece's Third Way in Prof. Tushnet's Distinction Between Strong-Form and Weak-Form Judicial Review, and What We May Learn from It' (2014) 13 *Jus Politicum* <https://ssrn.com> accessed 23 February 2017

Kelemen K, 'A bírói különvélemény története a nyugati jogrendszerekben' (2008) 9 *Jogtudományi Közlöny* 413

——— 'The Road from Common Law to East-Central Europe. The Case of the Dissenting Opinion' (2010) in P Cserne and M Könczöl (eds), *Legal and Political Theory in the Post-National Age* (Peter Lang 2011) 118–134

——— 'Appointment of constitutional judges in a comparative perspective – with a proposal for a new model for Hungary' (2013) 54 *Acta Juridica Hungarica* 5

——— 'Dissenting opinions in constitutional courts' (2013) 14 *German Law Journal* 1345

——— 'Opinion 2/13 of the CJEU: Whose Opinion?' *Diritti Comparati* (4 June 2015) <www.diritticomparati.it> accessed 19 January 2017

——— and Fekete B, 'How Should the Legal Systems of Eastern Europe Be Classified Today?' in A Badó et al (eds), *International Conference for the 10th Anniversary of the Institute of Comparative Law, Lectiones Iuridicae 11* (Universitätsverlag 2014) 197

Kelman M, 'The Forked Path of Dissent' (1985) *The Supreme Court Review* 227

Kelsen H, *Pure Theory of Law* (tr Max Knight, University of California Press 1967)

——— *Introduction to the Problems of Legal Theory* (B Litschewski Paulson and SL Paulson trs, Clarendon Press 1992)

Kenney SJ, 'Beyond Principals and Agents: Seeing Courts as Organizations by Comparing *Référendaires* at the European Court of Justice and Law Clerks at the U.S. Supreme Court' (2000) 33 *Comparative Political Studies* 593

Kirby MD, 'Judicial Dissent – Common Law and Civil Law Traditions' (2007) 123 *Law Quarterly Review* 379

Kirman I, 'Standing Apart to Be a Part: The Precedential Value of Supreme Court Concurring Opinions' (1995) 95 *Columbia Law Review* 2083

Kommers DP, *Judicial Politics in West Germany: A Study of the Federal Constitutional Court* (Sage 1976)

——— *The Constitutional Jurisprudence of the Federal Republic of Germany* (Duke UP 1997)

——— 'The Federal Constitutional Court: The Guardian of German Democracy' (2006) 603 *Annals of the American Academy of Political and Social Science* 111

——— and Miller R, 'Das Bundesverfassungsgericht: Procedure, Practice and Policy of the German Federal Constitutional Court' (2009) 3 *Journal of Comparative Law* 194

Kornhauser LA and Sager LG, 'The One and the Many: Adjudication in Collegial Courts' (1993) 81 *California Law Review* 1

Kowalczyk A, 'Crisis over the Constitutional Tribunal in Poland' *KOD* (17 October 2016) <www.kod.ngo/crisis-constitutional-tribunal-poland/> accessed 19 January 2017

Kuijer M, 'Voting Behaviour and National Bias in the European Court of Human Rights and the International Court of Justice' (1997) 10 *Leiden Journal of International Law* 49

Kurland PB, 'The Supreme Court and the Attrition of State Power' (1958) 10 *Stanford Law Review* 274

Kühn Z, 'The Authoritarian Legal Culture at Work: The Passivity of Parties and the Interpretational Statements of Supreme Courts' (2006) 2 *Croatian Yearbook of European Law and Policy* 19

——— and Kysela J, 'Nomination of Constitutional Justices in Post-Communist Countries: Trial, Error, Conflict in the Czech Republic' (2006) 2 *European Constitutional Law Review* 183

Laffranque J, 'Dissenting Opinion in the European Court of Justice. Estonia's Possible Contribution to the Democratisation of the European Union Juridical System' (2003) 9 *Juridica International* 14

——— 'Dissenting Opinion in the European Court of Justice' (2004) 9 *Juridica International* 14

Lambert É, *Le gouvernement des juges et la lutte contre la législation sociale aux États-Unis* (Giard 1921)

Lane D, '*Bush v. Gore*, Vanity Fair, and a Supreme Court Law Clerk's Duty of Confidentiality' (2005) 18 *Georgetown Journal of Legal Ethics* 863

Lange F, 'American Liberalism and Germany's Rejection of the National-Socialist Past – The 1973 *Roe v. Wade* Decision and the 1975 German *Abortion I Case* in Historical Perspective' (2011) 12 *German Law Journal* 2033

Lasser M, *Judicial Deliberations: A Comparative Analysis of Judicial Transparency and Legitimacy* (Oxford UP 2004)

Lauterpacht H, *The Development of International Law by the International Court* (Cambridge UP 1982)

Lazarus E, 'The Supreme Court's Excessive Secrecy: Why It Isn't Merited' *FindLaw Legal News and Commentary* (30 September 2004) <http://writ.news.findlaw.com> accessed 19 January 2017

Le Sueur A, 'A Report on Six Seminars About the U.K. Supreme Court' (2008) Queen Mary University of London, Legal Studies Research Paper 1/2008 <http://ssrn.com> accessed 18 January 2017

Lencsés K, 'Paczolay: Az Alkotmánybíróság döntései mindenkire kötelezőek' [Paczolay: The decisions of the Constitutional Court bind everyone] *Népszabadság* (Budapest, 29 July 2012) <http://nol.hu> accessed 16 January 2017

Lerner CS and Lund N, 'Judicial Duty and the Supreme Court's Cult of Celebrity' (2010) 78 *George Washington Law Review* 1255

Levy P, 'This Is How the Supreme Court Decides Which Cases to Announce When' *Mother Jones* (24 June 2015) <www.motherjones.com> accessed 19 January 2017

Little RK, 'Reading Justice Brennan: Is There a "Right" to Dissent?' (1999) 50 *Hastings Law Journal* 683

Lively DE, *Foreshadows of the Law. Supreme Court Dissents and Constitutional Development* (Praeger 1992)

Llewellyn KN, *The Common Law Tradition: Deciding Appeals* (Little 1960)

——— and Gewirtz P, 'The Case Law System in America' (1988) 88 *Columbia Law Review* 989

Luatti L, *Profili costituzionali del voto particolare. L'esperienza del tribunale costituzionale spagnolo* (Giuffrè 1995)

Luther J, 'L'esperienza del voto dissenziente nei paesi di lingua tedesca' (1994) *Politica del diritto* 241

Lynch A, 'Is Judicial Dissent Constitutionally Protected?' (2004) 4 *Macquarie Law Journal* 81

Magyar Helsinki Bizottság, TASZ, Eötvös Károly Intézet, *Egypárti alkotmánybírák a kétharmad szolgálatában* (2015) <http://tasz.hu> accessed 19 January 2017

Mak E, *Judicial Decision-Making in a Globalised World* (Hart 2013)

Margolick D, Peretz E and Shnayerson M, 'The Path to Florida' *Vanity Fair* (October 2004) 310

Malecki M, 'Do ECJ judges all speak with the same voice? Evidence of divergent preferences from the judgments of chambers' (2012) 19 *Journal of European Public Policy* 59

Mastor W, *Les opinions séparées des juges constitutionnels* (Presses Universitaires d'Aix-Marseille 2005)

Mayer FC, 'Constitutional Comparativism in Action. The Example of General Principles of EU Law and How They Are Made – A German Perspective' (2013) 11 *International Journal of Constitutional Law* 1003

McGlynn Gaffney E Jr, 'The Importance of Dissent and the Imperative of Judicial Civility' (1994) 28 *Valparaiso University Law Review* 583

McLauchlan WP, 'Assignment and Writing of Opinions' in KL Hall (ed), *The Oxford Companion to the Supreme Court of the United States* (2nd edn, Oxford UP 2005) 705

McWhinney E, 'Judicial Concurrences and Dissents: A Comparative View of Opinion-writing in Final Appellate Tribunals' (1953) 31 *Canadian Bar Review* 595

Merrills JG, *The Development of International Law by the European Court of Human Rights* (2nd edn, Manchester UP 1993)

——— *International Dispute Settlement* (5th edn, Cambridge UP 2011)

Merryman JH, *The Italian Style I: Doctrine* (1965) 18 *Stanford Law Review* 39

——— *The Italian Style II: Law* (1966) 18 *Stanford Law Review* 396

——— *The Italian Style III: Interpretation* (1966) 18 *Stanford Law Review* 583

——— and Pérez-Perdomo R, *The Civil Law Tradition* (3rd edn, Stanford UP 2007)

Mieres Mieres LJ, 'Votos particulares y Derechos fundamentales en la práctica del Tribunal Constitucional español (1981–1991)' (1995) 15 *Revista Española de Derecho Constitucional* 349

Mink A, 'Interview with László Sólyom' (1997) 6 *East European Constitutional Review* 71

Montesquieu C de, *The Spirit of the Laws* (first published 1748, Cambridge UP 1989)

Moreso JJ, *Legal Indeterminacy and Constitutional Interpretation* (Springer 1998)

Morgan DG, 'Mr. Justice William Johnson and the Constitution' (1944) 57 *Harvard Law Review* 328

——— 'The Origin of Supreme Court Dissent' (1953) 10 *The William and Mary Quarterly* 353

Mortati C, *Le opinioni dissenzienti dei giudici costituzionali ed internazionali* (Giuffrè 1964)

——— *Prefazione*, in C Mortati (ed), *Le opinioni dissenzienti dei giudici costituzionali ed internazionali* (Giuffrè 1964) III

Nadelmann KH, 'The Judicial Dissent: Publication v. Secrecy' (1959) 8 *American Journal of Comparative Law* 415

Newman JO, 'Between Legal Realism and Neutral Principles: The Legitimacy of Institutional Values' (1984) 72 *California Law Review* 200

Noland JD, 'Stare Decisis and the Overruling of Constitutional Decisions in the Warren Years' (1969) 4 *Valparaiso University Law Review* 101

Novak L, 'The Precedential Value of Supreme Court Plurality Decisions' (1980) 80 *Columbia Law Review* 756

Oneto LP, 'Le opinioni dissenzienti dei giudici della Corte costituzionale tedesca', *Annali della Facoltà di Scienze Politiche di Genova* (1976–77) 1093

Onida V, *La giustizia costituzionale nel 2004* (Palazzo della Consulta, Rome, 20 January 2005) <www.cortecostituzionale.it> accessed 18 January 2017

Palandri L, 'Theoretical Reflections on Legal Pluralism and Global Constitutionalism: Their Possible Reconciliation in an Alternative Model of Plural Constitutionalism' (2013) 54 *Acta Juridica Hungarica* 58

Panizza S, *L'introduzione dell'opinione dissenziente nel sistema di giustizia costituzionale* (Giappichelli 1998)

——— 'Composizione, organizzazione e funzionamento della Corte costituzionale' in R Romboli (ed), *Aggiornamenti in tema di processo costituzionale (2002–2004)* (Giappichelli 2005)

Panza SC and Reposo A, 'Le "dissenting opinions" ancora alla ribalta' (1981) *Quaderni costituzionali* 595

Passaglia P, 'La giustizia costituzionale in Francia' in J Luther, R Romboli and R Tarchi (eds), *Esperienze di giustizia costituzionale*, Vol 1 (Giappichelli 2000) 199

Paterson A, *The Law Lords* (McMillan 1982)

——— *Final Judgment. The Last Law Lords and the Supreme Court* (Hart 2013)

Pecorario A, 'Il rovescio del giudizio della *Grand Chamber*, in tema di violazione dell'art 3 primo protocollo e degli articoli 10 e 11 della convenzione, svela la complessità della transizione lettone' (2006) <http://archivio.rivistaaic.it> accessed 19 January 2017

Pederzoli P, *La Corte costituzionale* (Il Mulino 2008)

Perju VF, 'Reason and Authority in the European Court of Justice' (2009) 49 *Virginia Journal of International Law* 307

Pernice I, 'Multilevel Constitutionalism in the European Union' (2002) 27 *European Law Review* 511

———, Kokott J and Saunders C (eds), *The Future of the European Judicial System in a Comparative Perspective* (Nomos 2005)

Peterson MD (ed), *Writings. Thomas Jefferson* (Library of America 1984)

Pizzorusso A, 'Dal "relatore" al "redattore" delle sentenze della Corte costituzionale' (1988) *Il Foro italiano*, I, cols 2–3

'Plurality Decisions and Judicial Decisionmaking' (1981) 94 *Harvard Law Review* 1127

Pokol B, 'Az alkotmánybíráskodás szociológiai megfigyelése' (2014) 3 *Alkotmánybírósági Szemle* 158

Popelier P, 'An Italian or a European Style of Judicial Review? Setting the Agenda for Comparative Research on Courts' (2016) 8 *Italian Journal of Public Law* 72

Posner EA and Figueiredo MFP de, 'Is the International Court of Justice Biased?' (2005) 34 *Journal of Legal Studies* 599

Posner RA, 'Judges' Writing Style (And Do They Matter?)' (1995) 62 *University of Chicago Law Review* 1420

——— *How Judges Think* (Harvard UP 2008)

Pound R, 'Judges Holmes's Contributions to the Science of Law' (1921) 34 *Harvard Law Review* 449

Procházka R, *Mission Accomplished. On Founding Constitutional Adjudication in Central Europe* (Central European UP 2002)

Přibaň J, 'Judicial Power vs. Democratic Representation: The Culture of Constitutionalism and Human Rights in the Czech Legal System' in W Sadurski (ed), *Constitutional Justice, East and West* (Kluwer Law International 2002) 373

Quint PE, 'Leading a Constitutional Court: Perspectives from the Federal Republic of Germany' (2006) 154 *University of Pennsylvania Law Review* 1853

Rasmussen H, 'Present and Future European Judicial Problems After Enlargement and the Post-2005 Ideological Revolt' (2007) 44 *Common Market Law Review* 1661

——— 'Legal Opinion About the European Court of Justice's Competence Transgressions, Poor Reasonings and the Complete Non-Transparency of *Willensbildung*' (2009) <http://curis.ku.dk> accessed 16 January 2017

——— and Rasmussen LN, 'Comment on Katalin Kelemen – Activist EU Court "Feeds" on the Existing Ban on Dissenting Opinions: Lifting the Ban is Likely to Improve the Quality of EU Judgments' (2013) 14 *German Law Journal* 1373

Relazione illustrativa della proposta di emendamenti dell'art 18 Norme integrative (Quaderno n 13 dell'Ufficio studi della Corte costituzionale, 1965)

Reynold F, *Disagreement and Dissent in Judicial Decision-making* (Wildy, Simmons & Hill 2013)

Rivière F, *Les opinions séparées des juges à la Cour Européenne des Droits de l'Homme* (Bruylant 2004)

Rodotà S, 'Corte costituzionale. Abolire il segreto sul voto dei giudici' *Il Giorno* (31 March 1973)

——— 'L'opinione dissenziente dei giudici costituzionali' (1979) *Politica del diritto* 637

Rolla G, *Indirizzo politico e Tribunale costituzionale in Spagna* (Jovene 1986)

Romboli R and Tarchi R, 'La giustizia costituzionale in Spagna' in J Luther, R Romboli and R Tarchi, *Esperienze di giustizia costituzionale*, Vol 2 (Giappichelli 2000) 285

Rosenfeld M, 'Constitutional Adjudication in Europe and the United States: Paradoxes and Contrasts' in G Nolte, *European and US Constitutionalism* (Cambridge UP 2005) 184

Rörig MT and Guerrero Picó C, *L'opinione dissenziente nella prassi del* Bundesverfassungsgericht*e del* Tribunal Constitucional *spagnolo* (2009) 23 <www.cortecostituzionale.it> (January 2017)

Sadurski W, 'Introduction' in W Sadurski (ed), *Constitutional Justice, East and West* (Kluwer Law International 2010) 3

——— 'Constitutional Courts in Transition Processes: Legitimacy and Democratization' (2011) Sydney Law School Legal Studies Research Paper No. 11/53

——— *Rights Before Courts: A Study of Constitutional Courts in Postcommunist States of Central and Eastern Europe* (2nd edn, Springer 2014)

Sajó A, 'Reading the Invisible Constitution: Judicial Review in Hungary' (1995) 15 *Oxford Journal of Legal Studies* 253

Salzberger EM and Voigt S, 'On the Delegation of Powers: With Special Emphasis on Central and Eastern Europe' 82002) 13 *Constitutional Political Economy* 25

Samuel G, 'Common law' in JM Smits (ed), *Elgar Encyclopedia of Comparative Law* (2nd edn, Edward Elgar 2012) 169

——— *A Short Introduction to the Common Law* (Edward Elgar 2013)

Sandulli A, 'Voto segreto o palese dei giudici costituzionali' *Corriere della sera* (8 May 1973)

Scalia A, 'Remarks on Dissenting Opinions' in A Anzon (ed), *L'opinione dissenziente* (Giuffrè 1995) 411

Schmidt FF, 'The Ratio Decidendi. A Comparative Study of a French, a German, and an American Supreme Court Decision' (1965) 6 *Acta Instituti Upsaliensis Iurisprudentiae Comparativae* 12

Schubert G, 'Judicial Behavior' (1968) 8 *International Encyclopedia of the Social Sciences* 307

Schütze R, *European Constitutional Law* (2nd edn, Cambridge UP 2016)

Schwartz H, *The Struggle for Constitutional Justice in Post-Communist Europe* (University of Chicago Press 2000)

Sereni AP, 'Le opinioni separate dei giudici dei tribunali internazionali' in C Mortati, *Le opinioni dissenzienti dei giudici costituzionali ed internazionali* (Giuffrè 1964) 144

Shetreet S, 'Judicial Independence and Accountability: Core Values in Liberal Democracies' in HP Lee (ed), *Judiciaries in Comparative Perspective* (Cambridge UP 2011) 3

Smith JE, *John Marshall: Definer of a Nation* (H Holt 1998)

Solum LB, 'On the Indeterminacy Crisis: Critiquing Critical Dogma' (1987) 54 *University of Chicago Law Review* 462

Sólyom L, *Az alkotmánybíráskodás kezdetei Magyarországon* (Osiris 2001)

——— 'The Role of Constitutional Courts in the Transition to Democracy: With Special Reference to Hungary' (2003) 18 *International Sociology* 133

Spiliotopoulos E, 'Judicial review of legislative acts in Greece' (1983) 56 *Temple Law Quarterly* 463

Staugaitytė V, 'Dissenting opinion in the constitutional justice: collegiality of the court *vs.* personal independence of the judge' (2008) 9(111) *Jurisprudencija* 125

Stone A, *The Birth of Judicial Politics in France: The Constitutional Council in Comparative Perspective* (Oxford UP 1992)

——— (as Stone Sweet A), *Governing With Judges: Constitutional Politics in Europe* (Oxford UP 2000)

——— (as Stone Sweet A) 'Why Europe Rejected American Judicial Review: And Why It May Not Matter' (2003) 101 *Michigan Law Review* 2744

——— (as Stone Sweet A) and Burnell TL, 'Constructing a Supranational Constitution: Dispute Resolution and Governance in the European Community' (1998) 92 *American Political Science Review* 63

Sturley MF, 'Cert pool' in KL Hall (ed), *The Oxford Companion to the Supreme Court of the United States* (2nd edn, Oxford UP 2005) 155

Sunstein CR, *Why Societies Need Dissent* (Harvard UP 2005)

——— 'Where are the liberal visionaries on the Supreme Court?' *The New Republic* (15 May 2007)

Takács A, 'Egy alkotmányos forradalmár. Sólyom László – a tudós, az alkotmánybíró, az elnök' in Gábor Halmai, *A megtalált alkotmány? A magyar alapjogi bíráskodás első kilenc éve* (INDOK 2000) 99

Tatham AF, *Central European Constitutional Courts in the Face of EU Membership* (Brill 2013)

Tega D, 'La Corte costituzionale vista da vicino Intervista di Diletta Tega a Gaetano Silvestri' (2014) 3 *Quaderni costituzionali* 757

Teitel R, 'Transitional Jurisprudence: The Role of Law in Political Transformation' (1997) 106 *Yale Law Journal* 2031

Tridimas T, 'The Role of the Advocate General in the Development of Community Law: Some Reflections' (1997) 34 *Common Market Law Review* 1349

Tversky A and Kahneman D, 'The Framing of Decisions and the Psychology of Choice' (1981) 211 *Science* 453

Verdugo RS, 'Aportes del Modelo de Disidencias Judiciales al Sistema Político' (2011) 18 *Revista de Derecho Universidad Católica del Norte* 217

Voeten E, 'The Politics of International Judicial Appointments: Evidence from the European Court of Human Rights' (2006) SSRN <https://ssrn.com> accessed 18 January 2017

Vörös I, *Dixi et salvavi. Különvélemények, párhuzamos indokolások* (Logod Bt 2000)

——— 'The Impartiality of International Judges: Evidence from the European Court of Human Rights' (2008) 102 *American Political Science Review* 417

Von Mehren A, 'The Judicial Process: A Comparative Analysis' (1956) 5 *American Journal of Comparative Law* 197

Waldron J, *Law and Disagreement* (Oxford UP 1999)

Walker TG and Epstein L, *The Supreme Court of the United States: An Introduction* (St Martin's Press 1993)

Ward A and Weiden DL, *Sorcerers' Apprentices. 100 Years of Law Clerks at the United States Supreme Court* (New York UP 2006)

Watts A, 'The International Court of Justice: Efficiency of Procedures and Working Methods – Report of the Study Group with additional comments' in Derek W Bowett et al (eds), *The International Court of Justice: Process, Practice and Procedure* (British Institute of International and Comparative Law 1997) 27

Weber R, 'The Romanian Constitutional Court: In Search of its Own Identity' in W Sadurski (ed), *Constitutional Justice, East and West* (Kluwer Law International 2002) 283

Weiler JHH, 'Epilogue: The Judicial Après Nice' in Gráinne de Búrca and JHH Weiler (eds), *The European Court of Justice* (Oxford UP 2001) 215

Wetter JG, *The Styles of Appellate Judicial Opinions* (Sythoff 1960)

White GE, 'The Canonization of Holmes and Brandeis: Epistemology and Judicial Reputations' (1995) 70 *New York University Law Review* 576

White RCA and Boussiakou I, 'Separate Opinions in the European Court of Human Rights' (2009) 9 *Human Rights Law Review* 37

Woodhouse D, 'The Constitutional Reform Act 2005 – Defending Judicial Independence the English Way' (2007) 5 *International Journal of Constitutional Law* 153

Woodward B and Armstrong S, *The Brethren: Inside the Supreme Court* (Simon and Schuster 1979)

Zagrebelsky G,*Il diritto mite* (Einaudi 1992)

——— *La giustizia costituzionale nel 2003* (Palazzo della Consulta, Rome, 2 April 2004) 5 <www.cortecostituzionale.it> accessed 18 January 2017

——— 'La Corte costituzionale italiana' in P Pasquino and B Randazzo (eds), *Come decidono le corti costituzionali (e altre Corti). How Constitutional Courts Make Decisions* (Giuffrè 2009) 59

Zhang AH, 'The Faceless Court' (2015) King's College London Law School Research Paper No 2015-45 <https://ssrn.com> (January 2017)

Zo Bell KM, 'Division of opinion in the Supreme Court: A history of judicial disintegration' (1958–59) 44 *Cornell Law Quarterly* 186

Zweigert K and Kötz H, *An Introduction to Comparative Law* (Weir tr, 3rd edn, Oxford UP 1998)

Zypries B, 'The Basic Law at 60 – Politics and the Federal Constitutional Court' (2010) 11 *German Law Journal* 87

Index

For Product Safety Concerns and Information please contact our EU representative GPSR@taylorandfrancis.com
Taylor & Francis Verlag GmbH, Kaufingerstraße 24, 80331 München, Germany

www.ingramcontent.com/pod-product-compliance
Ingram Content Group UK Ltd.
Pitfield, Milton Keynes, MK11 3LW, UK
UKHW021303190926
475701UK00009B/617